Progress in

EXPERIMENTAL PERSONALITY RESEARCH

VOLUME 5

CONTRIBUTORS TO THIS VOLUME

RUE L. CROMWELL

GEORGE H. FRANK

ANDREW McGHIE

JOHN M. NEALE

ARTHUR W. STAATS

BERNARD WEINER

PROGRESS IN
Experimental
Personality Research

Edited by Brendan A. Maher

DEPARTMENT OF PSYCHOLOGY
BRANDEIS UNIVERSITY
WALTHAM, MASSACHUSETTS

VOLUME 5

 1970

ACADEMIC PRESS   New York San Francisco London

A Subsidiary of Harcourt Brace Jovanovich, Publishers

ACADEMIC PRESS, INC.
111 Fifth Avenue, New York, New York 10003

United Kingdom Edition published by
ACADEMIC PRESS, INC. (LONDON) LTD.
24/28 Oval Road, London NW1

LIBRARY OF CONGRESS CATALOG CARD NUMBER: 64-8034

PRINTED IN THE UNITED STATES OF AMERICA

CONTRIBUTORS

RUE L. CROMWELL,[1] *Departments of Psychology and Psychiatry, Vanderbilt University, Nashville, Tennessee*

GEORGE H. FRANK, *Department of Psychology, New York University, New York, New York*

ANDREW McGHIE,[2] *Department of Clinical Psychology, Royal Dundee Liff Hospital, and Department of Psychiatry, University of Dundee, Dundee, Scotland*

JOHN M. NEALE,[3] *Departments of Psychology and Psychiatry, Vanderbilt University, Nashville, Tennessee*

ARTHUR W. STAATS, *Department of Psychology, University of Hawaii, Honolulu, Hawaii*

BERNARD WEINER, *Department of Psychology, University of California, Los Angeles, California*

[1]Present address: Lafayette Clinic, Detroit, Michigan.
[2]Present address: Department of Psychology, Queen's University, Kingston, Ontario, Canada.
[3]Present address: State University of New York, Stony Brook, New York.

PREFACE

More than five years have passed since the first volume in this serial publication was published. The contents of this fifth volume indicate that certain problems in personality research are of perennial significance; among these the role of attention in psychopathology is one of the most prominent. In part this may be understood as a consequence of the impact of the generally renewed interest of psychologists in the process of attention. In part it may be a reaction to the inadequacy of more motivational approaches to the study of psychosis.

This decline in the popularity of dynamic psychology is also evidenced in the increasing impact of the behavioral approaches to problems of personality and psychopathology. A contribution in this volume, dealing with social behaviorism and behavior therapy, presents an unambiguous example of this trend.

Other contributions deal with theoretical issues in the study of achievement motivation and problems of personality assessment from measures of intellectual functioning. All in all the contemporary scene in personality research continues to be vigorous and contentious. It continues to give good grounds for optimism about our present and future progress.

Weston, Massachusetts   BRENDAN A. MAHER
November, 1969

CONTENTS

Attention and Perception in Schizophrenia

ANDREW MCGHIE

Attention and Schizophrenia

JOHN M. NEALE AND RUE L. CROMWELL

New Conceptions in the Study of Achievement Motivation

BERNARD WEINER

ix

Social Behaviorism, Human Motivation, and the Conditioning Therapies

ARTHUR W. STAATS

The Measurement of Personality from the Wechsler Tests

GEORGE H. FRANK

CONTENTS OF PREVIOUS VOLUMES

xi

Progress in

EXPERIMENTAL PERSONALITY RESEARCH

VOLUME 5

ATTENTION AND PERCEPTION IN SCHIZOPHRENIA

Andrew McGhie[1]

DEPARTMENT OF CLINICAL PSYCHOLOGY, ROYAL DUNDEE LIFF HOSPITAL, AND
DEPARTMENT OF PSYCHIATRY, UNIVERSITY OF DUNDEE,
DUNDEE, SCOTLAND

I. Introduction

The last ten years has produced a bewildering array of psychiatric, bio-chemical, neurophysiological, and psychological research on schizo-phrenia. Among the often contradictory findings in the literature one common area of agreement has emerged: namely, that there is no such thing as schizophrenia. In spite of a continuing tendency to refer to schiz-ophrenia as if it represented a clear-cut disease entity, both research and clinical experience point to the essential plurality of this condition. In his original formulation of the concept of schizophrenia Bleuler (1911) care-fully referred to "the group of schizophrenias," and subsequent enquiries have served to underline heavily the heterogeneous nature of this diag-nostic grouping. In his initial classification Bleuler sought to reduce this heterogeneity by developing further the original Kraepelinian subdivision of hebephrenic, catatonic, and paranoid forms of the illness and adding the additional subcategory of "simple" schizophrenia. Although this method of "fractionating" schizophrenia into four more cohesive compo-

---

[1]Present address: Department of Psychology, Queen's University, Kingston, Ontario, Canada.

1

nents is still in use, it has become increasingly obvious that the amount of overlap between the subcategories greatly lowers their diagnostic reliability. The category of simple schizophrenia is particularly ambiguous and may easily lead to confusion in the case of nonpsychotic patients who have a markedly inadequate personality structure. Many clinicians have suggested that catatonia represents a transient symptom which can occur during any schizophrenic illness rather than a separate diagnostic subcategory. Only the paranoid and hebephrenic categories remain as reasonably stable subdivisions. The clear-cut clinical differences between the paranoid schizophrenic and all other schizophrenic patients have led many workers to suggest the paranoid-nonparanoid dichotomy as one of the most viable methods of demarcating within the schizophrenic group. It has been suggested (Venables & Wing, 1962) that this division may be rendered more stable if the paranoid category is restricted to so-called "coherent" paranoid patients. Under this diagnostic label only those patients who show a high level of coherent delusions, in the absence of primary schizophrenic symptoms such as thought disorder and loss of affect, would be accepted as paranoid. However, some psychiatrists would argue that to diagnose as schizophrenic patients who have none of the primary symptoms associated with this syndrome makes poor clinical logic. They would advocate that the coherent paranoid patients be allocated to a separate diagnostic category of "paranoid psychoses."

The term hebephrenia has much in common with the original Kraepelinian (1896) concept of "dementia praecox," the forerunner of Bleuler's concept of schizophrenia. It is usually applied to patients whose premorbid history, current symptomatology, and poor response to treatment imply a more malignant form of the illness. The use of malignancy as a criterion for subdividing the schizophrenic group is evident in more recent distinctions between process and reactive forms of the illness. The process category is applied to patients who show a poorly integrated, usually schizoid prepsychotic personality, an insidious onset to their illness, and a poor prognosis regardless of treatment. In contrast, the reactive category is applied to patients who have a relatively good premorbid personality, whose illness has shown a rapid acute onset, and whose prognosis is relatively good. The process-reactive dimension has some similarity to Langfeldt's (1939) distinction between "nuclear" schizophrenia and the "schizophreniform" psychosis, the latter term being applied to patients whose illness is less severe and runs a more benign course than that of the classical schizophrenic illness. In a follow-up study of a mixed group of patients (Eitinger, Laane, & Langfeldt, 1958) it was shown that whereas only 50% of those patients diagnosed as schizophrenic were eventually able to lead a normal independent social life, 75 % of those diagnosed as schizophreni-form subsequently reached this level.

Another frequently used method of subdividing schizophrenia is to di-chotomize on the basis of length of illness to distinguish the two catego-ries of acute and chronic schizophrenia. Since Brown (1960) showed that schizophrenics have a significantly poorer likelihood of improvement af-ter a continuous stay in hospital of 2 years or more, most recent workers have adopted the 2-year hospitalization period as a convenient, although arbitrary method of denoting the onset of chronicity.

There is obviously a great deal of overlap among the systems of sub-classification. Process schizophrenics, with their poorer response to treat-ment are likely to spend longer in hospital and thus fall into the chronic category. Furthermore, by the very nature of their symptoms, they are likely to fit into the nonparanoid grouping.

All attempts to classify schizophrenia or its components are still hind-ered by an almost total ignorance of the etiology of this condition. Oppos-ing assumptions regarding the basic causes of schizophrenia are implicit in many of the suggested systems of subclassification. Studies of the dis-turbed family background of schizophrenic patients (Lidz & Lidz, 1949; Bateson, Jackson, Haley, & Weakland, 1956; Laing, 1960) have sug-gested a predominantly psychogenic etiology in the case of some schizo-phrenic patients.

In contrast to this approach, others have emphasized the organic and constitutional determinants of schizophrenia, seeking evidence of a bio-logical disorder which causes a malfunctioning of the brain and nervous system. This approach has led to a number of hypotheses suggesting a biochemical pathology in which schizophrenia is seen as the end result of a toxic process produced by a metabolic disorder (Hoffer & Osmond, 1959; Heath, 1960; Toderick, Tait, & Marshall, 1960; Smythies, 1967). A further extension of this approach is seen in the many genetic studies which aim at identifying the mode of transmission of the pathological or-ganic process.

Such uncompromising etiological views merely hamper progress by causing research workers to don blinkers which effectively screen out any findings not supportive of their own (organic *or* psychogenic) assump-tions. The weakness of this "either" or "or" approach to schizophrenic etiology has been clearly put by Maher (1966) in discussing genetic stud-ies. "As long as the question is posed as being whether schizophrenic behaviour is genetically determined *or* environmentally determined there seems to be little prospect that we shall advance much further in our un-derstanding of any of its determinants. We do have ample evidence that manipulations of biological variables produce changes in behaviour; we also have ample evidence that manipulating the environment changes behaviour. The important problem is the discovery of the processes by which these influences operate and the nature of the interaction between them." (Maher, 1966)

If schizophrenia is a blanket term enclosing a number of separate pathological conditions, any etiological arguments which ignore this heterogeneity are likely to end in confusion. The establishment of a reliable system of subclassifying the schizophrenias would appear to be a necessary precursor to etiological studies. This position has been stated by Tait (1958) who, in reviewing the physiopathology of schizophrenia wrote: "I do not personally believe that one single biochemical answer to what we call schizophrenia will be found. The biochemist and the electrophysiologist are more likely to give us a set of answers, and I could wish we were in a position to give them a set of questions which were equally precise and clearly defined. I feel that we must exploit old or develop new methods of defining and measuring our schizophrenic states." (Tait, 1958) Psychological studies may contribute to this process of delineating schizophrenia by producing reliable measurements of the changes in mental functioning occurring in different forms of the psychosis.

The remainder of this chapter is devoted to a summary of some of the psychological findings related to the processes of attention and perception. Unfortunately the psychological boundaries between different mental processes are every bit as permeable as those which exist in psychiatric classification. A review which restricted itself exclusively to studies of attentional and perceptual changes would be forced to neglect consideration of studies of other related cognitive processes. In reviewing the work in this field in an earlier volume of this series Venables (1964) avoided such artificial restrictions in widening his brief to cover "input dysfunction" in schizophrenia. The present review will also touch upon a number of aspects of schizophrenic performance which seem pertinent to our understanding of attentional dysfunction.

II. Observational Studies

Disturbances of attentional behavior have been noted by numerous clinical observers of schizophrenic patients. Bleuler (1911) described many such instances and some of his comments bear a striking similarity to more recently reported clincial observations: "Even although uninterested and autistically encapsulated patients appear to pay little attention to the outside world, they register a remarkable number of events of no concern to them. The selection which attention exercises over normal sensory impressions may be reduced to zero so that almost everything that meets the senses is registered." However, Bleuler appeared to disregard the importance of such observations and his final conclusion of a "clear sensorium" in schizophrenia caused subsequent clinicians to neglect any pathological variations in attention demonstrated by schizophrenic patients. More recently a number of clinical studies of acute schizophrenic patients have stressed the frequency with which patients include attentional changes as one of their earliest and most disturbing symptoms. A study by McGhie and Chapman (1961), in which young schizophrenic patients were encouraged to describe their difficulties contain the following reports from different patients:

I can't concentrate. It's diversion of attention that troubles me — the sounds are coming through to me but I feel my mind cannot cope with everything. It is difficult to concentrate on any one sound — it's like trying to do two or three different things at one time.

It's as if I'm too wide awake — very, very alert. I can't relax at all. Everything seems to go through me. I just can't shut things out.

Everything seems to grip my attention although I am not particularly interested in anything. I'm speaking to you just now but I can hear noises going on next door and in the corridor. I find it difficult to shut these out and it makes it more difficult for me to concentrate on what I am saying to you. Often the silliest things going on seem to interest me. That's not even true; they won't interest me but I find myself attending to them and wasting a lot of time this way. I know that sounds like laziness but it's not really.

A number of these patients also described allied perceptual changes involving an increase in sensory vividness of hitherto peripheral features in the perceptual field:

During the last while back I have noticed that noises all seem to be louder to me than they were before. It's as if someone had turned up the volume — I notice it most in background noises. — you know what I mean, noises that are always around you but you don't notice them. Now they seem to be just as loud and sometimes louder than the main noises that are going on — It's a bit alarming at times because it makes it difficult to keep your mind on something when there's so much going on that you can't help listening to.

Have you ever had wax in your ears for a while and then had them syringed? That's what it's like now, as if I had been deaf before. Everything is much noisier and it excites me.

The colours of things seem much more clearer and brighter — maybe it's because I notice so much more about things and find myself looking at them for a long time. Not only the colour of things fascinate me but all sorts of little things like markings on the surface, pick up my attention too.

Similar descriptions have been noted by others who have studied the self-reports of schizophrenic patients. Bowers and Freedman (1966) quote the following example:

> My senses were sharpened, I became fascinated by the little insignificant things around me — sights and sounds possessed a keenness that I had never experienced before — my senses were sharpened, sounds were more intense and I could see with great clarity, everything seemed very clear to me. Even my sense of taste seemed more acute.

Another patient, now recovered, described her illness in the following manner:

> What I do want to explain if I can is the exaggerated state of awareness in which I lived before, during, and after my acute illness. It was as if parts of my brain awoke which had been dormant, and I became interested in a wide assortment of people, events, places and ideas which normally would make no impression on me (McDonald, 1960).

The last patient quoted was able to offer the following interesting interpretation of her own experiences during the acute stage of her illness:

> Each of us is capable of coping with a large number of stimuli, invading our being through any of the senses — It's obvious that we would be incapable of carrying on any of our daily activities if even one hundredth of all these available stimuli invaded us at once. So the mind must have a filter, which functions without our conscious thought, sorting stimuli and allowing only those which are relevant to the situation in hand to disturb consciousness. What happened to me in Toronto was a breakdown of the filter, and a hodge-podge of unrelated stimuli were distracting me from things that should have held my undivided attention — I had very little ability to sort the relevant from the irrelevant — Completely unrelated events became intricately connected in my mind (McDonald, 1960).

This model of schizophrenic breakdown accords well with that put forward by many trained observers of schizophrenic behavior. For example, in attempting to unify their own observations McGhie and Chapman (1961) postulated along the following lines:

> By the process of attention we thus break down and effectively categorise both the information reaching us from the environment, and that which is internally available in the form of stored past experience. By such processes we reduce, organize, and interpret the otherwise chaotic flow of information reaching consciousness to a limited number of differentiated, stable and meaningful precepts from which reality is constructed. Now let us suppose that there is a breakdown in this selective-inhibitory function of attention. Consciousness would be flooded with an undifferentiated mass of incoming sensory data, transmitted from the environment via the sense organs. To this involuntary tide of impressions there would be added

the diverse internal images, and their associations, which would no longer be co-ordinated with incoming information. Perception would revert to the passive and involuntary assimilative process of early childhood, and, if the incoming flood were to carry on unchecked, it would gradually sweep away the stable constructs of a former reality.

Such observations suggest that schizophrenic patients experience a widening of attention which affects many other areas of their behavior. However, these descriptions also raise many questions, some of which are difficult to answer by direct observation. Are such impairments of attention specific to schizophrenia or do they occur in other psychiatric states — or for that matter, in normal subjects in certain conditions? Is the schizophrenic disorder of attention unitary or does it vary with other situational factors? Thus, for example, does attention fluctuate with the modality in which stimuli are presented? What is the effect of disturbance of selective attention on other mental functions, such as perception, memory, motor performance, language and so on? To what extent is the quality and degree of attentional impairment associated with the severity, the duration, or the form of the schizophrenic illness? In order to answer these and other related questions we turn next to studies which have employed the experimental approach.

III. Psychological Studies

A. OVERINCLUSIVE THINKING

Since Cameron (1938, 1939) first described the "overinclusive" aspects of schizophrenic thinking, a number of psychological studies have sought to explore and clarify the schizophrenic patient's inability to preserve conceptual boundaries. Although several earlier investigations attempted to measure overinclusive thinking (Zaslow, 1950; Chapman, 1956), the most intensive series of studies in this area are those reported by Payne and his colleagues. By employing a large battery of psychological tests with mixed groups of psychiatric patients, Payne and Hewlett (1960) were able to show that although various factors influenced the thinking of psychotic patients, only that of overinclusion was specific to schizophrenic patients. In a later study Payne (1966) investigated the association between overinclusive thinking and the span of attention. Groups of patients were presented with brief tachistoscopic exposures of pictures and invited to identify the picture as early as possible in a series of exposures of increasing length. Payne postulated that overinclusive schizophrenics would have a widened span of attention and thus process more information than others on each exposure. Taking the earliest point in the exposure series where the patient attempts to identify the picture as an index of the amount of information being processed, he found a very high correlation (+0.90) between this measure of "perceptual overinclusion" and his standard measures of overinclusive thinking.

Unlike some previous investigators who had considered overinclusion as purely a form of thought disorder, Payne suggested that it was a secondary elaboration of a more fundamental disturbance of attention. "The mechanism of attention itself seems to become defective. Whatever filtering mechanism ensures that only the stimuli (internal or external) that are relevant to the task enter consciousness and are processed, seems no longer able to exclude the irrelevant. This has numerous repercussions. Thinking becomes distracted by external events. It also becomes distracted by irrelevant personal thoughts and emotions which may even become mixed up with the problem. Selective perception becomes impossible so that instead of dealing with the essence of the problem, irrelevant aspects are perceived and thought about. . . ." (Payne, 1966)

Payne had already noted that only around half of schizophrenic patients were overinclusive in their thinking, the remainder being predominantly retarded. First on purely theoretical and observational grounds (Payne, 1961) and later on the basis of experimental findings (Payne, Caird, & Laverty, 1964; Payne & Caird, 1967), it was suggested that overinclusion is associated mainly with the paranoid subclass of schizophrenia. In one of these experimental studies (Payne *et al.*, 1964) it was demonstrated that deluded (paranoid) patients were significantly more overinclusive than nonschizophrenic patients. However, no significant differences in overinclusion were apparent when deluded and nondeluded (nonparanoid) schizophrenic groups were compared. Payne's suggestion that this absence of any clear-cut differences was probably due to some of his high overinclusive-scoring, nonparanoid patients being secretly deluded is not entirely convincing. In a more recent study of the relationship between overinclusion and distractibility Payne and Caird (1967) have produced further support of the suggested association between overinclusion and paranoid symptomatology. Adopting an earlier suggestion (Rodnick & Shakow, 1940) that the slow reaction times of schizophrenic patients is due to their being distracted by irrelevant stimuli, it was suggested that the latency time of paranoid patients would progressively increase in the presence of experimentally imposed distractions. The results of this study confirmed that the R.T. of highly overinclusive schizophrenics was more susceptible to distraction, although this effect varied widely with different types of distracting conditions. When the schizophrenic group was subdivided into paranoid and nonparanoid categories, and an analysis of variance carried out on both simple and choice reaction time scores, no significant interaction could be established between paranoid diagnosis and distraction effect, although the mean scores tended in this direction. Payne and Caird considered that the failure of this analysis to fully support their hypotheses was probably due to the heterogenity of the nonparanoid group and repeated the analysis without these patients. On this occasion the relevant interactions were significant, thus supporting their view that paranoid schizophrenia is associated with high distractibility and overinclusiveness. However, the high variance of their nonparanoid group scores suggests that some nonparanoid schizophrenic patients were more distractible than some paranoid patients.

Payne has also considered the relationship between overinclusion and the acute-chronic dichotomy. The findings from two separate investigations (Payne, 1962; Payne & Freidlander, 1962) have demonstrated that overinclusion is associated mainly with acute patients and that the overinclusive scores of chronic schizophrenic patients tend to fall within the normal range.

To briefly recapitulate then, Payne's studies suggest that overinclusive thinking (as measured by his tests) is one aspect of a general deficit of selective attention which is more evident in acutely ill patients of the paranoid subtype, although the evidence for this latter association is less clear cut.

B. DISTRACTION STUDIES

A number of studies of the effects of distraction on various aspects of schizophrenic performance have been reported by McGhie and his colleagues. Some of their investigations (Chapman & McGhie, 1962; McGhie, Chapman, & Lawson, 1965a) have been concerned with the effect of experimentally imposed distraction upon the psychomotor performance of schizophrenic patients. For this purpose a battery of tests selected from Fleishman's (1954) standard psychomotor tasks was modified to allow the effect of both auditory and visual distraction to be examined independently. The test battery was presented to matched groups of schizophrenic patients, nonschizophrenic psychotic patients, and a normal control group. In the absence of distraction all psychotic patients showed a low level of psychomotor performance, this being in accordance with the findings of a variety of other studies (Shakow & Huston, 1936; King, 1954; Hall & Stride, 1954; Huston & Senf, 1952). When the tests were repeated with experimentally induced distraction, the performance of most patients deteriorated slightly but this decline was no more evident in the schizophrenic than in any other diagnostic group. The majority of the tests employed in this study were simple speed tests involving a motor response to a predictable stimulus. In a few of the tests demanding the processing of unpredictable signals, distraction did lead to a performance decrement in the schizophrenic group. Thus, in a signal tracking task, involving the tracking of a variable visual signal, the level of schizophrenic performance fell sharply when either visual or auditory distraction was introduced.

In a later series of investigations (McGhie, Chapman, & Lawson, 1965b; Lawson, McGhie, & Chapman, 1966) the same workers examined the effect of distraction on tasks involving the processing, storage, and recall of information. The main technique here was to present the patient with information, usually consisting of a series of rapidly presented letters or digits, together with a similar series of irrelevant information. The patient's task was to observe and report the relevant series, while ignoring the irrelevant information. In some of the tests the relevant and irrelevant information was presented in the same sensory modality, while in others two sensory modalities were involved. Although the findings of these investigations confirmed the susceptibility of schizophrenic patients to distraction, they also indicated that this effect varied greatly with the nature of the task and with the sensory modality involved. Compared with other psychotic patients, the schizophrenic group were seen to have considerable difficulty in coping with tasks which demanded the integration of information from two different sensory modalities. It was also noticeable that, when presented with a task of this nature, the schizophrenic patient fared most poorly in processing visual information. Furthermore, in a number of tasks requiring the perception and recall of either auditory or visual information, in the absence of distraction, schizophrenic patients showed themselves capable of processing auditory information reasonably well, but performed badly with an equivalent task in the visual modality. It was further demonstrated (McGhie, Chapman, & Lawson, 1964) that elderly normal subjects showed a similar deficiency in processing visual information. This suggestion of a specific modality difference in schizophrenia has been advanced by other workers, particularly Venables (Venables & O'Connor, 1959, Venables, 1960, 1963) but in an apparently opposite direction. Venables' studies indicate that schizophrenic patients show a disturbance of information processing in the auditory rather than the visual modality. Several possible explanations may be advanced to account for the apparent contradictions in these findings. The poor visual performance of the schizophrenic patients in the studies reported by McGhie and his colleagues was most apparent in tasks involving short-term retention, whereas storage was not involved in Venables' reaction time studies. Another likely source of these antagonistic findings is to be found in the different clinical state of the schizophrenic patients participating in the investigations. The poor visual performance observed by McGhie and his colleagues was confined to deteriorated or nuclear schizophrenics while the poor auditory performance noted by Venables involved mainly nondeteriorated paranoid patients.

In the studies reported by McGhie and his colleagues the effects of distraction on schizophrenic performance were found to be relatively slight in the case of visual tasks. In such tasks the basic performance of schizophrenic patients was so low that it is possible that any effects of distraction would not be evident. However, on tasks requiring the processing of auditory information, the effect of distraction on schizophrenic performance was very marked. These effects were independent of the sensory modality in which the distracting stimuli were presented. This finding of a modality-specific effect of distraction on schizophrenic performance is again evident in a more recent investigation by the same team of workers (Lawson *et al.*, 1966).

These workers have interpreted their experimental findings in a model of disturbed attention which leans heavily on Broadbent's (1958) theory of a limited capacity decision channel. Studies of normal information processing have already made it clear that the limitation of the human communication channel is an informational one, so that the number of stimuli which can be responded to at any time is determined by the amount of information they contain. It is thus possible to deal with more than one set of data at a time only if the informational demands of each task are small. In order to function effectively, the individual is forced to perform a selective filtering operation on the input to ensure that his limited capacity is not overloaded. McGhie and his colleagues interpret their findings as indicating that in schizophrenia this normal filtering process has broken down so that the patients are less able to attend selectively and to process only relevant information. This defect may be expected to have varying effects depending upon the nature and demands of any task. In dealing with a situation requiring a response to simple predictable stimuli, overloading will be less likely and the patient's deficit is less obvious. In tasks demanding the monitoring of a range of stimuli involving more complex decision making and fully occupying the limited decision channel, the failure in selective attention is more likely to lead to overloading and consequent breakdown in performance. In dealing with visual data the relatively slow rate of recoding information into the auditory modality increases the likelihood of overloading.

Yates (1966) has suggested that these findings might be interpreted in a slightly different manner to suggest that the primary schizophrenic deficit lies in slowing down in the rate at which the primary processing channel

deals with information. This formulation would imply that more information would be passed to the short-term memory system, leading to overloading and loss of information. Yates sees part of the schizophrenic patient's confusion as being a result of his registering only a small part of the
relevant environmental input.

The communication difficulty observed so clearly in schizophrenic patients has focused a great deal of clinical interest upon the patient's inability to express his thoughts in speech and to assimilate in a meaningful way
the speech of others. In spite of the clearly observable language deficiency of the schizophrenic, relatively few attempts have been made to
systematically examine schizophrenic language disturbance. The majority
of studies which have been reported have been concerned with a psycholinguistic analysis of the content of schizophrenic speech. In their first
clinical study McGhie and Chapman (1961) noted many examples of the
patient's inability to process incoming verbal material and suggested that
at least part of this deficiency could be regarded as a secondary consequence of the attentional deficit. The following extract is characteristic of
the reports given by a number of young schizophrenic patients of their
inability to comprehend the speech of others.

> When people talk to me now it's like a different kind of language. It's too much to
> hold at once. My head is overloaded and I can't understand what they say. It makes
> you forget what you've just heard because you can't get hearing it long enough. It's
> all in different bits which you have to put together again in your head — just words in
> the air unless you can figure it out from their faces.

An examination of such reports suggested to these workers that the patient's difficulties arise, not from an inability to perceive the individual
words comprising a connected discourse, but from an inability to perceive
the words in meaningful relationship to each other as part of an organized
pattern. Studies of normal speech (Shannon, 1951; Miller, 1963; Goldman-Eisler, 1961) have made it clear that speech processing is facilitated
by the "redundancy" in normal language structure. Such redundancy
makes it possible for a passage of speech to be adequately comprehended
without necessarily processing every word contained in it.

Investigations of normal subjects (Miller, 1963; Goldman-Eisler, 1961)
suggest that speech is usually assimilated in phrase units of three to four
words. Listening to speech is essentially a matter of making decisions
about what is being said and storing these decisions in short-term memory
to allow the communication to be subsequently understood in its entirety.
Our ability to organize incoming speech into small phrase units ensures
that, in listening to normal speech (at a rate of approximately 150 words
per minute), the decision rate is reduced to a comfortable level

(approximately 1 second), well within our capacity for processing information. The reports of schizophrenic patients suggested that their difficulty in assimilating speech is due both to a deficiency in the screening out of "redundant" information, and to an inability to organize the incoming verbal data in an economical way.

As a preliminary test of this hypothesis Lawson, McGhie, and Chapman (1964) presented schizophrenic patients, patients suffering from other psychiatric conditions, and normal subjects with passages of English prose of different degrees of internal organization (Miller & Selfridge, 1950). These varied from collections of random unrelated words (zero constraint) to standard English text. The intervening passages were graded according to the degree of contextual constraint involved in their structure. The results clearly indicated that, although the schizophrenic patients were able to perceive and recall sentences of low contextual constraint as well as the controls, they fared badly in comparison with nonschizophrenics, in dealing with sentences of higher constraint. In other words, the schizophrenic patient seems unable to utilize the transitional bonds between words which normally facilitate our perception of the passage as an organized whole. By processing speech in single words rather than in phrase units, they must make decisions about what is being said at the rate of three to four per second. It was also theorized that, if the deficiency in speech perception of schizophrenic patients was due in part to an inability to screen out irrelevant information, there should be a direct connection between poor performance on the speech test and a high distraction scores on the previously mentioned tests of distraction. A high positive and significant correlation between these two measures was found (Lawson, 1965), and taken to support this interpretation that the poor speech perception of some schizophrenic patients was a consequence of a breakdown in selective attention.

Although these findings were independently replicated by Nidorf (1964), a more recent study by Raeburn and Tong (1968) failed to substantiate some of the findings reported by Lawson et al. The results of this investigation suggest that both speed of response and verbal ability are related to the recall of contextually constrained passages and that the effect observed by Lawson et al. is confined to certain schizophrenics.

Like Payne, McGhie and his colleagues found heightened distractibility to be characteristic of only some of their schizophrenic patients. However, according to their data, the paranoid patients were the least distractible of any of the clinical groups tested. Indeed, patients with a predominantly paranoid symptomatology were found to be less distractible than normal control subjects. These findings were confirmed in a later study (Lawson, 1965) where a significantly negative biserial correlation was found between a rating of paranoid symptoms and distractibility scores. The patients who were markedly distractible had all been diagnosed within the hebephrenic subtype. McGhie and his colleagues failed to find any significant differences in distractibility between acute and chronic patients although they did observe acute patients to react with more affect to their changing experiences.

C. PERCEPTUAL CONSTANCY

Further experimental evidence of an attentional deficit in schizophrenia may be derived from a series of studies by Weckowicz and his colleagues of perceptual anomalies in psychotic patients. These investigations (Weckowicz, 1957; Weckowicz, Sommer, & Hall, 1958) have demonstrated a reduction in both size and distance constancy in schizophrenic patients. This finding is in accordance with the reports of schizophrenic patients (McGhie & Chapman, 1961) that their world now seemed flat, lacking in depth, and that approaching objects appeared to change in size in an alarming manner. Such changes in the perceptual constancy of schizophrenic patients were confirmed and elaborated by other investigators (Crookes, 1957; Hamilton, 1963). Weckowicz and Whitney (1960) have also demonstrated an increase of the illusory effect in the Muler-Lyer illusion with schizophrenic patients. Susceptibility to the illusion was presumed to indicate a reduced ability to ignore the irrelevant lines and to attend selectively to the irrelevant part of the figure. In another study Weckowicz (1960) found schizophrenic patients to perform considerably poorer than other psychiatric patients on a task involving the identification of forms embedded in an irrelevant background.

Weckowicz suggested that these and other findings of perceptual anomalies in schizophrenic patients were all related to a deficit in perceptual selectivity and that this failure should also be evident in thought process where abstract thinking is dependent upon a high degree of selectivity. Some support for this hypothesis was found in an investigation (Weckowicz & Blewett, 1959) into the association between reduced perceptual constancy and impaired concept formation. Here it was found that schizophrenic patients with poor perceptual constancy performed very poorly on tests of conceptual thinking.

Such findings led these workers to formulate the following model of attentional breakdown in schizophrenia.

> There is a redundancy of information in the sensory input from the environment to the organism. The "cognitive process" is to a great extent concerned with the reduction of this redundancy and with "selection" or "abstraction" of some infor-

mation according to certain principles and suppression of all other information. In the perceptual process it will manifest itself in the ability to see stable "things" or objects in spite of a constant change in the sensory input — the ability which is usually described as "constancy of perception". . . . . Their (schizophrenic's) perception is more influenced by the here and now factors of the immediate situation and less by the experience of the past and the anticipation of the future. . . . There is some change in the filtering of stimulation. . . . The gates are open wide, the cortex is flooded with irrelevant information so that maintenance of set becomes difficult! (Weckowicz & Blewett, 1959).

In examining intragroup differences Weckowicz found that it was the nonparanoid, usually hebephrenic patients who demonstrated the greatest reduction in both size and distance constancy (Weckowicz, 1957; Weckowicz *et al.,* 1958). Patients with predominantly paranoid symptoms were sharply distinguished by showing either normal constancy or overestimation of size and distance. In the later studies by Weckowicz and Blewett (1959) showing a positive correlation between perceptual anomalies and poor conceptual thinking, both these impairments were found to be most evident in the hebephrenic, nonparanoid patient. Similar results have been found by Raush (1952) in his investigations of size estimation in paranoid and nonparanoid groups. In another study of size constancy Lovinger (1956) found that schizophrenic patients with poor contact with reality (predominantly hebephrenic type) showed less constancy than schizophrenic patients in good contact with their environment. As the majority of these constancy experiments have been restricted to chronic patients, it is uncertain to what extent the findings also apply to acutely ill patients.

D. MENTAL SET

Shakow (1963) has put forward a model of the schizophrenic deficit, which embraces disturbances in both attentional and intentional behavior. He suggests that the schizophrenic is impaired in his ability to maintain major sets so that his behavior is controlled by a number of independent and isolated segmental sets. Goldstein (1944) had already referred to the schizophrenic patient's inability to hold the mental set required to maintain an adequate state of readiness to respond to stimuli. Shakow's concept of major or generalized sets is a more complex one involving some aspects of Coghill's theory of integrated action and Cameron's concept of homeostasis. He suggests that one of the main functions of the cortex is to control, integrate, and organize current input and past experience in such a way as to produce goal-directed, integrated behavior. In the schizophrenic patient, the failure of the central mechanism to control and integrate input results in areas of behavior being segmentalized or dissociated, and thus functioning independently. One effect of this lack of integration is that the schizophrenic patient becomes preoccupied with the mechanics of processes rather than with their unified ends.

> There is increased awareness and preoccupation with the ordinarily disregarded details of existence—the details which normal people spontaneously forget, train themselves, or get trained rigorously to disregard. He is (the schizophrenic), as in the case of the centipede of the fable, so deeply concerned about the way his feet move that he loses sight of where they should be going (Shakow, 1962).

In his discussion of the consequences of this failure of cortical integration Shakow (1962) comes close to the view of a breakdown in selective attention advanced by those who have studied overinclusiveness, disturbed perceptual constancy, and distractibility in schizophrenic patients.

> It is as if, in the scanning process which takes place before the response to a stimulus is made, the schizophrenic is unable to select out the material relevant for optimal response. He apparently cannot free himself from the irrelevant among the numerous possibilities available for choice. In other words, that function which is of equal importance as a response *to* stimuli, namely the protection *against* the response to stimuli, is abeyant (Shakow, 1962).

Later he goes on to comment that

> these irrelevant associations to which the normal is also subject but to a much lesser degree would appear to arise from three sources: chance distractors from the environment; irrelevancies from the stimulus situation; and irrelevancies from past experience—the mere presence of these irrelevant factors—seems to lead the schizophrenic to give them focal rather than ground significance, signal rather noise import (Shakow, 1962).

Many of Shakow's ideas on the schizophrenic deficit have been gathered from repeated studies of the reaction time performance of these patients. In accordance with others who have used this procedure, Shakow finds that schizophrenic patients demonstrate considerably slower simple reaction times than do other patients and normal subjects (Huston, Shakow, & Riggs, 1937). Normal performance on reaction time improves if the subject is aware that the preparatory interval is regular and therefore predictable. Shakow's work illustrates that the schizophrenic patient is unable to take advantage of this predictability to improve his performance unless the preparatory interval is a very brief one (not more than 6 seconds). He is also greatly affected by the immediately preceding interval so that when a series of longer preparatory intervals, giving longer reaction times, precedes a series of shorter ones his reaction times for the shorter series are markedly lengthened (Zahn, Rosenthal, & Shakow, 1961). In a choice reaction time situation the performance of the schizophrenic patient is significantly affected by the presence of irrelevant stimuli which do not evoke a response. In one of these reaction time studies Rodnick and Shakow (1940) developed a "set index" based upon the length of reaction time and its relationships with regular and irregular preparatory periods. This index successfully differentiated schizophrenic and normal groups without any degree of overlap.

Shakow and his colleagues have interpreted the "set index" as a reliable measure of the patient's inability to maintain a required mental set. It has been suggested by Knehr (1954) that the set index in reaction time studies is contaminated by intelligence and that differences in the set index between schizophrenic and nonschizophrenic subjects may merely reflect the lower intellectual level of the former group. This possibility was considered by Tizard and Venables (1956) who repeated the Rodnick and Shakow experiment with groups of schizophrenics, normals, and a group of intellectually subnormal adults. Their results tend to refute Knehr's criticism in that the subnormal subject's set indices were comparable to those of the normal subjects, while those of the schizophrenic patients were significantly reduced. Later the Worcester group (Rosenthal, Lawlor, Zahn, & Shakow, 1960) found no correlation between the set index and a performance test of intelligence but a highly significant positive correlation between the index and a rating of schizophrenic disorganization.

Although Shakow's studies have been concerned mainly with chronic patients, he is of the opinion that acute patients show the same type of attentive difficulties. The main difference between these two subgroups noted by Shakow is in the patient's affective reaction to the involuntary broadening of his attention. Shakow suggested that acute patients are at first excited by this wider area of experience and react to it with the same fascinated delight as the LSD subject reacts to a somewhat similar experience. The chronic patient, who has become more adapted to such changes in his attention, shows no particular affective reaction. However, Shakow (1963) does report clear-cut differences between paranoid and hebephrenic patients:

> In 58 measurements which we made on groups of normal, paranoid and hebephrenic subjects, we found the paranoid to be nearer than normal in 31 instances and the hebephrenic nearer the normal in only 7 instances. In 20 instances in six quite varied experiments, however, the paranoid and hebephrenic subjects' scores fell on either side of the normals. Thus, these two groups seem consistently to deal with situations in distinctive ways, giving quite different "styles of response."

Shakow (1962) summarizes his observations on these intragroup differences in a vivid analogy of the schizophrenic patient walking through a wood.

> If he is of the paranoid persuasion he sticks even more closely than the normal person to the path through the forest, examining each tree along the path, and sometimes even each tree's leaves, with meticulous care—if at the other extreme, he follows the hebephrenic pattern then he acts as though there were no paths for he strays off the obvious ones entirely, . . . he is attracted—by any and all trees, and even the undergrowth and floor of the forest in a superficial, flitting way, apparently forgetting in the meantime about the place he wants to get to—my impression is that the acute patient in the same forest undergoes a multitude of fairly new experiences reacting highly effectively, for instance, to new and unusual patterns of light on the leaves, or to novel and subtle patterns of form in the branches.

A commonly reported feature of the clinical behavior of chronic schizophrenic patients is their tendency to perseverate, offering responses which are appropriate to preceding rather than to current stimuli. This aspect of mental set has been explored in recent studies by Soviet psychologists. In a recent paper Bzhalava (1965) used a technique suggested by Uznadze's concept of fixated set. The initial procedure involves placing two balls of markedly different size on the open hand of blindfolded subjects and requesting them to indicate which hand holds the larger ball. If repeated rehearsals of this procedure are followed by the presentation of balls of equal size, it is found that most subjects will continue for some time to perceive the balls as being of unequal size. Continued presentation of the equal balls ultimately results in an abandonment of this fixated set and a regaining of correct perception. The number of presentations of equal stimuli required to extinguish the formerly established mental set provides a measure of its strength. The procedure may also be repeated in other modalities, using for example, tachistoscopic presentations of circles to examine fixation of set in the visual modality. With epileptic patients Bzhalava found that a strongly fixated set was established in the tactile modality but only a small minority of patients showed a fixated set in the visual modality. However, in schizophrenic patients a fixated set was easily and quickly established in either modality. Furthermore, once a fixated set is established to stimuli in one modality it is immediately transferred to stimuli in any other modality without additional rehearsal in the second modality. Thus, a set quickly established to perceive two equal circles as unequal was carried over when the patient was subsequently presented with pairs of lines or triangles. This diffuseness of sensory adaptation of the schizophrenic patients is interpreted by Bzhalava (1965) as indicative of volitional impairment:

> The patient strives to dispense with the necessity of having recourse to a volitional act required for the overcoming of an experimentally set-up difficulty. . . . A clear impression is produced that for schizophrenics, fixation of *intention* is unattainable, i.e. they cannot be brought to act on the basis of a specifically volitional set and thus to switch over from the first level of activity to the second.

This type of inability to switch from one mental set to another has been observed in other studies of schizophrenic performance. Huston, Cohen, and Senf (1955) found that schizophrenic subjects had great difficulty in shifting attention between different types of tasks under different conditions of distraction. Their observations led them to conclude that the fixated set of schizophrenics was more evident in situations demanding the shifting of attention between stimuli open to personal and social interpretations, and less evident in more objective tasks (e.g., arithmetical calculations). Shakow also refers to the motivational deficit in schizophrenic patients in his concept of neophobia:

> Curiosity and search for stimulation seem particularly weak in the schizophrenic. He appears to suffer from the kind of neophobia I have alluded to—the disturbance that results from entry into new settings, from contact with the uncertain. He seems to prefer old already experienced situations. His lack of involvement with his environment, seen for example, in his poor co-operation, is another aspect of this deficit.

Other workers (e.g., Hunt & Cofer, 1944) have also suggested that the results of most reaction time studies of schizophrenic patients may simply reflect the patient's reduced responsiveness to social situations and to a general lack of volition rather than to a specifically cognitive impairment. A somewhat similar view has been put by Morris (1963) who has criticized the assumption made by McGhie and Chapman (1961) that the reports of their schizophrenic patients refer only to disturbed attention. In her own similar study she finds that the reports of schizophrenic patients suggest a disturbance of what she terms intentional as well as attentional behavior. Intentional behavior refers to reduced volition, poor responsiveness to social stimulation, and a general low level of motivation.

While it is thus well established that schizophrenic patients have difficulty in maintaining or switching required mental sets, it is less certain whether this is cognitive or motivational in origin.

E. Attention and Cognitive Control

The work of the Menninger group (Gardner, Holzman, Klein, Linton, & Spence, 1959) on cognitive attitudes has thrown some light on individual strategies in processing the external environment. Among the various cognitive strategies which have been examined by Gardner and others, two in particular are directly related to attentive behavior. One of these, scanning control, reflects differences in the extensiveness with which stimuli are sampled when attention is directed to any perceptual field. This factor is used to explain over and underestimations of the distance of objects in the center or periphery of the perceptual field. Such errors of judgment of apparent size or distance have been found to be related to the amount of time during which subjects "center" upon the stimuli in the course of making their judgments. Long centrations (extensive scanning) have been shown to be related to underestimation of the stimulus, while minimal scanning is associated with overestimation of the stimulus. The other attentive principle of cognitive control, field articulation, refers to differences in attending to complex perceptual fields and particularly to the inhibition of other nonessential aspects of the perceptual field. Factor analytic study of scores on tests measuring scanning and field articulation principles (Gardner & Long, 1962) have indicated that these two cognitive control principles are independent measures of attentional behavior.

Silverman (1964a,b) has attempted to apply this approach to the problem of attentional dysfunction in schizophrenia. Surveying a number of perceptual studies of schizophrenic patients, Silverman (1964a) concludes that nonparanoid patients show a tendency toward underestimation of stimuli and a heightened autokinetic effect, both of which have been shown by Gardner to be associated with minimal scanning. On tests which purport to measure the field articulation factor these patients show undifferentiated and poor field articulation. Paranoid schizophrenics tend, in contrast, to be excessive scanners and have high field articulation scores (Silverman, 1964b). Although Silverman's results give a picture of the paranoid patient as hyper-alert and excessively scanning his environment, this is not taken to mean that he is cortically "overloaded." Silverman employs Brunner's (1957) concept of "cognitive filtering" to suggest that the sensory input of the paranoid patient is excessively scanned only to facilitate the rejection of input likely to be disturbing to the patient. This process of "ideational gating" ensures that only stimuli which are acceptable to the paranoid patient's thinking are allowed to enter consciousness at a cortical level:

Things and events either fit the paranoid schizophrenic's delusional system or they do not exist. Under these conditions, a state of information overload—a state which appears to characterise certain other schizophrenias—is not possible. For there are only two kinds of information to be processed—that which is congruent with one's delusional system and that which is not (Silverman, 1964b)

Silverman's conclusions are thus to some extent congruent with those of others in their differentiation of the paranoid and nonparanoid groups. However, in contrast to most other theories, Silverman sees the schizophrenic patient as actively monitoring out stimuli to defend himself against a hostile environment. In searching for the genesis of this defensive system which ultimately corrupts the attentive process, Silverman looks toward the early social experiences of the schizophrenic patient. His interpretation thus lines up with other theories, such as Bannister's (1962) serial invalidation hypothesis, which regard schizophrenia as a product of intrapsychic conflict and repeated environmental trauma. Some of Silverman's (1964b) work suggests that the extensive field scanning shown by paranoid patients lessens as the patients become more chronic. Silverman has also made the suggestion that some of the differences in attentional behavior of acute and chronic patients may be a consequence of the chronic patient adopting certain strategies which enables him to deal more effectively with an environment which threatens to overload and engulf him. A similar point has been made by McGhie and his colleagues who noted that their chronic patients often resorted to protective activities (such as plugging their ears and sitting with their eyes closed) to reduce the amount of environmental stimulation and aid their concentration. Other studies (Harris, 1957; Bryant, 1961) suggest that minimal scanning behavior is more typical of process schizophrenia, and that extensive scanning behavior is more prominent in reactive patients.

F. SUSTAINED ATTENTION

As an inability to sustain attention over a period of time has often been observed to be a characteristic feature of the clinical picture of schizophrenia, it might be expected that vigilance studies would be a rewarding area of research. That there have been very few systematic investigations of schizophrenic vigilance performance may possibly reflect the acceptance of the fact that such patients are less likely to be highly enough motivated to cooperate on such relatively lengthy tasks. One of the few reports of research in this area is that by Claridge (1960, 1967) using a psychotic group composed mainly of schizophrenic patients. Claridge used an auditory vigilance task consisting of a 30-minute recording of random digits read out at the rate of one per second. The signals to be detected were runs of three consecutive odd digits. Although the overall vigilance performance of the psychotic group was found to be significantly poorer than that of the normal subjects, the score variance of the psychotic group was twice that of the normal controls. In seeking to reduce the heterogenity of the schizophrenic group scores, Claridge found that the vigilance performance of process schizophrenics was greatly inferior to that of reactive schizophrenics. Vigilance performance has frequently been accepted as an indirect measure of arousal level, on the grounds that a falling rate of signal detection is due to reduced arousal consequent upon the monotonous conditions of the task. Such studies therefore link up with the growing number of investigations of variations of arousal level in schizophrenia.

G. Arousal Level

Investigations of the arousal level of schizophrenic patients have been well reviewed by Venables (1966), and more extensively by Claridge (1967) in his recent book on the subject. This discussion will be limited to a brief summary of the results of some studies which have a particular bearing upon attentional deficit in schizophrenia.

Although EEG studies of schizophrenic patients have produced discouragingly ambiguous results, agreement has been reached that fast or choppy records are characteristic of some schizophrenic patients (Davis & Davis, 1939; Jasper, Fitzpatrick, & Solomon, 1939; Davis, 1942; Hill, 1957). Such EEG findings have suggested that some schizophrenic patients function at an abnormally high level of cortical activation.

Further indirect support for this suggestion comes from the work of Mirsky and his colleagues in the U.S.A. (Mirsky, Primac, Ajmone Marsan, Rosvold, & Stevens, 1960). Mirsky has used a signal detection task developed by Rosvold et al. (1956) as a means of measuring variations of attention in brain-damaged patients. This test, the Continuous Performance Test (CPT) employs the visual presentation, by means of a revolving drum, of single letters, briefly exposed one at a time through a small aperture. The test has two conditions, the first requiring the subject to respond by key pressing only when the letter X is exposed and the second requiring a response only when the X appears following an A. Previous use of this test in the assessment of brain-damaged patients had already suggested that performance on the CPT is particularly vulnerable to damage to the midbrain centers assumed to mediate arousal. Further support for this interpretation was given by Kornetsky and Mirsky's (1966) finding that drugs such as Chlorpromazine, which are known to act upon the midbrain reticular system, directly affect performance on the CPT. The Wechsler Digit Symbol Substitution Test (DSST) was selected by Mirsky as representing a task dependent upon cortical, but independent of sub-cortical midbrain structures. The validity of this contrast between these two tests is supported by Kornetsky and Mirsky's (1966) study which showed that moderate doses of barbiturates, known to act mainly at a cortical level, impair the performance on the DSST and not on the CPT. On the basis of such inferences from previous findings it was postulated that schizophrenic patients would do badly on the CPT but reasonably well on the DSST, which does not depend upon arousal level for its exe-cution. This was confirmed by Orzack and Kornetsky (1966) and their results would appear to support further the hypothesis that the schizo-phrenic patient is overaroused. However, Orzack and Kornetsky noted that this indirect evidence of a higher level of activation was true only of some schizophrenic patients, others displaying no such signs of high arousal levels.

Another test which has been taken to provide an indirect measure of the level of cortical activation is the Spiral After Effect (SAE). When a rotating spiral is fixated for some time it produces an aftereffect of appar-ent movement in the opposite direction. This visual illusion has been for long of interest to psychologists interested in perceptual anomalies and recently a detailed review of its use has been published by Holland (1965). Its main interest to clinical psychologists has been its application in measuring changes due to brain damage, but more recently it has been employed as a correlative measure of arousal. Several investigations have found a significant correlation between the SAE and alpha blocking, sug-gesting that longer aftereffects are indicative of high arousal levels (Claridge & Herrington, 1963).

The application of the SAE to schizophrenic patients has produced conflicting results. Whereas some studies (Price & Deabler, 1955; Krish-namoorti & Shagass, 1964) have found no differences between schizo-phrenic and normal groups, others (Claridge, 1960; Herrington & Clar-idge, 1965) have reported a significantly longer aftereffect in schizophrenic patients. In a more recent investigation, using a larger group of 67 psychotic patients (all but 5 of whom were schizophrenic), Claridge (1967) replicated his previous findings which support the hy-pothesis of a higher level of arousal in schizophrenia. However, the use of the spiral aftereffect as an indirect measure of arousal level should be viewed with some caution. In his review of the literature on the SAE Hol-land (1965) raises the possibility that variations in the effect may reflect more superficial aspects of behavior such as eye movement rate or the ability to fixate the moving spiral. The findings of a recent investigation, using the SAE with brain-damaged subjects (Efstathiou & Morant, 1966) suggests that failure to experience the effect may be due to inattentiveness rather than to the influence of any specific neurological damage on the experience of movement aftereffect.

As there is much in common between both the operational definitions and techniques of measuring the arousal level and the orienting response as used in Russian psychology, any information on variations of orienting responses in schizophrenics would appear to be relevant to the present issue. Most of the Russian work reports that the majority of schizophrenic patients are characterized by a weakness or absence of the orienting response, indicating a low arousal level. Studies by Stretslova (1955), based mainly on measurement of variations of pupil dilation under stimulation, found that about two thirds of the schizophrenics examined gave weak or absent orienting responses. Other investigations (Traugott, Balonov, Kauffman, & Luchko, 1958; Gamburg, 1958) report reduced orienting responses of schizophrenic patients to a variety of visual, auditory, and tactile stimuli. However, most of these workers have also noted that some schizophrenic patients show unusually strong orienting responses which are difficult to extinguish.

As in considering all other aspects of schizophrenic performance, it is obvious that the interpretation of arousal studies is made more difficult by ignoring intragroup differences.

Venables and Wing (1962) have employed the technique of measuring the fusion threshold of paired light flashes as an indication of arousal. This method of assessment is based upon the earlier findings (Lindsley, 1958; Steriade & Demetrescu, 1962) that the ability to differentiate light flashes presented in close temporal proximity increases with a heightening of the level of activation. Using this method Venables and Wing (1962) found nonparanoid patients to have an abnormally high fusion threshold, indicating a state of overarousal. In his use of the SAE, Claridge (1967) found nonparanoid patients to have a higher aftereffect than paranoid patients, again indicating a higher arousal in the former group. However, this relationship does not appear to hold where measures of autonomic arousal are used. Claridge (1967) has reviewed his own and other related findings which suggest that paranoid patients are overaroused on tests purporting to measure autonomic arousal such as the Sedation Threshold.

Comparisons between acute and chronic patients also fail to yield any clear-cut conclusions. Using the EEG coefficient of variation as an inverse measure of cortical arousal, Goldstein and his colleagues (Goldstein, Murphe, Sugarmann, Pfeiffer, & Jenney, 1963; Goldstein, Sugarmann, Stolberg, Murphe, & Pfeiffer, 1965) found the activation level of chronic schizophrenics to be unusually high. In the Venables and Wing (1962) study and in a later study by Venables (1967) a positive association was established between schizophrenic social withdrawal and a high threshold for the resolution of paired light flashes and paired auditory clicks (both indicating overarousal). These findings might be taken to indicate that chronic or process schizophrenic patients (who would be expected to be more withdrawn) are at a higher level of arousal. This view is given added support by the findings of Venables and Wing (1962) that chronic schizophrenics show a high level of autonomic arousal (as indicated by the level of skin potential) and that again these measures are correlated with clinical ratings of social withdrawal.

The use of the Sedation Threshold Test as a measure of arousal also supports the view that chronic schizophrenic patients are overaroused and acute patients underaroused. Shagass, who originally developed the technique, reported (1960) that acute schizophrenics who had been ill for less than 6 months had the lowest sedation thresholds of any clinical group studied. In this and other studies (Boudreau, 1958; Krishnamoorti & Shagass, 1964) more chronically ill schizophrenics were reported to have high thresholds (indicating an overaroused state). Claridge's (1967) study of a large group of schizophrenic patients used a somewhat different technique of assessing sedation thresholds but arrived at the same findings of low thresholds for acutely ill patients. Some workers have produced further evidence of such arousal differences by assessing the effects of depressant drugs on the level of attention and general clinical state of schizophrenic patients. This approach has indicated that chronic patients improve and show a nearer normal level of attention under such drugs which are known to lower arousal levels (Fulcher, Gallagher, & Pfeiffer, 1957; Stevens & Derbyshire, 1958). Work repeated by Williams (1953), Malmo, Shagass, and Davies (1951), and Venables and Wing (1962) adds further support to the view that autonomic arousal is higher in chronic patients.

Findings related to the arousal level of schizophrenic patients are complicated by the somewhat ambiguous nature of the concept of arousal itself and particularly by the variety of techniques used in its assessment. Some workers (e.g., Sternbach, 1960) have found no association between EEG measures of cortical arousal and other measures of autonomic reactivity in normal subjects. Hume and Claridge (1965) found only a slight and insignificant positive correlation between autonomic arousal as measured by skin potential and a two-flash threshold measure of cortical arousal.

In contrast to this Venables (1963) has found a negative correlation between skin potential and two-flash threshold measures of arousal in normal subjects. Other workers (Darrow, Pathman, & Kronenberg, 1946; Stennett, 1957) suggest that the association between autonomic and EEG activity may depend on the existing arousal level, positive correlations between the two being more likely at high levels of arousal. It would therefore appear unwise at this stage to readily equate results of investigations using different measurements of arousal as if they represented a unified measure of one specific arousal process.

The interrelation of arousal measures in schizophrenic patients is perhaps even more ambiguous. Venables (1963) has found that the skin potential and paired light flash thresholds are positively associated in schizophrenic subjects in contrast to his own findings with normal subjects where he reports a dissociation between these two aspects of arousal. Venables (1967) suggests that these findings might be interpreted to suggest that in some (more chronic) schizophrenic patients, autonomic and cortical systems of arousal operate in parallel, cortical activity being uncontrolled by the normal regulatory action of the reticular system. In this view the schizophrenic patient is seen to suffer from an inability to control selectively his responsiveness to significant stimuli, resulting in an indiscriminate arousal reaction to all stimuli.

Claridge (1967) has used the distinction between cortical and autonomic measures of arousal in a somewhat different way to produce a more comprehensive psychophysiological model of arousal. The model proposed by Claridge involves two functionally related arousal mechanisms which he terms the tonic arousal system and the arousal modifying system. The function of the former tonic system is to maintain the individual's overall level of arousal while the second modifying system regulates the activity level of the tonic arousal system and guards the central nervous system from overstimulation. Apart from this homeostatic role, the modulating system also filters incoming information to facilitate the reception of relevant and inhibit the reception of irrelevant data. Claridge's diagnostic representation of the two linked systems is illustrated in Fig. 1.

It is postulated that in schizophrenia the two systems become functionally dissociated due to a breakdown in the feedback mechanisms preserving the normal balance. The effects of such imbalance will depend upon which of the two systems are predominant in their function. If the dissociation results in a weakening of the modulating system, disinhibition of the tonic system would cause an abnormally high level of arousal. As incoming information would no longer be monitored, attention would become less selective and directed in its operation. However, if imbalance resulted in a weakening of the tonic system and strengthening of the modulating system's functions, arousal level would fall and attention would become severely narrowed.

This model helps to clarify the conflicting and often contradictory findings that schizophrenic patients are over- or underaroused. In this formu-

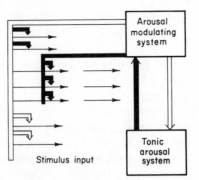

FIG. 1. Diagnostic representation of the two linked systems – tonic arousal and arousal modifying system. The thick black arrows represent activating or facilitating influences and the white arrows represent inhibitory processes (from Claridge, 1967, p. 187).

lation all schizophrenics suffer from both high and low levels of arousal, depending upon the arousal components being considered. Although the two systems are obvious parallels to the cortical and subcortical centers proposed in neurophysiological models, Claridge wisely refuses to use such terms on the grounds that they would imply a localization of function which would be out of context in a model based upon psychophysiological findings. While Claridge's dual arousal model has a certain theoretical appeal in its ability to resolve some of the hitherto discrepant findings, much of his evidence is based on the rather tenuous association between the spiral aftereffect and cortical arousal.

IV. Summary and Conclusions

There seems little doubt that the mechanisms responsible for the direction and control of attention are disrupted in many schizophrenic patients. This disturbance may manifest itself in heightened distractibility, failure to hold and pursue required mental sets, abnormal levels of arousal, or in other directions considered in this review. As attention is the first essential stage in coming to terms with the environment, it seems likely that a disturbance at this level will have a reverberating effect on all other mental functions involved at later stages of the learning process. To this extent, the attentional deficit may be regarded as a basic part of schizophrenic psychopathology, although its underlying cause remains obscure. The closer study of intragroup differences provides a slightly clearer picture of the clinical significance of the attentive deficit. However, many of the pieces are still missing and a great deal more research is obviously necessary before a clear picture emerges of the attentional dysfunction which appears to be a prominent feature of at least some varieties of schizophrenia.

There is clear experimental support for those clinicians who would mark off the paranoid group from that of all other forms of schizophrenia. Patients with a predominantly paranoid symptomatology demonstrate a highly selective type of attention which enables them to screen out extraneous stimulation more efficiently than normal subjects. It is possible that the suggestion made by such workers as Silverman is correct and that the filter mechanism of the paranoid patient is set to attend selectively only to events which might interfere with the rationale of his delusional system. Some years ago Cameron (1951) described how the paranoid patient restricts himself

> to watching with his newly acquired reaction sensitivity and making selections which confirm his favoured hypotheses — the patient excludes whatever he cannot handle regardless of its importance — everything that can be made congruent gets absorbed into the sectors of the developing (delusional) system, even although this system may not correspond with the social fact.

However, this distinction is blurred by the ambiguous nature of the criteria used for diagnosing the paranoid group. Many schizophrenics entertain transient delusions during the course of their illness although these may be embedded in a welter of other schizophrenic symptoms. In other patients, a highly elaborated system of delusional thinking is a prominent feature of the illness and may exist in the absence of other schizophrenic symptoms. Some clinicians would feel that the inclusion of such paranoid patients within the schizophrenic group merely obscures the clinical picture, and that they should be regarded as constituting an entirely separate psychotic group. The findings of most studies of disturbed attention in schizophrenic patients would support such a conclusion.

Consistent findings have also been reported in respect of another subgroup of schizophrenia which stands in vivid contrast to the paranoid group. It is probably of little importance whether we label this subgroup "hebephrenic," "nuclear" or "process." The patients in this category show an insidious onset to their illness, marked thought disorder, loss of affect, and a tendency to progress to a chronic deteriorating state. The clinical picture is almost identical with the original Kraepelinian description of dementia praecox. The experimental work with this group suggests that the normal processes of selection and inhibition governing attention have broken down so that the patients suffer from a marked inability to attend selectively to stimuli in such a way that only relevant information is processed. The effect of this impairment of selective attention on the performance of the schizophrenic patients will vary with a number of factors, including the amount of information to be processed, in any situation, the particular modality in which the information is presented, and the rate of arrival of information. There is some suggestion that the breakdown in selective attention exhibited by these patients is the result of a state of overarousal of the reticular activating system, or of a failure in the normal homeostatic control between subcortical and cortical centers. There is also some suggestion that this group of patients may have an underlying organic pathology.

The issue regarding changes in attention between the acute and chronic phases of the illness is more obscure. There is some evidence that during the acute phase, selective attention is less impaired and that any impairment is variable so that the patient's behavior may fluctuate widely from one time to another. Measures of arousal suggest that the basic level of activation changes during the progress of the illness. Most psychological measurements of attentional dysfunction, with the exception of paranoid patients, demonstrate a widening of attention. It is possible that any differences which do exist might reflect various behavioral strategies adopted by the chronic patient to reduce the flow of stimulation to a more tolerable level. Another source of difficulty in making comparisons of the acute and chronic patient lies in the fact that chronic patients are more likely to show behavioral changes induced by institutionalization. Such changes are notoriously difficult to distinguish from changes which might be an inherent part of the disease process. Apart from differences in the social environment of the two groups, chronic patients are exposed to a different diet, different pharmacological regimes, and different therapeutic attitudes. They are likely to be considerably older than acute patients so that the aging process may itself act as an uncontrolled variable. The general motivation of the more recently ill acute patient is likely to be considerably higher than his chronic counterpart who may value less the reinforcement of pleasing the investigator by cooperating well. Indeed, in a modern research and teaching hospital the chronic patient may be rendered "test-sophisticated" and blasé by repeated investigations at the hands of a changing parade of enthusiastic research workers. All such factors may easily interact to confuse the picture of acute/chronic differences. The overlapping between the acute/chronic dichotomy and other subclassifications of schizophrenia is likely to confound the picture even more. There is a clear need for prospective longitudinal studies, to examine changes in attentional behavior of patients from the early acute stages of their illness through to the more chronic phase.

References

Bannister, D. The nature and measurement of schizophrenic thought disorder. *Journal of Mental Science*, 1962, **108**, 825.

Bateson, G., Jackson, D. D., Haley, J., & Weakland, J. H. Toward a theory of schizophrenia. *Behavioral Science*, 1956, **1**, 251, 264.

Bleuler, E. *Dementia praecox or the group of schizophrenias.* New York, International Universities Press, 1950.

Boudreau, D. A valuation of the sedation threshold test. *A.M.A. Archives of Neurology and Psychiatry*, 1958, **80**, 771.

Bowers, M. V., & Freedman, D. Psychedelic experiences in acute psychoses. *A.M.A. Archives of General Psychiatry*, 1966, **15**, 240.

Broadbent, D. E. *Perception and communication.* New York: Macmillan (Pergamon), 1958.

Brown, G. W. Length of hospital stay in schizophrenia: A review of statistical studies. *Acta Psychiatrica et Neurologica Scandinavica*, 1960, **35**, 414, 430.

Bruner, J. S. On perceptual readiness. *Psychological Review,* 1957, **64**, 123.

Bryant, A. R. P. An investigation of process-reaction schizophrenia with relation to perception of visual space. Unpublished doctoral dissertation, University of Utah, 1961.

Bzhalava, I. T. On the psychopathology of fixated set in epilepsy and schizophrenia. *Cortex,* 1965, **1**, 4, 493.

Cameron, N. Reasoning, regression and communication in schizophrenics. *Psychological Monographs*, 1938, **50** (*1*, Whole No. 221).

Cameron, N. Deterioration and regression in schizophrenic thinking. *Journal of Abnormal and Social Psychology*, 1939, **34**, 265.

Cameron, N. Perceptual organisation and behaviour pathology. In R. R. Blacke and G. V. Ramsey (Eds.), *Perception: An approach to personality.* New York: Ronald Press, 1951.

Chapman, J., & McGhie, A. A comparative study of disordered attention in schizophrenia. *Journal of Mental Science*, 1962, **108**, 487.

Chapman, L. J. Distractibility in the conceptual performance of schizophrenics. *Journal of Abnormal and Social Psychology*, 1956, **53**, 286.

Claridge, G. S. The excitation-inhibition balance in neurotics. In H. J. Eysenck (Ed.), *Experiments in personality.* London: Routledge & Keegan Paul, 1960.

Claridge, G. S. *Personality and arousal. A psychophysiological study of psychiatric disorder.* New York: Macmillan (Pergamon), 1967.

Claridge, G. S., & Herrington, R. N. An E.E.G. correlate of the Archimedes spiral aftereffect and its relationship with personality. *Behaviour Research and Therapy*, 1963, **1**, 217.

Crookes, T. G. Literalness in schizophrenia. *British Journal of Medical Psychology*, 1957, **30**, 99.

Darrow, C. W., Pathman, J., & Kronenberg, G. A level of autonomic activity and electroencephalogram. *Journal of Experimental Psychology*, 1946, **36**, 355.

Davis, P. A. Comparative study of the E.E.G.'s of schizophrenic and manic-depressive patients. *American Journal of Psychiatry*, 1942, **99**, 210.

Davis, P. A., & Davis, H. The electroencephalograms of psychotic patients. *American Journal of Psychiatry*, 1939, **95**, 1007.

Efstathiou, A., & Morant, R. B. Persistence of the waterfall illusion after-effect as a test of brain damage. *Journal of Abnormal Psychology*, 1966, **71**, 300.

Eitinger, L., Laane, C. J., & Langfeldt, G. The prognostic value of the clinical picture and the therapeutic value of physical treatment in schizophrenia and the schizophrenoform states. *Acta Psychiatrica Neurologica Scandinavica*, 1958, **33**, 33.

Fleishman, E. A. Dimensional analysis of psychomotor abilities. *Journal of Experimental Psychology*, 1954, **48**, 54.

Fulcher, J. H., Gallagher, W. H., & Pfeiffer, C. C. Comparative lucid intervals after amobarbitol, CO_2, and arecoline in chronic schizophrenia. *American Medical Association of Neurological Psychiatry*, 1957, **75**, 392.

Gamburg, A. L. The orienting and defensive reactions in simple and paranoid forms of schizophrenia. In L. G. Voronin (Ed.), *The orienting reflex and orienting-investigating behaviour*. Moscow: Moscow Acad. Pedagogical Sci., 1958.

Gardner, R. W., Holzman, P. S., Klein, G. S., Linton, H. B., & Spence, D. P. Cognitive control; A study of individual consistencies in cognitive behaviour. *Psychological Issues*, 1959, **1**, 4.

Gardner, R. W., & Long, R. I. Control, defence, and centration effects; A study of scanning behaviour. *British Journal of Psychology*, 1962, **53**, 129.

Goldman-Eisler, F. The distribution of pause durations in speech. *Language and Speech*, 1961, **4**, 232.

Goldstein, K. Die Lokalisation in der Grosshirnrinde. In A. Bethe and E. Fisher (Eds.), *Hanbuch der normale und pathologischen physiologie*. Berlin: Springer, 1927.

Goldstein, K. Methodological approach to the study of schizophrenic thought disorder. In J. S. Kasanin (Ed.), *Language and thought in schizophrenia*. Berkeley: University of fornia Press, 1944.

Goldstein, L., Murphe, H. B., Sugarmann, A. A., Pfeiffer, C. C., & Jenney, E. H. Quantitative electroencephalographic analysis of naturally occurring schizophrenia and drug induced psychotic states in human males. *Clinical Pharmacology and Therapeutics*, 1963, **4**, 10.

Goldstein, L., Sugarmann, A. A., Stolberg, H., Murphe, H. B., & Pfeiffer, C. C. Electrocerebral activity in schizophrenics and non-psychotic subjects; Quantitative E.E.G. amplitude analysis. *Electroencephalography and Clinical Neurophysiology*, 1965, **19**, 350.

Hall, K. R. L., & Stride, E. Some factors affecting the reaction times to auditory stimulation in mental patients. *Journal of Mental Science*, 1954, **100**, 462.

Hamilton, V. Size constancy and cue responsiveness in psychoses. *British Journal of Psychology*, 1963, **54**, 25.

Harris, J. G. Size estimation of pictures as a function of thematic content for schizophrenic and normal subjects. *Journal of Personality*, 1957, **25**, 651.

Heath, R. G. A biochemical hypothesis on the aetiology of schizophrenia. In D. D. Jackson, (Ed.), *The aetiology of schizophrenia*. New York: Basic Books, 1960.

Herrington, R. N., & Claridge, G. S. Sedation threshold and Archimedes spiral effect in early psychoses. *Journal of Psychiatric Research*, 1965, **3**, 159.

Hill, D. Electroencephalogram in schizophrenia. In D. Richter (Ed.), *Schizophrenia: Somatic aspects*. New York: Macmillan (Pergamon), 1957.

Hoffer, A., & Osmond, H. The adrenochrome model and schizophrenia. *Journal of Nervous and Mental Diseases*, 1959, **128**, 18.

Holland, H. C. *The spinal after effect*. New York: Macmillan (Pergamon) 1965.

Hume, W. I., & Claridge, G. S. A comparison of two measures of arousal in normal subjects. *Life Sciences*, 1965, **4**, 545.

Hunt, J. McV., & Cofer, C. N. Physiological deficit. In J. McV. Hunt (Ed.), *Personality and behaviour disorders*. Vol. 2. New York: Ronald Press, 1944.

Huston, P. E., Cohen, B. D., & Senf, R. Shifting of set and goal orientation in schizophrenia. *Journal of Mental Science*, 1955, **101**, 423.

Huston, P. E., & Senf, R. Psychopathology of schizophrenia and depression; 1. Effect of amytal and amphetamine sulphate on level and maintenance of attention. *American Journal of Psychiatry*, 1952, **109**, 139.

Huston, P. E., Shakow, D., & Riggs, L. A. Studies of motor function in schizophrenia: II. Reaction time. *Journal of General Psychology*, 1937, **16**, 39.

Jasper, H. H., Fitzpatrick, C. P., & Solomon, P. Analogies and opposites in schizophrenia and epilepsy: Electroencephalographic and clinical studies. *American Journal of Psychiatry*, 1939, **95**, 835.

King, H. E. *Psychomotor aspects of mental disease*. Boston: Harvard University Press, 1954.

Knehr, C. A. Schizophrenic reaction time responses to variable preparatory intervals. *American Journal of Psychiatry*, 1954, **110**, 585.

Kornetsky, C., & Mirsky, A. F. On certain psychopharmacological and physiological differences between schizophrenic and normal persons. *Psychopharmacologia*, 1966, **8**, 309.

Kraepelin, E. *Lehrbuch der psychiatrie*. Leipzig: Barth, 1896.

Krishnamoorti, S. R., & Shagass, C. Some psychological test correlates of sedation threshold. In J. Wartis (Ed.), *Recent advances in biological psychiatry*. Vol. 6. New York: Plenum Press, 1964.

Laing, R. O. *The divided self*. London: Tavistock, 1960.

Langfeldt, G. *The schizophreniform states*. Copenhagen: Munksgaard, 1939.

Lawson, J. S. Disorders of attention and language in schizophrenia. Unpublished doctoral dissertation, University of St. Andrews, 1965.

Lawson, J. S., McGhie, A., & Chapman, J. Perception of speech in schizophrenia. *British Journal of Psychiatry*, 1964, **110**, 375.

Lawson, J. S., McGhie, A., & Chapman, J. Distractibility in schizophrenia and organic cerebral disease. *British Journal of Psychiatry*, 1966, **113**, 527.

Lidz, R. W., & Lidz, T. The family environment of schizophrenic patients. *American Journal of Psychiatry*, 1949, **106**, 332.

Lindsley, D. B. The reticular formation and perceptual discrimination. In H. H. Jasper *et al.* (Eds.), *Reticular formation of the brain*. London: Churchill, 1958.

Lovinger, E. Perceptual contact with reality in schizophrenia. *Journal of Abnormal and Social Psychology*, 1956, **52**, 87.

McDonald, N. Living with schizophrenia. *Canadian Medical Association Journal*, 1960, **82**, 218.

McGhie, A., & Chapman, J. Disorders of attention and perception in early schizophrenia. *British Journal of Medical Psychology*, 1961, **34**, 103.

McGhie, A., Chapman, J., & Lawson, J. S. Disturbances in selective attention in schizophrenia. *Proceedings of the Royal Society of Medicine*, 1964, **57**, 419.

McGhie, A., Chapman, J., and Lawson, J. S. The effect of distraction on schizophrenic performance: 1. Psychomotor ability. *British Journal of Psychiatry*, 1965, **111**, 391.

McGhie, A., Chapman, J., and Lawson, J. S. The effect of distraction on schizophrenic performance: 2. Perception and immediate memory. *British Journal of Psychiatry*, 1965, **111**, 383. (b)

Maher, B. A. *Principles of psychopathology*. New York: McGraw-Hill, 1966.

Malmo, R. B., Shagass, C., & Davies, F. H. Electromyographic studies of muscular tension in psychiatric patients under stress. *Journal of Clinical and Experimental Psychopathology*, 1951, **12**, 45.

Miller, G. A. Decision units in the perception of speech. *IRE (Institute of Radio Engineers), Transactions On Informal Theory*, 1963, **It-8**, 81.

Miller, G. A., & Selfridge, J. A. Verbal content and the recall of meaningful material. *American Journal of Psychology*, 1950, **63**, 176.

Mirksy, A. F., Primac, D. W., Ajmone Marsan, C., Rosvold, H. E., & Stevens, J. R. A comparison of patients with focal and non-focal epilepsy on a test of attention. *Experimental Neurology* 1960, **2**, 75.

Morris, J. An analysis of schizophrenic interviews. *British Journal of Medical Psychology,* 1963, **36**, 283.

Nidorf, L. J. The role of meaningfulness in the serial learning of schizophrenics. *Journal of Clinical Psychology,* 1964, **20**, 92.

Orzack, M. H., & Kornetsky, C. Attention dysfunction in schizophrenia. *Archives of General Psychiatry,* 1966, **14**, 323.

Payne, R. W. Cognitive abnormalities. In H. J. Eysenck (Ed.), *Handbook of abnormal psychology.* New York: Basic Books, 1961.

Payne, R. W. An object classification test as a measure of overinclusive thinking in schizophrenic patients. *British Journal of Social and Clinical Psychology,* 1962, **1**, 213.

Payne, R. W. The measurement and significance of overinclusive thinking and retardation in schizophrenic patients. In P. Hoch & J. Zubin (Eds.), *Psychopathology of Schizophrenia.* New York: Grune & Stratton, 1966.

Payne, R. W., & Caird, W. K. Reaction time, distractability and overinclusive thinking in psychotics. *Journal of Abnormal Psychology,* 1967 **72**, 112.

Payne, R. W., Caird, W. K., & Laverty, S. G. Overinclusive thinking and delusions in schizophrenic patients. *Journal of Abnormal and Social Psychology,* 1964, **68**, 562.

Payne, R. W., & Friedlander, D. A. A short battery of simply tests for measuring overinclusive thinking. *Journal of Mental Sciences,* 1962, **108**, 363.

Payne, R. W., & Hewlett, J. H. G. Thought disorder in psychotic patients. In H. J. Eysenck (Ed.), *Experiments on personality.* Vol. 2. London: Routledge & Kegan Paul, 1960.

Price, A. C., & Deabler, H. L. Diagnosis of organicity by means of spiral after-effect. *Journal of Consulting Psychology,* 1955, **19**, 299.

Raeburn, J. M., & Tong, J. E. Experiments on contextual constraint in schizophrenia. *British Journal of Psychiatry,* 1968, **114**, 43.

Raush, H. L. Perceptual constancy in schizophrenia. *Journal of Personality,* 1952, **21**, 176.

Rodnick, E. H., & Shakow, D. Set in the schizophrenic as measured by a composite reaction time index. *American Journal of Psychiatry,* 1940, **97**, 214.

Rosenthal, D., Lawlor, W. G., Zahn, P. P., & Shakow, D. The relationship of some aspects of mental set to degree of schizophrenic disorganisation. *Journal of Personality,* 1960, **28**, 26.

Rosvold, H. E., Mirsky, A. F., Sarason, I. G., Bransome, E. D., & Beck, L. H. A continuous performance test of brain damage. *Journal of Consulting Psychology,* 1956, **20**, 343.

Shagass, C. Drug thresholds as indicators of personality and affect. In L. Uhr and J. G. Miller (Eds.), *Drugs and behaviour.* New York: Wiley, 1954.

Shagass, C. The sedation threshold — a method for estimating tension in the psychiatric patient. *E.E.G. and Clinical Neurophysiology,* 1954, **6**, 221.

Shakow, D. Segmental set: A theory of the formal psychological deficit of schizophrenia. *Archives of General Psychiatry,* 1962, **6**, 1.

Shakow, D. Psychological deficit in schizophrenia. *Behavioral Science,* 1963, 8(4), 275.

Shakow, D., & Huston, P. E. Studies of motor function in schizophrenia. 1. Speed of tapping. *Journal of General Psychology,* 1936, **15**, 63.

Shannon, C. E. Prediction and entropy of printed English. *Bell System Technical Journal,* 1951, **30**, 50.

Silverman, J. Scanning control and cognitive filtering. *Journal of Consulting Psychology,* 1964, **28**, 385. (a)

Silverman, J. The problem of attention in the research and theory of schizophrenia. *Psychological Review,* 1964, **71**, 352. (b)

Smythies, J. R. Recent advances in the biochemistry of schizophrenia. In A. Coppen & A. Walk (Eds.), *Recent developments in schizophrenia.* London: Headley, 1967.

Stennett, R. G. The relationship of alpha amplitude to the level of palmar conductance. *Electroencephalography and Clinical Neurophysiology*, 1957, 9, 131.

Steriade, M., & Demetrescu, M. Reticular facilitation of responses to acoustic stimuli. *Electroencephalography and Clinical Neurophysiology*, 1962, 14, 21.

Sternbach, R. A. Two independent indices of activation. *Electroencephalography and Clinical Neurophysiology*, 1960, 12, 609.

Stevens, J. M. & Derbyshire, J. A. Shifts along the alert response continuum during remission of catatonic stupor with amobarbitol. *Psychosomatic Medicine*, 1958, 20, 99.

Stretslova, N. L. The characteristics of some unconditioned reflexes in schizophrenics. In *Proceedings of the all-union theoretical-practical conference dedicated to the centenary of S. S. Korsokov and to current psychological problems*. Moscow: Medgiz, 1955.

Tait, A. C. The physiopathology of schizophrenia. In T. F. Roger, R. M. Mowbray, and J. R. Roy (Eds.), *Topics of psychiatry*. London: Cassell, 1958.

Tizard, J., & Venables, P. H. Reaction time responses by schizophrenics, mental defectives and normal adults. *American Journal of Psychiatry*, 1956, 112, 803.

Toderick, A., Tait, A. C., & Marshall, E. F. Blood platelet 5-Hydroxytryptamine levels in psychiatric patients. *Journal of Mental Science*, 1960, 106, 884.

Traugott, N. N., Balonov, L. Y. A., Kauffman, D. A., & Luchko, A. E. O. On the dynamics of the destruction of orienting reflexes in certain psychotic syndromes. In *The orienting reflex and orienting investigating activity*. Moscow: Moscow Acad. Pedagogical Sci., 1958.

Venables, P. H. The effect of auditory and visual stimulation on the skin potential responses of schizophrenics. *Brain*, 1960, 83, 77.

Venables, P. H. The relationship between the level of skin potential and fusion of paired light flashes in schizophrenic and normal subjects. *Journal of Psychiatric Research*, 1963, 1, 279.

Venables, P. H. Input dysfunction in schizophrenia. In B. A. Maher (Ed.), *Progress in experimental personality research*. Vol. 1. New York: Academic Press, 1964.

Venables, P. H. The psychophysiological aspects of schizophrenia. *British Journal of Medical Psychology*, 1966, 39, 289.

Venables, P. H. The relation of two-flash and two-click thresholds to withdrawal in paranoid and non-paranoid schizophrenics. *British Journal of Social and Clinical Psychology*, 1967, 6, 60.

Venables, P. H., & O'Connor, N. Reaction times to auditory and visual stimulation in schizophrenic and normal subjects. *Quarterly Journal of Experimental Psychology*, 1959, 11, 175.

Venables, P. H., & Wing, J. K. Level of arousal and the sub-classification of schizophrenia. *Archives of General Psychiatry*, 1962, 7, 114.

Weckowicz, T. E. Size constancy in schizophrenic patients. *Journal of Mental Science*, 1957, 103, 432.

Weckowicz, T. E. Perception of hidden figures by schizophrenic patients. *Archives of General Psychiatry*, 1960, 2, 521.

Weckowicz, T. E., & Blewett, D. B. Size constancy and abstract thinking in schizophrenic patients. *Journal of Mental Science*, 1959, 105, 441.

Weckowicz, T. E., Sommer, R., & Hall, R. Distance constancy in schizophrenic patients. *Journal of Mental Science*, 1958, 104, 436.

Weckowicz, T. E., & Whitney, G. The Muller-Lyer illusion in schizophrenic patients. *Journal of Mental Science*, 1960, 106, 1002.

Williams, M. Psychophysiological responsiveness to psychological stress in early chronic schizophrenic reactions. *Psychosomatic Medicine*, 1953, 15, 456.

Yates, A. J. Data processing levels and thought disorder in schizophrenia. *Australian Journal of Psychology,* 1966, 18, 103.

Zahn, T. P., Rosenthal, D., & Shakow, D. Reaction time in schizophrenic and normal subjects in relation to the sequence of a series of regular preparatory intervals. *Journal of Abnormal and Social Psychology,* 1961, **63**, 161.

Zaslow, R. W. A new approach to the problems of conceptual thinking in schizophrenia. *Journal of Consulting Psychology,* 1950, **14**, 335.

ATTENTION AND SCHIZOPHRENIA

John M. Neale[1] *and Rue L. Cromwell*[2]

DEPARTMENTS OF PSYCHOLOGY AND PSYCHIATRY, VANDERBILT UNIVERSITY,
NASHVILLE, TENNESSEE

Impaired attention has been used in the past to describe a clinically prominent aspect of schizophrenia (Bleuler, 1951; McGhie & Chapman, 1961). For example, Bleuler referred to two distinct modes of attentional response among schizophrenics. Some schizophrenics were hypothesized to overemphasize pathologically their sense impressions, while others were hypothesized to ignore the outside world completely. Acute schizophrenic patients' descriptions of their attentional responses were reported by McGhie and Chapman (1961). Typical among these were statements such as:

> Everything seems to grip my attention although I am not particularly interested in anything (p. 104).

> Things are coming in too fast. I lose my grip of it and get lost. I am attending to everything at once and as a result I do not really attend to anything (p. 104).

[1]Present address: State University of New York, Stony Brook, New York.
[2]Present address: Lafayette Clinic, Detroit, Michigan.

Recently, the construct of attention has also been used to interpret some deficits shown by schizophrenics in experimental situations. For example, deviant perception (Silverman, 1964a; Venables, 1964a), idiosyncratic verbal associations (Cromwell & Dokecki, 1968), broadened conceptual performance (Payne, 1966), and slow reaction time (Shakow, 1962) have been viewed in terms of attentional deficit.

The papers of Venables (1964a) and Silverman (1964a) are especially important because they attempt to relate a wide range of findings to a single theoretical construction. The voluminous literature on deficit in schizophrenics has been sorely in need of such attempts at integration. Again and again it has been shown that schizophrenics perform less optimally than normals. However, these results have produced little increase in our understanding of schizophrenia.

The construct of schizophrenia itself, however, stands as a major obstacle confronting researchers dealing with deviant populations. As has often been noted, the reliability and validity of this construct leave much to be desired. At the present time, however, the construct of schizophrenia is so embedded in the research literature that it cannot be ignored. Thus, the construct provides the basis around which the present paper will be organized.

A recent trend toward more detailed reporting of the differential characteristics of schizophrenic subjects has facilitated attempts to integrate research findings. Some inconsistencies in the research literature have been resolved and more replicable research findings have been produced, no small accomplishment when dealing with the highly variable performance of schizophrenics. Furthermore, results have been found which could not have been demonstrated if differential characteristics of the patients had not been noted. For example, Harris (1957) in an initial analysis of size estimation performance of schizophrenics and normals found no significant differences. However, when the schizophrenics were divided according to good vs. poor premorbid adjustment, it was found that the goods and poors differed significantly from each other with the goods underestimating and the poors overestimating size.

The notion that schizophrenia is a heterogeneous construct has been adopted very slowly in the laboratory. This slowness is somewhat surprising in view of Kraepelin's (1919) early classification system and Bleuler's work on "the group of schizophrenias." The acute-chronic and good-poor premorbid (or process-reactive) dimensions have been demonstrated to have considerable utility. Although some of Kraepelin's system has not proved useful for research, the paranoid-nonparanoid dimension has proved especially useful. While these dimensions cannot be taken as final criteria on which to subclassify schizophrenics, they have served an important function. Since the research to be reported in this paper depends heavily on these dimensions, a more detailed description of them is needed.

I. Individual Difference Constructs in Schizophrenia

A. ACUTE-CHRONIC

Researchers have usually defined the acute-chronic dimension in terms of length of hospitalization. Most typically, less than three years in the hospital has been taken to designate an acute and greater than 6 years a chronic. In contrast, the use of acute-chronic in formal psychiatric classi-fication has symptomatology as its primary referent. Since this usage al-lows overlapping between the chronicity dimension and other dimensions of schizophrenia, most current researchers have chosen to avoid it.

The use of acute-chronic in reference to length of hospitalization in-volves a number of gratuitous assumptions. It assumes, first, that some dimension of schizophrenia begins upon first admission and, second, that the transition to the other pole of the dimension is uniformly time-bound. While both these assumptions may be convenient for the description of large patient groups, neither is tenable when applied to the individual case. Furthermore, this definition implicitly assumes that the patient was not schizophrenic for very long prior to his hospitalization. This is seldom true.

Ideally, the acute-chronic dimension should perhaps be bound initially by the onset of psychotic symptoms. However, this also has its difficul-ties. While patients with sudden onset would present no definitional prob-lem, the patients with slow onset would. The time at which psychotic symptoms began would often be a matter of subjective judgment by unso-phisticated observers.

As presently used, the length of hospitalization definition of the chro-nicity dimension has a twofold function. First, it allows the assessment of the effects of prolonged hospitalization and chemotherapy. Second, it al-lows the assessment of the temporal changes which would occur in schiz-ophrenic disturbances independently of hospital treatment. Unfortunate-ly, these factors of chronicity cannot be separated in the individual hospitalized patient. With this time-bound definition, statements concern-ing chronicity are probabilistic and not absolute. Nevertheless, separate investigations have demonstrated the utility of the acute-chronic dimen-sion in each of the preceding senses (Johannsen & O'Connell, 1965; Sil-verman, Berg, & Kantor, 1965).

If a time-bound definition of chronicity is to be used, however, the cut-off points employed must be given more careful consideration. Epidemiological research (e.g., Brown, 1960) indicates that a criterion of less than 2 years since first admission is preferable for specifying a patient as acute. From his review of the relevant literature, Brown (1960) concluded that if a patient had not been discharged within 2 years following admission, his probability of subsequent discharge was very small. That is, if discharges are plotted cumulatively, an inflection in the curve appears at the 2-year point. Following this, the probability of discharge levels off and shows minimal subsequent increase.

Additionally, selection of groups of acute *vs.* chronic schizophrenics should take premorbid adjustment into account. That is, since poor premorbid patients have poor prognosis, a sample of chronics will likely be biased toward including more patients with poor premorbid adjustment. Also, the poor premorbid patient is more likely to have been psychotic for some time prior to hospitalization. Thus, if symptom onset is the critical referent for defining chronicity, many poor premorbid patients could be considered chronic upon their first admission.

B. PREMORBID ADJUSTMENT

The good-poor premorbid and process-reactive dimensions are currently viewed as continua and are frequently used interchangeably. The scales typically used to measure these dimensions have recently been compared (Solomon & Zlotowski, 1964). The relationship between the premorbid adjustment counterparts of the Phillips and Elgin scales was found to be .80. In addition, no experimental differentiation between good and reactive or poor and process patients has been reported. Thus, for the purpose of the present paper, these dimensions will be used interchangeably.

Premorbid adjustment has usually been determined by utilizing information concerning social and sexual adjustment obtained from the patient's case file (e.g., Phillips, 1953). Recently self-report measures of premorbid adjustment have also been developed (e.g., Ullmann & Giovannoni, 1964). These scales have the advantages of ease of administration and less reliance on the patient's case file. The Ullmann-Giovannoni scale has been found to compare quite favorably with the Phillips scale (Held & Cromwell, 1968; Johnson & Ries, 1967). The validity of both the case file and self-report measures seems to be dependent on a single item: "Have you ever been married?" (Held & Cromwell, 1968). Subjects with good premorbid adjustment have been or are now married, while those with poor premorbid adjustment have never been married. More completely, the modal patient with good premorbid adjustment is defined as having many friends, history of regular dating, and rapid onset of psychosis with precipitating stress. The modal patient with poor premorbid adjustment is defined as having little social or sexual interest, and insidious development of the psychosis. Good premorbid patients have been found to have better prognosis than poor premorbid patients (Farina & Webb, 1956).

Although this classification scheme has proved useful, it is not without its problems. For example, although currently viewed as a continuum, the most prevalent research practice has been to dichotomize patients into goods and poors. Usually, median splits or the upper and lower thirds of the distribution have been employed. However, if premorbid adjustment is taken seriously as a continuum, a correlation or correlation ratio logic would appear to be appropriate for research. Certainly, groups of "average premorbid adjustment" patients with scores in the middle of the distribution should also be investigated.

As discussed previously, the good-poor dimension is expected to be confounded with chronicity.

The good-poor dimension is also not independent of the paranoid-nonparanoid dimension. In separate studies, Goldstein, Held, and Cromwell (1968) have found that while good premorbid schizophrenics tend to be either paranoid or nonparanoid, the poor premorbid schizophrenics tend in the vast majority to be nonparanoid.

Another possible criticism of the good-poor dimension is that it measures only severity of illness. In order for the good-poor dimension to be useful it must be shown to have meaning over and above a simple severity of illness criterion. For example, it has often been shown that groups are ordered on some performance criterion as follows: normals > goods > poors. This is hardly surprising given the data on which the groups were selected. More convincing evidence for the utility of the good-poor dimension is found in cases where goods and poors differ from normals in opposite directions (e.g., Harris, 1957; Neale & Cromwell, 1968).

Finally, social class should be given greater attention in selecting goods and poors. Nuttall and Solomon (1965) have reported that some of the factors extracted from the Phillips scale had a differential prognostic significance depending on the patient's social class.

C. PARANOID-NONPARANOID

The final dimension which has been widely employed is the presence or absence of paranoid symptomatology, i.e., whether delusions are or are not the primary symptom feature. Unlike the first two dimensions this one depends heavily on psychiatric observation or diagnosis. A critical problem with this dimension concerns the frequently noted change in symptoms which patients characteristically exhibit. Reliance on symptomatology at admission for subject classification clearly does not allow for the changes which may occur, especially after being hospitalized for several years under heavy doses of medication. Many paranoid schizophrenic patients tend to become less "paranoid" over time. Furthermore, the mere use of presence of delusions does not appear to do justice to some clinical aspects of the paranoid syndrome. The florid suspiciousness and ideas of reference often found in acute paranoid patients appear to be quite different from the crystallized delusions often found in more chronic patients (e.g., a patient's belief that he is Christ). The relevance of these differences to performance in laboratory tasks has not been fully investigated.

II. Theories of Attentional Deficit in Schizophrenia

The present paper will focus on the theories proposed by Venables (1964a) and Silverman (1964a). These have been major attempts to gather evidence and provide formulations for viewing schizophrenic deficits in terms of an attention construct. The theories and the data on which they are based will be carefully scrutinized. Where possible, additional information will be utilized to accomplish an evaluation of the hypothesis of attentional deficit in schizophrenia.

A problem of considerable importance which has not yet been mentioned concerns the delineation of the meaning of attention. Clearly, it is difficult to evaluate research and theory on attention in schizophrenia unless one has a good working definition of attention. Unfortunately, no such definition is available. Attention has been applied to an extremely wide range of phenomena. These have varied from observables such as eye movements (Faw & Nunnally, 1967), and the orienting response (Berlyne, 1960), to constructs such as the central inhibition of irrelevant information (Broadbent, 1958). In global terms, attention refers here to the behaviors which an organism employs to direct his receptors to particular inputs, and the central processes by means of which these inputs may be modified. Long-term storage and response generation is therefore excluded. The term attention itself has been primarily used as a construct to organize research findings. That is, none of the studies attempt to quantify attention as such. Instead, other variables are operationally defined and studied which are then viewed as being subsumed by the attention construct. Thus, from a philosophy of science viewpoint, attention is a generic construct with a finite amount of utility. The use of other constructs to deal with the same subject matter is not precluded.

A. Venables

Venables (1964a) has presented a formulation relating arousal to attention in schizophrenic patients. His notions concerning attention and arousal were derived primarily from Callaway's work on drugs and attention.

Callaway and Thompson (1953) proposed a negative feedback mechanism to reduce threatening input. More specifically, threat was hypothesized to lead to sympathetic nervous system arousal which is followed by narrowed attention. This theory was tested by employing a cold pressor test and the inhalation of amyl nitrate to produce arousal. Size constancy was chosen as the response system on which the effects of arousal would be examined. Size constancy refers to the degree to which objects are matched according to their physical dimensions (distal match; constancy) as opposed to being matched according to subtended size on the retina (proximal match; underconstancy). Size constancy was assumed to be related to attention in the following manner: if narrowed attention reduces the reception of information which subjects use to make distal matches, then narrowed attention should produce reduced constancy or underconstancy (i.e., a tendency toward proximal matches). As predicted, both arousal treatments were found to produce underconstancy.

Callaway (1959) studied the effects of drug-induced arousal on the Stroop test. In the critical phase of this test, a subject is confronted with a competing cue situation. Subjects must name the color of the ink used to print the name of a different color, e.g., "RED" printed in blue ink calls for the response "BLUE." Callaway predicted that narrowed attention would facilitate performance on this test. As predicted, subjects treated with a stimulating drug (methamphetamine) exhibited less interference. To further support his formulation Callaway (1959) examined the possibility that a drug which produces the opposite of arousal would produce broadened attention. The Stroop test was again employed. It was found that subjects who had previously been administered amobarbital exhibited greater interference. Callaway's research on drug-manipulated arousal and the Stroop test, however, has failed to be replicated (Quarton & Talland, 1962).

A thorny problem in Callaway's research lies in the interpretation of his measures in terms of an attention construct. Certainly, drug-produced arousal has been shown to produce performance changes on certain tasks. However, the drugs involved may reasonably be assumed to have effects in addition to a negative feedback to narrow or broaden attention. The Stroop test used by Callaway not only demands attention response to separate relevant from irrelevant cues but also the suppression of a learned habit to read instead of to name color. For this reason, attention may or may not be the mediating factor. Callaway himself later gave up using size constancy because of the possibility of alternative explanations.

The attempt to demonstrate a relationship between arousal and attention has also been taken up by investigators with a more psychological bent. In these investigations it has been assumed that arousal and the Hullian construct of drive are identical. While this assumed identity may be challenged, to do so would be beyond the scope of the present paper. Agnew and Agnew (1963) used threat of shock and failure feedback in an attempt to manipulate drive. It was found that under high drive conditions, performance on the Stroop test was indicative of narrowed attention. That is, subjects in the high drive condition showed less interference. On the other hand, Miller and Cromwell (1961) using the Taylor manifest anxiety scale (1953) found high anxiety subjects to do more poorly than low anxiety subjects upon initial examination with the Stroop test. However, after subjects were more accustomed to the testing situation, the high anxiety subjects improved and the significant difference was no longer present. From these two studies the notion of generality between threat of shock and failure feedback, on the one hand, and Taylor anxiety, on the other, must be rejected.

Evidence in favor of the attention-arousal formulation is found in a recent investigation by Zaffy and Bruning (1966). Position response learning was studied in high and low anxious subjects selected on the basis of Manifest Anxiety scores. Three conditions were employed: no-cue, relevant cue, and irrelevant-cue. Their results indicated that the performance of the low anxious subjects was significantly influenced by the cues, whether relevant or irrelevant. The high anxious subjects, on the other hand, were uninfluenced by either the relevant or the irrelevant cues.

In summary, research on normal subjects has demonstrated that arousal (drive) and performance are related. However, whether or not attention mediates this effect would appear to be an as-yet unsolved issue. The work of investigators such as Callaway would be greatly furthered by utilizing dependent variables which are more interpretable. Tasks which lend themselves more readily to an attentional interpretation should be employed. Also, multiple dependent variables should be considered since attentional components can account for only part of the variance in any given single task. Even if an attentional construct is appropriate, its utility would seem to be severely hampered due to the imprecision with which it has been employed. For example, assuming that "narrowed attention" exists, to what is attention narrowed? The critical question of the parameters influencing which cues are attended to and which are ignored has been neglected.

Venables (1964a) related the attention-arousal theory to schizophrenics in the following manner:

> Chronic schizophrenics—and possibly included in this category are process patients—tend to be characterized by a state of restriction of the attentional field resulting from elevated states of sympathetic and cortical activation. . . . In contrast to the chronic patient, the acute (and possibly the reactive and paranoid) patient is characterized by an inability to restrict the range of his attention so he is flooded by sensory impressions from all quarters. . . . The acute patient's broadened level of attention would appear to arise from a low level of cortical activation or possibly the parasympathetic imbalance which he displays (pp. 41–42).

Venables' theory can be seen to rest on three major points. The first has already been discussed in this section and concerns the validity of the proposed relationship between attention and arousal. Second, it must be shown that chronic and process patients have supernormal arousal levels, while acute and reactive patients have subnormal levels. Third, these arousal differences in schizophrenics must be shown to be relevant to performance in experimental tasks related to narrowed or broadened attention.

The relevant literature on arousal in schizophrenic patients has been reviewed in detail elsewhere (Lang & Buss, 1965; Maher, 1966; Buss, 1966). In partial support of Venables' theory, all three reviews concluded that the habitual level of activity is generally higher in chronic schizophrenics than in normals. This finding holds especially for the cardiovascular and muscle tension systems. However, the results of investigations in which different groups of schizophrenics have been studied have yielded no consistent pattern of findings. For example, Devault (reported in Lang & Buss, 1965) found higher than normal resting heart rate levels in chronic reactive but not chronic process patients. Reynolds (reported in Lang & Buss, 1965) found process schizophrenics to have higher than normal pulse rate, blood pressure, and resting electromyograph response. The reactive patients in Reynolds' study were consistently above the normals but below the process patients, rather than being below normal as Venables' theory would assert.

B. SILVERMAN

Silverman's (1964a) theory represents an attempt to extend cognitive control principles (e.g., Klein, 1954; Witkin, Lewis, Hertzman, Machover, Meissner, & Wapner, 1954; Gardner, Holzman, Klein, Linton, & Spence, 1959) to attention in schizophrenia. Following Solley and Murphy (1960), attention is divided into extensive and intensive aspects. The former refers to the sampling of environmental cues; the latter to the articulation of the sampled cues into relevant and irrelevant aspects. The measurement of the extensive aspects of attention has been related to the cognitive control construct of scanning (Gardner *et al.*, 1959) and the measurement of the intensive aspects of attention to the field articulation control principle (e.g., Witkin *et al.*, 1954).

The scanning construct was developed from a combination of an earlier "focusing" principle (Schlesinger, 1954) and Piaget's perceptual research (e.g., Piaget, 1950). Size estimation has been the main behavior from which differences in scanning have been inferred. Gardner *et al.*'s (1959) formulation stated that extensive scanners, i.e., those subjects who repeatedly look about the visual field, should show underestimation or else minimal overestimation of a standard stimulus. Minimal scanners, on the other hand, should show size overestimation due to their excessive "centration" on the standard stimulus.

Gardner and Long (1962a) attempted a more direct test of this theory by recording eye movements during size estimation. This study has been a major basis for relating the scanning construct to size estimation. Three different size estimation tasks were employed and seven measures derived from the eye movement recordings were correlated with size estimation performance. Of the resulting 21 correlations, only two reached significance. However, only one of these was interpretable within the scanning construct — that is, if one dares to reject chance as an interpretation. This was an inverse relationship between number of fixations on the standard stimulus and estimated size on the first size estimation task ($r = -.32$).

Since the proposed relationship between scanning and size estimation was found for only one of the three size estimation tasks, more description of this particular task is warranted. Subjects adjusted a circular patch of light to match the size of a disk held at arm's length. Three disks varying in color and weight were utilized. These varying colors and weights and the kinesthetic-tactile stimulation from holding the disks may have introduced irrelevant variation to the test of the scanning-size estimation relationship.

In another attempt to delineate the relationship between eye movement and size estimation, subjects' eye movements were observed and recorded by the experimenter (Gardner & Long, 1962b). Again the relationship found was disappointingly small. The correlations between number of centrations on the standard and five measures of size estimation ranged from .04 to −.49. Two of these (−.49 and −.29) reached significance.

These small relationships and the lack of systematic means to predict why three of the five measures fail to relate to eye movement, while two do relate to eye movement, leave the results equivocal with respect to support of the scanning construct. While reliable individual differences in size estimation have been found, the interpretation to be placed on these differences is unclear.

Field articulation has been investigated primarily by Witkin (Witkin *et al.*, 1954; Witkin, Dyk, Faterson, Goodenough, & Karp, 1962). The constructs of field independence and dependence were introduced by Witkin to explain individual differences in performance on tasks such as the rod-and-frame and embedded figures. The rod-and-frame consists of a luminous rod inside a luminous frame placed in an otherwise darkened room. With the rod and frame tilted, subjects are asked to adjust the rod to a vertical position. On the embedded figures test, subjects are asked to pick out a smaller figure which is hidden in a larger, more complex one. Supposedly, both these tasks involve the separation of figure from ground (or the articulation of the stimulus field into its relevant and irrelevant aspects). Subjects who are overly influenced by the tilt of the frame and do not adjust the rod to a near-vertical position are designated as field-dependent. Conversely, those who can set the rod close to the true upright are designated field-independent. Similarly, field-independent subjects take less time to locate embedded figures than do field-dependent subjects (Witkin *et al.*, 1954).

Witkin's interpretation of rod-and-frame performance has recently been challenged (Brosgole & Cristal, 1967). According to Witkin, subjects in the rod-and-frame test have two cues available, their own kinesthetic feedback which provides information concerning the true upright and the tilted frame which adds an irrelevant cue to vertical position. Within Witkin's framework, the field-independent subject sets the rod more in accord with his own kinesthetic cues, while the field-dependent subject is influenced to a greater extent by the tilted frame. Witkin's theory must, then, assert that if kinesthetic feedback concerning the upright were reduced, subjects would tend to perform in a field-dependent manner. Brosgole and Cristal (1967) accomplished the reduction of kinesthetic cues by having subjects perform the rod-and-frame while reclining with the apparatus suspended horizontally above them. Although this treatment led to a decrement in performance accuracy, the effect did not reach significance. It should be noted, however, that subjects in the reclining condition still would have body alignment available as a referent for verticality.

Similarly, it has recently been concluded that measures of field articulation do not appear to be differentiable from general spatial factors e.g. the

Primary Mental Abilities Space Test (Sherman, 1967). That is, performance on rod-and-frame and embedded figures is highly related to other spatial tasks which do not involve conflicting cues.

Thus, the research on field articulation control appears to be in a position similar to that of the scanning control. Reliable individual differences can be elicited on the tests employed, but the interpretability of these differences is questionable.

Various measures of scanning and field articulation have been employed with schizophrenics. Silverman (1964a) reviewed this literature and generated the following formulation. Acute paranoid and good premorbid patients were hypothesized to be extensive scanners, while acute poor premorbid and nonparanoid patients were hypothesized to be minimal scanners. In the chronic phase of the illness these scanning response dispositions were hypothesized to reverse. With reference to field articulation, acute paranoid and good premorbid patients were assumed to be field-independent, while acute nonparanoid and poor premorbid patients were assumed to be field-dependent. No clear formulation was offered concerning field articulation and the acute-chronic dimension.

Silverman's theory can be seen to rest on two major points. The first has been discussed above and concerns the validity of the cognitive controls approach to the study of attention. The second concerns the finding of reliable differences between specific subgroups of schizophrenics on these cognitive control tasks.

III. Research Findings with Schizophrenics

A. SIZE CONSTANCY

As noted previously, size constancy was hypothesized to be related to narrowed attention (or minimal scanning) in that these phenomena should reduce the reception of the information necessary for a distal match. Silverman further asserted that broadened attention (excessive scanning) should produce overconstancy, that is, a larger than distal match. Silverman's proposed relationship between scanning and size constancy, however, does not appear to fit the earlier research employing size constancy as a measure of scanning (Gardner *et al.*, 1959). Although Gardner *et al.* found that size constancy loaded on the scanning factor, the size constancy measure employed was the reverse of the usual situation. That is, subjects were instructed to attempt to make proximal rather than distal matches. Their findings indicated that subjects who were high scanners were more efficient; that is, they could come closer to making proximal size matches.

Constancy has been shown to be reduced when distance cues are removed (Holway & Boring, 1941). Therefore, it does seem reasonable to assert that if the information relevant to distal matching is not given attention, underconstancy should result. However, Silverman's assertion that broadened attention produces overconstancy does not appear to follow from this formulation. Why should a supernormal sampling of cues produce overconstancy? Rather, if the information necessary for distal matching is attended to, distal size matches should occur.

Venables' and Silverman's theories make partially similar predictions concerning the size constancy performance of schizophrenics. Venables asserted that the hyperaroused, chronic, and process schizophrenic patients with narrowed attention should sample fewer cues and hence should show underconstancy. Silverman's scanning theory predicts that the extensive cue-sampling acute good premorbid and paranoid patients should show overconstancy, while the minimal cue-sampling acute poor premorbid and nonparanoid patients should show underconstancy. However, in the chronic phase of the illness, these relationships should be reversed due to the crossover in scanning which Silverman has postulated.

Two investigators have reported overconstancy in schizophrenics (Raush, 1952; Sanders & Pacht, 1952). Since Sanders and Pacht (1952) give no further information concerning their subjects, their findings are of little direct relevance to the theories being examined here. Raush (1952) tested groups of normals and relatively acute paranoid and nonparanoid schizophrenics under full cue and reduced cue situations (well illuminated *vs.* darkened room, respectively). All three groups exhibited overconstancy. In the full cue condition the paranoids were significantly more overconstant than the normals. The nonparanoids were between the paranoids and normals but did not differ significantly from either. In the reduced cue situation, the paranoids were significantly more overconstant than both the normals and the nonparanoids. The latter two groups did not differ. However, the overconstancy found in Raush's experiment was most likely due to the spatial arrangement of standard and variable. That is, the standard stimulus was located at right angles to the variable in his testing situation. Holway and Boring (1941) reported overconstancy employing a similar arrangement of standard and variable. Given the tenuous relation between attention and overconstancy, Raush's findings may be more parsimoniously interpreted to indicate that the performance of paranoid patients is more greatly influenced by the spatial location of standard and variable.

It should also be noted that both investigations which reported over-constancy in schizophrenia were carried out prior to the widespread adoption of chemotherapy. The next studies to be reviewed were completed later and the patients involved were thus more likely to have been on phenothiazine medication. While no investigation employing schizophrenic patients has examined the relationship between drugs and size constancy, the possibility of such a relationship must loom large.

Underconstancy has been reported quite often by investigators who have employed various "types" of schizophrenics. Lovinger (1956) employed normals and groups of schizophrenics with either good or poor reality contact. Half of each schizophrenic group was diagnosed as paranoid. Unfortunately, no information concerning the degree of chronicity of the groups was presented. All groups were tested under each of three conditions: maximal cue-binocular vision, and well-illuminated viewing tunnel; minimal cue-binocular vision, and dimly lighted tunnel; no-cue-monocular vision, reduction screen, and darkened tunnel. Poor contact schizophrenics were found to show less constancy than the other two groups, but only in the minimal cue condition. No difference between the paranoid and nonparanoid patients was found. To interpret this finding as indicating underconstancy in schizophrenia begs the question: "Underconstant as opposed to what?" A distal match was represented by a choice of a 16-inch variable. Under the minimal cue condition the mean choices of the three groups were: normals—6.75 inches; poor contact schizophrenics—5.34 inches; good contact schizophrenics—7.21 inches. Thus, all three groups' performance was considerably underconstant, and the poor contact schizophrenics were only slightly "worse" than the other two groups.

In a series of investigations, Weckowicz has consistently reported underconstancy in chronic schizophrenics (Weckowicz, 1957, 1958; Weckowicz & Blewett, 1959). Crookes (1957) has also reported underconstancy in the performance of an unspecified group of schizophrenics. Finally, Hamilton (1963) compared the size constancy performance of groups of normals, chronic nonparanoid, and chronic paranoid schizophrenics in full cue (daylight) and reduced cue (dimly illuminated viewing tunnel) conditions. No significant differences were found between the paranoid and nonparanoid patients. However, the schizophrenic group as a whole showed less constancy than the normals, but only in the maximum cue condition.

Superficially, these studies appear to support Venables' contention that chronic schizophrenics are underconstant. However, the nature of the instructions given the subjects in these studies creates a problem in interpreting the results. All the investigators discussed above employed relatively ambiguous instructions. Although Joynson (1958) has demonstrated that normal subjects interpret ambiguous instructions as calling for a distal match, this may not be the case for schizophrenics. Hamilton (1963) reported that 13 of his subjects indicated that they made their size judgments in terms of apparent (proximal) size. Of these 13, 9 were schizophrenic. Hamilton further reported that there was no significant difference between the constancy ratios of his schizophrenic subjects who indicated they had attempted a proximal match and those who did not. Which response system are we to believe? The finding of no relation between the verbal report and actual constancy behavior in schizophrenics casts doubt on the validity of their verbal reports. The constancy ratios themselves, however, would appear to indicate that many of the schizophrenics may have been attempting a proximal match.

This instruction-interpretation view of underconstancy receives added support from a number of studies showing no differences between the size constancy performance of normals and schizophrenics (Leibowitz & Pishkin, 1961; Pishkin, Smith, & Leibowitz, 1962; Harway & Salzman, 1964; Perez, 1961). In contrast to many of the studies noted earlier, these investigations have utilized relatively unambiguous instructions which clearly emphasized distal matching. In Perez' (1961) study, subjects were given pretraining to accentuate the difference between making proximal vs. distal matches. It is notable that in this study, the schizophrenics performed slightly but not significantly better than the normals in making distal matches.

A recent size constancy study has made an important contribution to perceptual research employing abnormal populations (Price & Erikson, 1966). Size constancy was studied in normals, acute paranoid, and acute nonparanoid schizophrenics employing signal detection analysis (Swets, Tanner, & Birdsall, 1961). In an initial analysis of their data, Price and Erikson found no differences in the points-of-subjective equality of the three groups. However, a further analysis employing d_s (one of the sensitivity parameters of signal detection theory) revealed that the nonparanoids had significantly lower sensitivity than either of the other two groups. That is, nonparanoids were less sensitive in their ability to make distal matches.

These results indicate that caution should be exercised in interpreting the findings of any psychophysical experiment involving schizophrenics. The usual methods of analysis lump together both sensitivity and response or criterion factors. Thus, if an experimenter is concerned with sensitivity alone, the more usual methods of analysis are inappropriate. Recent papers by Clark (Clark, 1966; Clark, Brown, & Rutschmann, 1967) add further support to this position.

In summary, the size constancy data add little support to either Venables' or Silverman's theories and more generally contribute minimally to an understanding of attention in schizophrenia. Contrary to Venable's formulation, no clear differences between acute and chronic schizophrenics have emerged. With respect to Silverman's theory, premorbid adjustment effects on size constancy have not been investigated, so only the paranoid dimension need be discussed. Only one investigator found overconstancy in paranoid patients (Raush, 1952); however, the incomparability of this study has already been noted. The investigations of nonparanoid patients are about equally divided between those reporting no differences and those reporting underconstancy in these patients. However, the results of these studies are clearly vulnerable on methodological grounds.

B. Size Estimation

The data on size estimation in schizophrenics has been the prime basis for Silverman's theory concerning differences in scanning behavior in these patients. Size estimation differs primarily from size constancy in that in the former task the stimuli are both presented at the same distance from the subject. As noted earlier, size underestimation is supposedly related to extensive scanning and size overestimation to minimal scanning.

The initial study of size estimation in schizophrenia was that of Harris (1957). Groups of normals, acute good premorbid, and acute poor premorbid schizophrenics were studied. A method of adjustment was employed with subjects adjusting a variable to the remembered size of the standard stimulus. The schizophrenic groups differed significantly from each other with the goods underestimating and the poors overestimating. However, when the results were analyzed in terms of deviations from the criterion of correct performance, neither the goods nor the poors showed consistently significant over- or underestimation for each of the six stimuli employed. This indicates that the magnitude of size estimation error found in these groups is small when compared to optimal performance.

Zahn (1959) also investigated size estimation utilizing good and poor premorbid schizophrenics and following Harris' procedure quite closely. In addition, Zahn employed stimuli which had previously been associated with reward and punishment. It was found that all groups underestimated except the good premorbid schizophrenics on the "punished" picture. Thus, we see a result opposite to that reported by Harris. However, Zahn's subjects were more chronic in comparison to Harris'. Also, Zahn noted that in pilot work employing acute patients he had replicated Harris' earlier findings.

Two additional studies have been reported which are relevant to size estimation differences between acute and chronic schizophrenics. Mehl (1966) studied size estimation in chronic good and poor premorbid nonparanoid patients prior to and following each of three treatments. These were: sensory deprivation; sensory stimulation, and a control (on ward) condition. No overall difference was found between the goods and poors. Neale, Davis, and Cromwell (1967), as part of a larger investigation, examined size estimation in chronic and acute good premorbid paranoid and chronic and acute poor premorbid nonparanoid patients. No significant performance differences were found.

Silverman (1964b) investigated size estimation in paranoid and nonparanoid schizophrenics. Following Gardner et al.'s (1959) procedure, subjects adjusted a circular patch of light to match the size of each of three circular disks held by the subject at arm's length. As in the previous work of Gardner et al., the disks varied in both color and weight. Significant differences were found between the paranoid and nonparanoid patients. Paranoid patients underestimated on an average of 7.06 of the 12 trials, while nonparanoids overestimated on an average of 9.15 of the 12 trials. Unfortunately, no normal group was run for comparison purposes.

Davis, Cromwell, and Held (1967) investigated size estimation in acute patients selected on the basis of both paranoid symptomatology and premorbid adjustment. Each subject was presented with a standard stimulus followed by six comparison stimuli from which he was to choose the one which matched the standard. The comparison stimuli were in ordinal positions 1, 2, 3, 5, 6, and 7, with respect to size, while the six standard stimuli were always in the fourth ordinal position. Thus, no exact match was possible. Significant main effects were found for both paranoid symptomatology and premorbid adjustment. No interaction was found between these two dimensions. The only subjects to underestimate were the good premorbid paranoids. Increasing degrees of overestimation were shown by the poor-paranoids, good-nonparanoids, and poor-nonparanoids, respectively. However, when the performance of the various groups was analyzed with reference to absolute deviations from 4.0 (veridicality), no significant deviations were found.[3]

Neale and Cromwell (1968) examined whether eye movements are necessary for the occurrence of size estimation differences in schizophrenics. Groups of acute good premorbid paranoid and poor premorbid nonparanoid schizophrenics were studied as well as a group of hospital aides. In addition to the 10-second standard stimulus exposure time employed by Davis et al., Neale and Cromwell employed a presentation time

---

[3]D. Davis, personal communication, 1967.

of 100 msec and also a 10-msec blank flash. The former condition is too short to allow more than one fixation. Within Silverman's theory, it must be predicted that the previously noted differences in size estimation should not be present in this condition. The latter condition was included to examine a response bias interpretation of size estimation deviancy in schizophrenia. In contrast to Silverman's theory, which would predict no differences with 100 msec, the two schizophrenic groups differed from each other at both the 10-second and 100-msec presentation times. No such differences were found in the 10-msec blank flash condition. A further analysis of the data from this experiment examined the relative frequency of subjects' choices of comparison stimuli in ordinal positions 3 and 5. Since a choice of either of these stimuli represented minimal error, such choices were designated as hits. All three groups were virtually identical in their hit rates. Therefore, the between groups differences found in the earlier analysis result from differences in error patterns. That is, normals distribute their errors equally in directions of over- and underestimation, while the good paranoids and poor nonparanoids show patterns of error frequency which are skewed in directions of under- and overestimation, respectively.

Silverman and Gaarder (1967) studied size estimation in normals and acute and chronic schizophrenics and subsequently measured the microsaccadic rates of their subjects. Subjects' eye movements were recorded while they attempted to maintain fixation on a small target. For each group the mean size estimation level was subsequently correlated with eye movement. In the normal group eye movement was inversely related to level of size estimation. For the schizophrenics the relationship was reversed; eye movement was positively related to size estimation. Silverman and Gaarder interpreted their results in terms of a division of eye movement into two components—information search and physiological activation. Usually, these two components are positively correlated; however, in states of high arousal this relationship reverses. The finding of high microsaccadic rate in the overestimating schizophrenics was interpreted to indicate that in schizophrenics saccadic rate becomes dissociated from its information-search function and reflects a high arousal level. Certainly, more research is required to substantiate this post hoc formulation.

The results of the size estimation studies offer little support to Silverman's theory. The crossover effect which was postulated to occur between the acute and chronic phases of the illness has received no support beyond the original Zahn (1959) study (Mehl, 1966; Neale et al., 1967). Although the results of investigations employing acute patients are generally in agreement with Silverman's formulation, an interpretation of these differences solely in terms of gross eye movements appears untenable (Neale & Cromwell, 1968). Silverman and Gaarder's recent results add another dimension to the study of scanning and size estimation. While a substantial relationship between size estimation and saccadic eye movement has been found, a much tighter theoretical formulation is needed. This is especially true regarding whether microsaccadic movement, even in normals, is related to information search. Originally, scanning was a psychological construct inferred from size estimation behavior and information-search characteristics were ascribed to it. Later, gross eye movement was adopted as an empirical referent for the construct. Microsaccadic eye movements may or may not be relevant to the scanning construct as it has been used in the past.[4]

C. INCIDENTAL LEARNING

Studies of incidental learning were used by Venables to support his attention-arousal formulation. His theory asserts that chronic schizophrenics should show less incidental learning due to their narrowed attention (restricted range of cue utilization).

Venables (1964a) reported two unpublished investigations of incidental learning among schizophrenics. Greenberg (1953) found less incidental learning in chronic schizophrenics as compared to normals. Winer (1954) found less incidental learning in hebephrenics and catatonics, while a group of paranoids were equivalent to the normals. Topping and O'Conner (1960), however, found no differences in incidental learning among groups of normals, chronic paranoids, and chronic nonparanoids. Kar (1967) studied incidental learning in a Müller-Lyer task. In one condition of his study, the Müller-Lyer judgments were made with a number of irrelevant stimuli surrounding the figure. Acute good premorbid paranoid patients showed significantly more recall of these stimuli than did the acute poor nonparanoids and normals. The latter two groups did not differ. A study closely related to those discussed previously was performed by Venables (1963). Chronic schizophrenic patients sorted cards on the basis of either of two relevant letters in the presence of eight irrelevant letters. Following four such sorts, the irrelevant letters were changed without the subjects' knowledge. A predicted time for the fifth sort was made on the basis of individual regression lines. It was suggested that the

[4]Silverman (1964a) also presents data on the autokinetic effect in schizophrenics in support of his eye movement theory. However, since the importance of eye movement in the autokinetic effect has been recently challenged and the relevant evidence reviewed (Gregory, 1966), no discussion of the performance of schizophrenics on this task appears to be necessary.

discrepancy between the predicted and observed sorting times on the fifth trial would indicate the degree to which a subject had attended to the irrelevant cues. In partial support of Venables' theory, nonparanoid patients with high arousal, as measured by two-flash threshold, showed less disruption in sorting time on the fifth trial. This relationship did not obtain for the paranoid patients in the study.

The data reviewed above does not unequivocally support Venables' theory. His prediction of less than normal incidental learning in chronic and process patients was supported in only two of the four available investigations. Venables' own study (1963) provided no group of normals for comparison, and the relation between two-flash threshold and performance was significant only for the nonparanoid patients.

D. FIELD ARTICULATION

On tasks which have been used as measures of field articulation, Silverman predicts field-independent performance in acute good premorbid and paranoid patients and field-dependent performance in acute poor premorbid and nonparanoid patients. Silverman's field articulation formulation is given minimal support by the data of Witkin et al. (1954). Utilizing a score made up of performance on both the rod-and-frame and tilting-room-tilting-chair tests, paranoid schizophrenics showed a nonsignificant trend toward being field-independent. That is, of 12 paranoid patients, 7 were classified as field-independent.

Support for Silverman's theory comes from a study by Taylor (reviewed in Silverman, 1964a). He found that delusional schizophrenics were faster than hallucinatory schizophrenics on the embedded figures test. Faster performance on this test is hypothesized to be a referent of field independence. Similarly, Bryant (reviewed in Silverman, 1964a) found that on both the embedded figures and the rod-and-frame test, good premorbid patients tended to be field-independent while poors tended to be field-dependent. Kar (1967) investigated the Müller-Lyer illusion in acute good premorbid paranoid, acute poor premorbid nonparanoid, and normal subjects. Field-independent subjects have previously been shown to exhibit a smaller Müller-Lyer illusion effect (Gardner, 1961). In contrast to the earlier results, Kar found that the good-paranoid patients exhibited the greatest amount of illusion. The other two groups did not differ from each other.

Except for Kar's (1967) study, the performance of schizophrenics on field articulation tasks is consistent with Silverman's theory. As noted earlier, however, our understanding of the processes underlying performance on field articulation tasks is far from complete. Therefore, the relevance of these findings to a theory of attention in schizophrenia is not at all clear.

E. REACTION TIME

One of the largest bodies of experimental work on schizophrenics has dealt with reaction time (RT). This research differs from that reported earlier in two respects. First, it is not immediately relevant to either Venables' or Silverman's theories. Second, an attentional interpretation of RT involves the notion of the maintenance of a set (or readiness to respond). This is clearly a shift of emphasis from the literature previously reviewed which indicated little concern for temporal processes.

Schizophrenics have been consistently shown to have slower RTs in comparison with normal subjects. This slowness has been found to be proportionately greater in chronic and nonparanoid than in acute or paranoid patients (Shakow, 1962). The finding of slower RT does not, of course, point directly toward an attentional interpretation. However, other findings within the RT framework make an attentional interpretation of the deficit most plausible. It has been found that the preparatory interval (PI) is a highly significant determinant of RT performance. The PI refers to the interval between the onset of a warning signal and the actual RT stimulus. Chronic patients show great increases in RT when the PI is lengthened or is less than 2 seconds. This finding was interpreted by Shakow (1962) to indicate that the schizophrenic has difficulty in mobilizing and then maintaining a "major set" and instead is dominated by "minor sets." That is, schizophrenics do not appear to be able to maintain a readiness to respond to the appropriate stimulus. In Shakow's own words (1962):

> It is as if, in the scanning process which takes place before the response to a stimulus is made, the schizophrenic is unable to select the material relevant for optimal response (p. 25).

Schizophrenics are, then, hypothesized to be inordinately influenced by irrelevant, distracting stimuli. One source of irrelevant information which has been extensively investigated is the preceding preparatory interval (PPI). It has been found that schizophrenics are influenced by this source of stimulation to a greater extent than are normals (e.g., Zahn, Rosenthal, & Shakow, 1961). It appears that the schizophrenic goes on responding to a temporal configuration which is no longer relevant. In support of this interpretation, schizophrenics have been shown to be markedly less rapid in habituating to simple stimuli than are normals (Zahn, Rosenthal, & Lawlor, 1962).

F. COMPETING INFORMATION TASKS

A prediction which follows directly from the RT studies is that schizophrenics should exhibit their greatest deficit in situations where competing information is present. Rappaport, Rogers, Reynolds, and Weinmann (1966) and Rappaport (1967) have investigated the performance of schizophrenics and normals in a competing message task. The subjects were required to attend only to one message which was presented concurrently with others. The number of messages simultaneously presented varied from one to seven. Schizophrenics exhibited performance deficit only in those conditions in which more than one message was presented.

Polidoro[5] presented acute good paranoid and acute poor nonparanoid schizophrenics and normal controls a Staggered Spondaic Word test. Words such as "upstairs" were presented in one ear and "downtown" in the other ear with the last syllable of the first word overlapping with the first syllable of the second word. Both schizophrenic groups were found to have impaired reception only when the two competing syllables were presented.

Similarly, the visual and auditory recognition performance of schizophrenics has been found to be disrupted only under conditions when the judgments were made with the stimuli presented in a noise background (Stilson, Kopell, Vandenbergh, & Downs, 1966). Neale, McIntyre, Fox, and Cromwell (1969) investigated the perceptual span of schizophrenics employing tachistoscopically displayed elements presented either singly or in a matrix of other elements. The schizophrenics were found to perform more poorly than the normals only in the condition in which the critical elements were presented in a matrix of elements. Similar debilitating effects of distracting stimuli were reported by Chapman and McGhie (1962) and Shakow (1950).

Thus, it appears that schizophrenics perform least optimally when the task involves attending and responding to relevant input when that input is presented along with irrelevant input. It appears that the irrelevant input can produce its debilitating effects either by being temporally or spatially close to the relevant information.

Research on competing information does have some bearing on both Venables' and Silverman's theories. Venables' theory can be construed to predict that schizophrenics with broadened attention would be more debilitated by competing information than those with narrowed attention (assuming that attention is "narrowed" to the relevant and not the irrelevant information). Similarly, Silverman's theory may be construed to pre-

[5]L. G. Polidoro, personal communication, 1968.

dict that field-independent schizophrenics would show less debilitation than field-dependent schizophrenics.

Chapman and McGhie (1962) have found that process schizophrenics were especially susceptible to the effects of distractors. However, the chain of reasoning from process schizophrenia to field dependence or narrowed attention, to performance when irrelevant information is present, seems torturous. Additionally, in the Neale *et al.* and Polidoro studies no differences were found between acute good-paranoid and acute poor-nonparanoid schizophrenics.

Rappaport's (1967) study involved both acute and chronic schizophrenics. In support of prediction of Venables' theory, acute schizophrenics performed more poorly than chronics. However, more research is clearly needed to explicate further the relationship between individual difference constructs in schizophrenia and performance on competing information tasks.

G. Conceptual Performance

Studies of conceptual performance in schizophrenics have also been interpreted employing attentional constructs. Payne and his co-workers (e.g., Payne & Hewlett, 1960; Payne, 1966) have asserted that the overinclusive conceptual performance found in some schizophrenic patients is due to a defect in a hypothetical filter mechanism which normally serves to screen out irrelevant material. Paranoid patients have been found to be particularly overinclusive (Payne, Caird, & Laverty, 1964). Chapman (1956) has presented a similar notion to explain schizophrenics' deviant conceptual performance. Schizophrenics were required to form concepts between a stimulus word (e.g., horse) and one of three response words. One of the response words shared the concept (e.g., mule), another had an associative connection (shoe), and the third was irrelevant. The schizophrenics were found to exhibit more associative intrusions than the normal subjects (Chapman, 1956).

This research dovetails nicely with the work on RT and competing information. Again, it appears that schizophrenics perform especially poorly when the task involves response to relevant information presented along with irrelevant information. Chapman's research may provide an inroad into one of the processes which accounts for schizophrenic distractibility.

However, this research need not be interpreted with an attention construct (e.g., as by Cromwell & Dokecki, 1968). For example, Payne has used an object sorting task as a measure of overinclusion. Overinclusive schizophrenics were found to employ irrelevant details such as scratches and shadows in forming their concepts. Certainly this implies that schizophrenics are including as relevant that information which would usually be classified as irrelevant. But does this call for an attentional interpretation? Do normals not "see" the scratches and shadows? A response disorganization concept (Broen, 1966) appears to be just as adequate to handle these data.

H. TWO-FLASH THRESHOLD

As discussed earlier, Venables' attention-arousal formulation depends heavily on the assertion that chronic and process patients are characterized by a high state of arousal, while acute and reactive patients are found to have subnormal levels of arousal. Venables has used two-flash fusion threshold as a measure of cortical activation. Good temporal resolution, that is, a low threshold, was thought to be indicative of a high arousal level. In some support of this contention, Venables and Wing (1962) found a significant relationship between two-flash threshold and skin potential.

Venables has employed a modified method of limits in determining two-flash threshold. Starting with flash separations well above and below threshold, the range was gradually decreased until the subject's threshold was determined. Judging from a "typical record" presented by Venables (1964b), this procedure requires only about 17 trials. This number of trials would scarcely be considered as a "warm-up" in most psychophysical research. Furthermore, since Venables is interested only in sensitivity, his failure to consider the operation of response or criterion factors makes the interpretation of his results hazardous.

Borinsky, Neale, Cromwell, and Fox (1967) have recently investigated two-flash threshold in normals and acute good premorbid paranoid and acute poor premorbid nonparanoid schizophrenics. Two hundred and eighty-eight trials were administered to each subject employing a constant-stimulus forced-choice method. It was found that both schizophrenic groups had significantly lower sensitivity (d') than the normal group. Lowered sensitivity implies a higher threshold and hence less arousal in the schizophrenic groups.

More recently, a separate examiner in our laboratory has extended this research to chronic patients. The same apparatus and procedure as had been used by Borinsky et al., was employed. The d' of the chronics was then compared to the data obtained in the Borinsky et al. study. The chronic patients were found to have a significantly higher d' than either of the acute schizophrenic groups previously employed. However, in contrast to Venables' prediction, the chronic patients were not above the normals in d'. Thus, Venables' predictions concerning arousal and two-flash threshold were not supported.

IV. Conclusions

The literature on various deficits among schizophrenic patients does not point unequivocally toward an interpretation in terms of attention. The theories of Venables and Silverman fall short on two grounds. First, research findings exist which may be interpreted to indicate that their formulations have been contradicted. Second, the data which appear to provide support for their positions often are interpretable employing a construct other than attention. This problem arises for two reasons. First, neither Venables nor Silverman give a precise definition of attention. Due to this definitional looseness, precise measurement operations are lacking. Second, the tasks which have been employed to measure attention often have not isolated a given perceptual system so that the operation of alternative variables is untenable. Without such procedures little progress can be made in our study of perception and attention in schizophrenia.

In spite of the criticisms presented in this review, the theories of Venables and Silverman have made distinct contributions. Each of them has integrated aspects of research literature which previous writers had assumed to be alien or even contradictory. Each of them made effective arguments for meaningful differential constructs, such as acute-chronic, process-reactive, and paranoid-nonparanoid. In spite of the definitional looseness which has been described here, each author has advanced hypotheses which have met the criterion of falsifiability in comparison to earlier, more global theories.

Their theories, however, appear to reflect a transitional phase rather than the beginning of a new approach to research in this area. From the review just completed, a number of requirements for a new systematic approach to research in schizophrenia can be enumerated:

1. The construct of schizophrenia itself must be modified or discarded. Either a more specific set of operations must be developed or groups must be identified for study in terms of specific deficits without regard to conventional psychiatric diagnosis.

2. The recent emphasis upon specific subgroups of schizophrenia must give way to a more sophisticated approach. First, global dichotomies such as process-reactive, acute-chronic, and paranoid-nonparanoid, must be examined with regard to whether certain relevant components could be identified as having greater predictive utility. For example, why is marriage such an important item in the process-reactive distinction? What are the variables which affect the temporal course of schizophrenic disorder?

Do different kinds of delusions or factors associated with them have differential classification value? Second, once the differential constructs are refined to their optimal focus of convenience, a dimensional, as opposed to classification, logic should be examined. Third, the interrelations among the differential constructs should be more carefully explored. That is, research must consider all dimensions in the same study rather than just one dimension at a time.

3. More attention must be given to brain models and other tentative theoretical formulations by which behavioral, genetic, neurophysiological, biochemical, early history, and drug findings can be discussed within the same framework. For the present, the etiology of schizophrenia is often formulated within only a single restricted framework. Either the data of other frameworks are ignored or are construed as the secondary result of the framework considered as primary by the investigator. A major question in current research is whether a particular deficit is a primary symptom or is secondary to some other aspect of the disorder. Typically, the data of current studies cannot support one position or the other. Models and theories which cut across these different areas would help generate research to prevent this stalemate.

4. More attention must be given to the refinement of behavioral techniques which will reliably and validly measure aspects of the perceptual system being investigated. Choice of psychophysical method and more adequate screening of patients on visual parameters appear to be especially important. As such measures are developed and deficits are more clearly identified, new individual difference constructs can be formulated.

5. The behavioral scientist should not place all his hopes upon the "golden chalice," i.e., isolating a single highly reliable variable which explains everything about schizophrenia. Instead, he may have to resign himself to the reality that some factors, such as certain attentional ones, can only be measured and inferred amid a background of irrelevant variance. Multiple dependent variables must be employed. These should be selected so that they share the small but stable amount of variance common to the factor in question.

6. In terms of content, two aspects of research in schizophrenia appear to be especially in need of development. First, the data of the clinician (including attentional deficit, psycholinguistic dysfunction, and other aspects of schizophrenic disorder) are in need of integration with laboratory observations. Second, the understanding of and distinction between relevant and irrelevant informational cues need much more theoretical and empirical attention.

7. Finally, as the basic aspects of schizophrenic behavior become clarified, a more informed attack could then be made upon the etiology, prevention, and treatment of schizophrenic disorders.

References

Agnew, N., & Agnew, M. Drive level effects on tasks of narrow and broad attention. *Quarterly Journal of Experimental Psychology*, 1963, 15, 58–62.

Berlyne, D. *Conflict, arousal and curiosity.* New York: McGraw-Hill, 1960.

Bleuler, E. The basic symptoms of schizophrenia. In D. Rapaport (Ed.), *Organization and pathology of thought.* New York: Columbia University Press, 1951. Pp. 581–649.

Borinsky, M., Neale, J. M., Cromwell, R. L., & Fox, R. Two-flash threshold in schizophrenics using signal-detection methodology. Unpublished manuscript, Vanderbilt University, 1967.

Broadbent, D. E. *Perception and communication.* New York: Macmillan (Pergamon), 1958.

Broen, W. E. Response disorganization and breadth of observation in schizophrenia. *Psychological Review*, 1966, 73, 579–585.

Brosgole, L., & Cristal, R. M. The role of phenomenal displacement on the perception of the visual upright. *Perception and Psychophysics*, 1967, 2, 179–188.

Brown, G. W. Length of hospital stay and schizophrenia: A review of statistical studies. *Acta Psychiatry et Neurology Scandanavia*, 1960, 35, 414–430.

Buss, A. H. *Psychopathology.* New York: Wiley, 1966.

Callaway, E. The influence of amobarbital (amylobarbitone) and methamphetamine on the focus of attention. *Journal of Mental Science*, 1959, 105, 382–392.

Callaway, E., & Thompson, S. V. Sympathetic activity and perception. *Psychosomatic Medicine*, 1953, 15, 443–455.

Chapman, J. S., & McGhie, A. A comparative study of disordered attention in schizophrenia. *Journal of Mental Science*, 1962, 108, 487–500.

Chapman, L. J. The role of type of distractor in the "concrete" performance of schizophrenics. *Journal of Personality*, 1956, 25, 130–141.

Clark, W. C. The "psyche" in psychophysics: A sensory-decision theory analysis of the effect of instructions on flicker sensitivity and response bias. *Psychological Bulletin*, 1966, 65, 358–366.

Clark, W. C., Brown, J. C., & Rutschmann, J. Flicker sensitivity and response bias in psychiatric patients and normal subjects. *Journal of Abnormal Psychology*, 1967, 72, 35–42.

Cromwell, R. L., & Dokecki, P. R. Schizophrenic language: A disattention interpretation. In S. Rosenberg & J. H. Koplin (Eds.), *Developments in applied psycholinguistics research.* New York: Macmillan, 1968. Pp. 209–260.

Crookes, T. G. Size constancy and literalness in Rorschach Test. *British Journal of Medical Psychology*, 1957, 30, 99–106.

Davis, D., Cromwell, R. L., & Held, J. M. Size estimation in emotionally disturbed children and schizophrenic adults. *Journal of Abnormal Psychology*, 1967, 72, 395–401.

Farina, A., & Webb, W. W. Premorbid adjustment and recovery. *Journal of Nervous and Mental Disease*, 1956, 124, 612–613.

Faw, T. T., & Nunnally, J. C. The effects on eye movements of complexity, novelty, and affective tone. *Perception and Psychophysics*, 1967, 2, 263–267.

Gardner, R. W. Cognitive controls of attention deployment as determinants of visual illusions. *Journal of Abnormal and Social Psychology*, 1961, 62, 120–127.

Gardner, R. W., Holzman, P. S., Klein, G. S., Linton, H. B., & Spence, D. P. Cognitive control: A study of individual consistencies in cognitive behavior. *Psychological Issues*, 1959, 1(4); 186 pp.

Gardner, R. W., & Long, R. I. Control, defence and centration effect: A study of scanning behavior. *British Journal of Psychology*, 1962, 53, 129–140. (a)

Gardner, R. W., & Long, R. I. Cognitive controls of attention and inhibition: A study of individual consistencies. *British Journal of Psychology*, 1962, 53, 381–388. (b)

Goldstein, M. J., Held, J. M., & Cromwell, R. L. Premorbid adjustment and paranoid-non-paranoid status in schizophrenia. *Psychological Bulletin*, 1968, **70**, 382-386.

Greenberg, A. Directed and undirected learning in chronic schizophrenia. Unpublished PhD Thesis, Columbia University, 1953.

Gregory, R. L. *Eye and brain*. New York: McGraw-Hill, 1966.

Hamilton, V. Size constancy and cue responsiveness in psychosis. *British Journal of Psychology*, 1963, **54**, 64-74.

Harris, J. G. Size estimation of pictures as a function of thematic content for schizophrenic and normal subjects. *Journal of Personality*, 1957, **25**, 651-671.

Harway, N. I., & Salzman, L. F. Size constancy in psychopathology. *Journal of Abnormal and Social Psychology*, 1964, **69**, 606-613.

Held, J. M., & Cromwell, R. L. Premorbid adjustment in schizophrenia: An evaluation of a method and some general comments. *Journal of Nervous and Mental Disease*, 1968, **146**, 264-272.

Holway, A. H., & Boring, E. G. Determinants of apparent visual size with distance variant. *American Journal of Psychology*, 1941, **54**, 21-37.

Johanssen, W. J., & O'Connell, M. J. Institutionalization and perceptual decrement in chronic schizophrenia. *Perceptual and Motor Skills*, 1965, **21**, 244-246.

Johnson, M. H., & Ries, H. A. Validational study of the self-report scale for process-reactive schizophrenia. *Journal of Consulting Psychology*, 1967, **31**, 321-322.

Joynson, R. B. An experimental synthesis of the associationist and Gestalt accounts of the perception of size. *Quarterly Journal of Experimental Psychology*, 1958, **10**, 65-76.

Kar, B. C. Müller-Lyer illusion in schizophrenics as a function of field distraction and exposure time. Unpublished master's thesis, George Peabody College for Teachers, 1967.

Klein, G. S. Need and regulation. In M. R. Jones (Ed.), *Nebraska symposium on motivation*. Lincoln: University of Nebraska Press, 1954. Pp. 222-274.

Kraepelin, E. *Dementia praecox and paraphrenia*. (Transl. by R. M. Barclay) Chicago: Chicago Medical Book, 1919.

Lang, P. H., & Buss, A. H. Psychological deficit in schizophrenia: II. Interference and activation. *Journal of Abnormal Psychology*, 1965, **70**, 77-106.

Leibowitz, H. W., & Pishkin, V. Perceptual size constancy in chronic schizophrenia. *Journal of Consulting Psychology*, 1961, **25**, 196-199.

Lovinger, E. Perceptual contact with reality in schizophrenia. *Journal of Abnormal and Social Psychology*, 1956, **52**, 87-91.

McGhie, A., & Chapman, J. S. Disorders of attention and perception in early schizophrenia. *British Journal of Medical Psychology*, 1961, **34**, 103-116.

Maher, B. A. *Principles of psychopathology*. New York: McGraw-Hill, 1966.

Mehl, M. M. The effect of brief sensory deprivation and sensory stimulation on the cognitive functioning of schizophrenics. Unpublished doctoral dissertation, George Peabody College for Teachers, 1966.

Miller, M. B., and Cromwell, R. L. Response competition and the anxiety-as-drive concept: A direct study. Paper presented at the convention of the Southeastern Psychological Association Convention, Gatlinburg, Tenn., 1961.

Neale, J. M., & Cromwell, R. L. Size estimation in schizophrenics as a function of stimulus presentation time. *Journal of Abnormal Psychology*, 1968, **73**, 44-49.

Neale, J. M., Davis, D., & Cromwell, R. L. Size estimation in schizophrenia: A failure to replicate. Unpublished manuscript, Vanderbilt University, 1967.

Neale, J. M., McIntyre, C. W., Fox, R., & Cromwell, R. L. Span of apprehension in acute schizophrenics. *Journal of Abnormal Psychology*, 1969, **74**, 593-596.

Nutall, R. L., & Solomon, L. F. Factorial structure and prognostic significance of premorbid adjustment in schizophrenia. *Journal of Consulting Psychology*, 1965, **29**, 362-372.

Payne, R. W. The measurement and significance of overinclusive thinking and retardation in schizophrenic patients. In P. H. Hoch & J. Zubin (Eds.), *Psychopathology of schizophrenia*. New York: Grune & Stratton, 1966. Pp. 77–97.

Payne, R. W., Caird, W. K., & Laverty, S. G. Overinclusive thinking and delusions in schizophrenic patients. *Journal of Abnormal and Social Psychology*, 1964, 68, 562–566.

Payne, R. W., & Hewlett, J. A. G. Thought disorder in psychotic patients. In H. J. Eysenck (Ed.), *Experiments in personality*. Vol. II. London: Routledge & Kegan Paul, 1960. Pp. 3–104.

Perez, R. Size constancy in normals and schizophrenics. In W. H. Ittelson and S. B. Katush (Eds.), *Perceptual changes in psychopathology*. New Brunswick, N. J.: Rutgers University Press, 1961. Pp. 39–55.

Phillips, L. Case history data and prognosis in schizophrenia. *Journal of Nervous and Mental Disease*, 1953, 117, 515–525.

Piaget, J. *The psychology of intelligence*. London: Routledge & Kegan Paul, 1950.

Pishkin, V., Smith, T. E., & Leibowitz, H. W. The influence of symbolic stimulus value on perceived size in chronic schizophrenia. *Journal of Consulting Psychology*, 1962, 26, 323–330.

Price, R. H., & Erikson, C. W. Size constancy in schizophrenia: A reanalysis. *Journal of Abnormal Psychology*, 1966, 71, 155–161.

Quarton, G. C., & Talland, G. A. The effects of methamphetamine and pentobarbital on two measures of attention. *Psychopharmacologia*, 1962, 3, 66–71.

Rappaport, M. Competing voice messages: Effects of message load and drugs on the ability of acute schizophrenics to attend. *Archives of General Psychiatry*, 1967, 17, 97–103.

Rappaport, M., Rogers, N., Reynolds, S., & Weinmann, R. Comparative ability of normal and chronic schizophrenic subjects to attend to competing voice messages: Effects of method of presentation, message load and drugs. *Journal of Nervous and Mental Disease*, 1966, 143, 16–27.

Raush, H. L. Perceptual constancy in schizophrenia. *Journal of Personality*, 1952, 21, 176–187.

Sanders, R., & Pacht, A. R. Perceptual constancy of known clinical groups. *Journal of Consulting Psychology*, 1952, 10, 440–444.

Schlesinger, H. J. Cognitive attitudes in relation to susceptibility to interference. *Journal of Personality*, 1954, 22, 354–374.

Shakow, D. Some psychological features of schizophrenia. In M. L. Reymert (Ed.), *Feelings and emotions*. New York: McGraw-Hill, 1950. Pp. 383–390.

Shakow, D. Segmental set. *Archives of General Psychiatry, 1962,* 6, 1–17.

Sherman, J. A. Problems of sex differences in space perception and aspects of intellectual functioning. *Psychological Review*, 1967, 74, 290–299.

Silverman, J. The problem of attention in research and theory in schizophrenia. *Psychological Review*, 1964, 71, 352–379. (a)

Silverman, J. The scanning control mechanism and "cognitive filtering" in paranoid and nonparanoid schizophrenia. *Journal of Consulting Psychology*, 1964, 28, 385–393. (b)

Silverman, J., Berg, P. S., & Kantor, R. Some perceptual correlates of institutionalization. *Journal of Nervous and Mental Disease*, 1965, 141, 651–657.

Silverman, J., & Gaarder, K. Rates of saccadic eye movement and size judgements of normals and schizophrenics. *Perceptual and Motor Skills*, 1967, 25, 661–667.

Solley, C. M., & Murphy, G. *The development of the perceptual world*. New York: Basic Books, 1960.

Solomon, L. F., & Zlotowski, M. The relationship between the Elgin and the Phillips measures of process-reactive schizophrenia. *Journal of Nervous and Mental Disease*, 1964, 138, 32–37.

Stilson, D. W., Kopell, B. S., Vandenbergh, R., & Downs, M. P. Perceptual recognition in the presence of noise by psychiatric patients. *Journal of Nervous and Mental Disease,* 1966, **142**, 235-247.

Swets, J. A., Tanner, W. P., & Birdsall, T. G. Decision processes in perception. *Psychological Review,* 1961, **68**, 301-340.

Taylor, J. A. A personality scale of manifest anxiety. *Journal of Abnormal and Social Psychology,* 1953, **48**, 285-290.

Topping, G. G., & O'Connor, N. The response of chronic schizophrenics to incentives. *British Journal of Medical Psychology,* 1960, **33**, 211-214.

Ullmann, L. P., & Giovannoni, J. M. The development of a self-report measure of the process-reactive continuum. *Journal of Nervous and Mental Disease,* 1964, **138**, 38-42.

Venables, P. H. Selectivity of attention, withdrawal, and cortical activation. *Archives of General Psychiatry,* 1963, **9**, 74-78.

Venables, P. H. Input dysfunction in schizophrenia. In B. A. Maher (Ed.), *Progress in experimental personality research.* Vol. 1. New York: Academic Press. 1964. Pp. 1-47. (a)

Venables, P. H. Performance and level of activation in schizophrenics and normals. *British Journal of Psychology,* 1964, **55**, 207-218. (b)

Venables, P. H., & Wing, J. K. Level of arousal and the subclassification of schizophrenia. *Archives of General Psychiatry,* 1962, **7**, 114-119.

Weckowicz, T. E. Size constancy in schizophrenic patients. *Journal of Mental Science,* 1957, **103**, 475-486.

Weckowicz, T. E. Autonomic activity as measured by the mecholyl test and size constancy in schizophrenic patients. *Psychosomatic Medicine,* 1958, **20**, 66-71.

Weckowicz, T. E., & Blewett, D. B. Size constancy and abstract thinking in schizophrenic patients. *Journal of Mental Science,* 1959, **105**, 909-934.

Winer, H. R. Incidental learning in schizophrenics. Unpublished PhD Thesis, Purdue University, 1954.

Witkin, H. A., Dyk, R. B., Faterson, H. F., Goodenough, D. R., & Karp, S. A. *Psychological differentiation.* New York: Wiley, 1962.

Witkin, H. A., Lewis, H. B., Hertzman, M., Machover, K., Meissner, P. B., & Wapner, S. *Personality through perception.* New York: Harper & Row, 1954.

Zaffy, D. J., & Bruning, J. L. Drive and the range of cue utilization. *Journal of Experimental Psychology,* 1966, **71**, 382-384.

Zahn, T. P. Acquired and symbolic affective value as determinants of size estimation in schizophrenic and normal subjects. *Journal of Abnormal and Social Psychology,* 1959, **58**, 39-47.

Zahn, T. P., Rosenthal, D., & Lawlor, W. G. GSR orienting reactions to visual and auditory stimuli in chronic schizophrenic and normal subjects. Paper presented at the Society for Psychophysiological Research, Denver, October 1962.

Zahn, T. P., Rosenthal, D., & Shakow, D. Reaction time in schizophrenic and normal subjects in relation to the sequence of series of regular preparatory intervals. *Journal of Abnormal and Social Psychology,* 1961, **63**, 161-168.

NEW CONCEPTIONS IN THE STUDY OF ACHIEVEMENT MOTIVATION

Bernard Weiner[1]

DEPARTMENT OF PSYCHOLOGY, UNIVERSITY OF CALIFORNIA,
LOS ANGELES, CALIFORNIA

This paper focuses upon current conceptual issues within the domain of achievement-related behavior, and the interrelationship between theory and empirical evidence. First, a theory of achievement motivation formu-

[1]This paper was supported by a grant from the Graduate School of the University of California, Los Angeles. The author wishes to thank John Atkinson, Paul Feldman, Patrick Johnson, Penelope Potepan, Carol Price, Paul Slovic, and Anthony Stahelski for their many suggestions and aid in conducting the reported experiments.

lated by Atkinson in 1957 and the data supporting that theory will be examined. Continued analysis of Atkinson's 1957 model revealed certain conceptual inadequacies, and has resulted in important modifications of that theory (Atkinson, 1964; Atkinson & Cartwright, 1964; Weiner, 1965b). The conceptual changes and the data suggesting that such alterations are necessary will be discussed. Finally, research stimulated by the newer conceptions will be reviewed. Included in the review will be two previously unpublished experiments conducted by this writer.

I. The Initial Theory of Achievement Motivation

Atkinson (1957) conceives achievement-oriented behavior to be a resultant of an approach-avoidance conflict. The affect associated with approach to the goal is a hope of success; the affect inhibiting achievement-related behavior is a fear of failure (see Feather, 1963b). The resultant (approach-avoidance) achievement-oriented tendency (T_A) is conceptualized as:

$$T_A = (M_S \times P_s \times I_s) + (M_{AF} \times P_f \times -I_f)$$
$$(M_S \times P_s \times I_s) - (M_{AF} \times P_f \times I_f) \tag{1}$$

In this model, M_S represents a relatively stable personality disposition to strive for success. Operationally, the strength of M_S generally is determined by scoring a Thematic Apperception Test (TAT) according to a prescribed method of content analysis (see Atkinson, 1958a). The French Test of Insight (French, 1958), graphic expression (Aronson, 1958), and an Achievement Risk-Preference Scale (O'Connor, 1962) are among the other measures which have been employed with some success to assess the strength of the motive to succeed, or the need for achievement (n Ach). The probability of success, P_s, represents the probability that a given instrumental action will lead to the goal; P_s denotes a cognitive expectancy that a response made to a given stimulus will lead to the goal stimulus (Atkinson, 1954). P_s has been defined operationally by presenting subjects false norms (e.g., Feather, 1961), controlling reinforcement history (e.g., Weiner & Rosenbaum, 1965), having subjects compete against varying numbers of individuals (e.g., Atkinson, 1958b), or varying the actual (and perceived) difficulty of the tasks (e.g., Atkinson & Litwin, 1960). I_s symbolizes the incentive value of success. Within Atkinson's model for achievement-oriented behavior, I_s does not have independent operational existence; I_s is determined by the magnitude of P_s: $I_s = 1 - P_s$. Atkinson reasons that the incentive value of success is an affect often labeled "pride." It is postulated that the amount of pride experienced following goal attainment is inversely related to the subjective difficulty of the task, i.e., one experiences more pride following success at a task perceived as difficult than after success at a task perceived as easy. Because $I_s = 1 - P_s$, and I_s and P_s are multiplicatively related, the greatest approach tendency is derived when $P_s = .50$. In that condition $P_s \times I_s$ is maximum, or .25. As P_s increases or decreases from .50, approach motivation decreases. The approach tendency toward a goal, therefore, is portrayed by a bell-shaped curve relating P_s and the strength of approach motivation. The magnitude of M_s determines the absolute level and slope of that function.

The determinants of avoidance are analogous with those of the approach tendency. M_{AF} symbolizes a relatively stable personality disposition to avoid failure. Operationally, this component generally is determined by the score on the Mandler-Sarason Test Anxiety Questionnaire (TAQ) (Mandler & Sarason, 1952). Among the environmental determinants of avoidance behavior, P_f represents the subjective probability of failure, and I_f the incentive value of failure. The negative affect associated with nonattainment of an achievement-related goal is considered to be shame. Atkinson reasons that the easier the task, the greater the shame experienced following failure; $-I_f$, therefore, is conceived as $-(1 - P_f)$. It is further assumed that the subjective probabilities in the model total unity: $P_s + P_f = 1$. Inasmuch as $I_f = -(1 - P_f)$ and I_f and P_f are multiplicative, the maximum avoidance tendency is derived when $P_f = .50$, and decreases as P_f increases or decreases from the .50 level. The tendency to avoid failure also can be plotted as a bell-shaped curve relating strength of avoidance with task difficulty; the magnitude of M_{AF} determines the absolute level and slope of that function.

The strength of M_S relative to M_{AF} determines whether individuals will approach or avoid achievement tasks. The motive measures, therefore, may be considered weights given to the functions which relate motivation to task probability. If $M_S > M_{AF}$, then greater weight is given to the approach than avoidance tendency; and vice versa. When $M_S > M_{AF}$, resultant achievement motivation is positive and maximum when $P_s = .50$. Among these subjects resultant achievement motivation is positive but relatively weak when P_s is high or low. When $M_{AF} > M_S$, resultant achievement motivation is negative and most inhibitory when P_f (and P_s) = .50; among these subjects achievement motivation is negative but least inhibitory when P_s is very high or low. (The relative strengths of the empirically independent T A T and T A Q scores are compared by Z-scoring the test distributions; see Atkinson, 1964.)

The relationships enumerated above are clarified by making some simple mathematical transformations in the model. There is only one degree of freedom among the four environmental determinants of behavior (P_s, I_s, P_f, I_f). The model for achievement-related behavior therefore can be mathematically represented as:

$$T_A = (M_S - M_{AF}) [P_s \times (1 - P_s)] \tag{2}$$

Equation (2) clearly indicates that the strength of M_S relative to M_{AF} determines the positive or negative sign of the achievement tendency, and that the motive measures interact with situational determinants of behavior.

Equations (1) and (2) specify the magnitude of achievement motivation aroused in achievement-oriented situations. Behavior, however, is overdetermined; a response may be instigated by many sources of motivation. For example, an individual may engage in achievement activities because of the monetary rewards or potential friendships associated with goal attainment. To capture the overdetermination of behavior, Atkinson (1964) includes extrinsic (nonachievement-related) sources of motivation among the determinants of achievement activities:

$$T_A = \text{resultant achievement motivation} + \text{extrinsic motivation} \tag{3}$$

The magnitude of the extrinsic sources presumably is a function of individual differences, probabilities, and goal incentives. In an experiment investigating and measuring only achievement-related motivation, extrinsic motivations contribute error variance. They represent uncontrolled sources of motivation.

It is clear from Eq. (2) that when $M_{AF} > M_S$, T_A is negative. Individuals with this constellation of motives should avoid achievement-related activities. In situations where individuals low in resultant achievement motivation ($M_{AF} > M_S$) do engage in achievement behavior, the model specifies that this behavior must be attributed to extrinsic motivation. Further, Eq. (3) indicates that as the importance of the extrinsic motivation increases, the relative variance in behavior accounted for by the achievement source of motivation decreases. Differential predictions of behavior made only on the basis of differences in achievement motivation are not expected to be confirmed in situations which are influenced by many sources of motivation. Grades in school exemplify an overdetermined behavioral index which is not possible to predict with any accuracy, given only information relevant to achievement motivation (see McKeachie, 1961).

II. Evidence Supporting the Theory

A. Choice

Studies of choice can be categorized into two types. Selection either has been constrained within achievement-related options, or choice is between an achievement task and an unspecified or nonachievement-related alternative activity. As previously indicated, when $M_S > M_{AF}$, T_A is positive; these individuals should approach achievement tasks. Conversely, when $M_{AF} > M_S$, T_A is negative; these individuals should avoid achievement-related activities (assuming that extrinsic sources are minimal). Atkinson (1953) reports that subjects high in need for achievement are more likely to volunteer to undertake an apparent achievement activity than subjects low in need for achievement. That is, given a choice between an achievement-related activity and an unspecified alternative, subjects predictably differ in preference as a function of their motive score. Green (1963) indirectly replicated this finding. He demonstrated that volunteer subjects exhibit a greater Zeigarnik Effect than nonvolunteer subjects; Atkinson (1953) previously had found that high M_S subjects show a greater Zeigarnik Effect under achievement-oriented instructions than low M_S subjects. In a free choice situation which permitted the selection of a nonachievement-related activity, Weiner and Rosenbaum (1965) found that on the first trial subjects in whom $M_{AF} > M_S$ were less likely to undertake the achievement-related alternative than subjects considered to be high in resultant achievement motivation ($M_S > M_{AF}$). Further, French (1956) has shown that subjects high in M_S are more likely than low M_S subjects to choose work partners who would be instrumental to the attainment of achievement, as opposed to affiliative, goals.

Studies constrained within achievement-related contexts provide the best evidence for the validity of the 1957 conception of achievement motivation. In these studies subjects select a task to perform from a number of tasks which differ in reported or objective level of difficulty. The hypothesis generally tested has been that subjects in whom $M_S > M_{AF}$ will prefer tasks of intermediate difficulty more than subjects in whom $M_{AF} > M_S$. This prediction has been confirmed by many investigators (e.g., Atkinson, Bastian, Earl, & Litwin, 1960; Atkinson & Litwin, 1960; McClelland, 1958; Moulton, 1965; Raynor & Smith, 1966; Weiner, 1965b). In an extension of this finding to vocational aspiration, Mahone (1960) reports that subjects in whom $M_S > M_{AF}$ are more realistic in their vocational choice than subjects in whom $M_{AF} > M_S$. The latter subjects were prone to strive for goals which were too easy or too difficult relative to their level of ability. A similar finding has been reported by Morris (1966). In another study related to scholastic choice, Isaacson (1964) found that male students classified as high in achievement motivation were more likely to select major areas of study perceived as intermediate in difficulty than students classified as low in achievement motivation.

B. MAGNITUDE OF PERFORMANCE

Magnitude or intensity of performance has not been used frequently as a dependent variable in studies relevant to the validation of the 1957 model. Atkinson (1958b) reports that speed of performance at an arithmetic task was greater when the female subjects competed against only one other student, than when competing against 20 other students. However, in that study relatively similar performance was exhibited by the high and low M_S groups. More recently, Ryan and Lakie (1965) presented evidence that performance on a perceptual motor task increased under two-person competitive situations among subjects in whom $M_S > M_{AF}$. Among subjects classified as low in resultant achievement motivation, performance decreased when competition was against one other person. In an extension of this finding, Vaught and Newman (1966) found that motor steadiness was greater among low anxious than high anxious subjects in a competitive situation, while there were no significant differences in steadiness between the groups given noncompetitive instructions.

C. PERSISTENCE OF BEHAVIOR IN PROGRESS

Atkinson's 1957 model also has received support from studies employing persistence of behavior as the dependent variable. Atkinson and Litwin (1960) report that students high in resultant achievement motivation persist longer at a final exam than students low in resultant achievement motivation. Prior to that investigation, French and Thomas (1958) had discovered that high M_S subjects persist longer at an insoluble problem than low M_S subjects.

In the two studies cited above the nature of the alternative activity and the P_s at the activity in progress were not specified. These factors in part determine persistence of behavior. Persistence can be considered to be the repeated choice of the activity in progress, and implicitly involves a comparison between the strengths of motivation to perform any of the behaviors available to the person (see Feather, 1961).[2]

[2]Persistence of behavior and intensity of performance need not be positively related in investigations employing these two dependent variables. Consider a situation in which there is little motivation to perform the activity in progress, but no alternative activities available.

Feather (1961) specified the nature of the alternative activity and the P_s at the achievement task in his study of persistence. Subjects classified according to resultant achievement motivation were given an insoluble puzzle to complete. The alternative activity was another achievement-related puzzle task. In one condition subjects were told that the original puzzle was extremely difficult ($P_s = .05$); in a second condition the task was introduced as relatively easy ($P_s = .70$). It was assumed that the repeated failures would continually reduce the P_s values. When $P_s = .70$, achievement motivation was expected to increase initially following failure among subjects in whom $M_S > M_{AF}$. In that condition, during the first trials the P_s would approach the level of intermediate difficulty. However, when $P_s = .05$, achievement motivation was expected to decrease continually following failure; P_s was shifting further from the .50 level. Feather predicted, and found, that subjects in whom $M_S > M_{AF}$ persist longer in the $P_s = .70$ condition than in the $P_s = .05$ condition. On the other hand, among subjects in whom $M_{AF} > M_S$, achievement motivation was expected to be especially inhibited following failure when the P_s initially was .70. In that condition P_s approached closer to the level of intermediate difficulty. Following failure in the $P_s = .05$ condition, resultant achievement motivation was expected to be less inhibitory for these subjects; P_s and P_f were moving away from the .50 level. Feather hypothesized that when $M_{AF} > M_S$ there would be greater persistence in the .05 condition than in the .70 condition. This hypothesis also was confirmed. Feather (1963a) reports a replication of these findings when the P_s at the alternative achievement activity also was specified.

III. Weakness of the Model and a Conceptual Change

Although Atkinson's model for achievement-oriented behavior has received empirical support from many studies, it contains some conceptual difficulties (see Atkinson, 1964, pp. 295–298). Foremost among these is that the model, like other contemporary theories of motivation, is stimulus bound. The individual is viewed as inactive until a stimulus is presented which instigates behavior. It is assumed that the stimulus engages a motive and initiates a cognitive, inferential process. Other theorists, however, have accumulated evidence that behavior persists in the ab-

---

There should be great persistence, but poor performance. Conversely, one might be highly motivated to perform the activity in progress, but a very attractive alternative is available; poor persistence but high performance is expected. Given these circumstances, there will be a negative correlation between two dependent variables which presumably "measure the same thing."

sence of the instigating, external stimulus, and have postulated construct(s) to account for the maintenance of goal-seeking, purposive behavior. Freud (1915) cites clinical observations related to dreams, slips of the tongue, and symptom formation to support his notion of persisting internal wishes; Lewin (1935), supported by demonstrations of the recall and spontaneous resumption of previously interrupted tasks (Zeigarnik, 1927; Ovsiankina, 1928), postulated the concept of an enduring tense system which persists until an intention is fulfilled; Hebb (1949) discusses the organization and integration of behavioral sequences to support the concept of relatively autonomous phase sequence activity; and Peak (1958) utilizes concepts of psychological distance and feedback structure to account for assimilation and contrast phenomena which proceed in the absence of the instigating stimulus.

Atkinson and Cartwright (1964) recently also have attempted to account for the persistence of a goal-directed tendency. Using the language of Newtonian physics, they postulate "inertia" as a first principle of motivation. Atkinson and Cartwright assert that a goal-directed tendency, once aroused, will persist until the goal is attained. (This point is elaborated in Atkinson, 1964, p. 310.) The strength of the immediate tendency to act is conceived to be a function of the strength of the previously aroused but unsatisfied motivation, called the "inertial tendency," plus the strength of the tendency aroused by the immediate stimulus situation. They extended the formal model for achievement-oriented behavior to:

$$T_A = (M_S \times P_s \times I_s) - (M_{AF} \times P_f \times I_f) + T_{Gi} + \text{extrinsic motivation}$$

T_{Gi} symbolizes the inertial motivational tendency to strive for an achievement-related goal. The antecedent condition for the continuation of aroused motivation is nonattainment of an anticipated goal. Atkinson (1964) assumes that the inertial tendency is a general striving toward all goals relevant to a given motive. That is, following failure at one task, there is an inertial tendency to strive for any achievement-related activity.

A. DATA SUPPORTING THE EXTENDED MODEL

The persistence of aroused achievement motivation following nonattainment of a goal was demonstrated by this author (Weiner, 1965b) in a study guided by the experimental procedure developed by Feather. Individuals classified as high or low in resultant achievement motivation were given an achievement task to perform, knowing that they could shift to an activity unrelated to achievement motivation whenever they so desired. There were two experimental conditions. In one condition false norms conveyed that the achievement task was relatively difficult ($P_s = .30$); in the second condition the norms conveyed that the task was relatively easy ($P_s = .70$). Table I indicates the strength of motivation to undertake the achievement activity among the two motive groups. For illustrative purposes, it is assumed that when $M_S > M_{AF}$, $M_S = 2$ and $M_{AF} = 1$, and vice versa when $M_{AF} > M_S$. (For ease of illustration extrinsic sources of motivation are not included in the analysis, and on the initial trial T_{Gi} is assumed to be zero.) Table I indicates that on Trial One the strength of the achievement-oriented tendency is equal among subjects with similar motive constellations.

In this study, subjects in the $P_s = .30$ condition received repeated failure experiences; subjects in the $P_s = .70$ condition experienced continual success. It was assumed that the change in P_s following failure was equal but opposite in direction to the shift in P_s following success (e.g., .1). Table I shows that on Trial Two the strength of achievement motivation aroused by the immediate stimulus situation again is equal among subjects with similar motive dispositions. Therefore, Atkinson's 1957 model specifies that there should be equality in performance between conditions within the motive groups. However, the inertial model includes a component which captures previously aroused but unsatisfied motivation. T_{G_i} is greater after failure than success; the extended model leads to the prediction that in this situation subjects will perform with greater vigor following failure than after success (see Table I, 1957 and inertial approach models).[3]

The experimental design, therefore, permitted a critical comparison of the adequacy of the two models. The differential predictions were made possible by specifying the P_s at the achievement task, and having the P_s symmetrical around the level of intermediate difficulty. This allowed the motivational effects mediated by the expectancy of success to be disentangled from the influence of inertial motivation. In prior studies these two have been confounded because failure influences the magnitude of both situational and inertial sources of motivation.

The achievement activity employed in the study was a digit-symbol substitution task. There were two dependent variables: speed of performance (number of symbols substituted per unit of time), and persistence of behavior (number of digit-symbol tasks attempted). Failure and success were manipulated by interrupting subjects prior to task completion, or allowing them to finish the task before an artificial time limit.

---

[3]If one assumed that the change in P_s following success were greater than the change in P_s after failure an inertial conception would not be required to make this prediction. However, there is evidence (Feather & Saville, 1967) indicating that the probability shifts following failure are greater than the shifts after success.

TABLE I

STRENGTH OF ACHIEVEMENT MOTIVATION ACCORDING TO THREE MODELS OF ACHIEVEMENT-ORIENTED BEHAVIOR

Model	Trial	Condition	Motive classification	
			$M_S > M_{AF}$	$M_{AF} > M_S$
All	One	$P_s = .30$	$2 \times .3 \times .7 - (1 \times .7 \times .3) = .21^a$	$1 \times .3 \times .7 - (2 \times .7 \times .3) = -.21$
		$P_s = .70$	$2 \times .7 \times .3 - (1 \times .3 \times .7) = .21$	$1 \times .7 \times .3 - (2 \times .3 \times .7) = -.21$
1957 (no inertial component)	Two	$P_s = .30^b$	$2 \times .2 \times .8 - (1 \times .8 \times .2) = .16$	$1 \times .2 \times .8 - (2 \times .8 \times .2) = -.16$
		$P_s = .70^c$	$2 \times .8 \times .2 - (1 \times .2 \times .8) = .16$	$1 \times .8 \times .2 - (2 \times .2 \times .8) = -.16$
Inertial approach component	Two	$P_s = .30$	$2 \times .2 \times .8 - (1 \times .8 \times .2) + .42^d = .58$	$1 \times .2 \times .8 - (2 \times .8 \times .2) + .21 = .05$
		$P_s = .70$	$2 \times .8 \times .2 - (1 \times .2 \times .8) = .16$	$1 \times .8 \times .2 - (2 \times .2 \times .8) = -.16$
Resultant inertial component	Two	$P_s = .30$	$2 \times .2 \times .8 - (1 \times .8 \times .2) + .21^e = .37$	$1 \times .2 \times .8 - (2 \times .8 \times .2) - .21 = -.37$
		$P_s = .70$	$2 \times .8 \times .2 - (1 \times .2 \times .8) = .16$	$1 \times .8 \times .2 - (2 \times .2 \times .8) = -.16$

[a] Strength of resultant achievement motivation.
[b] Failure condition.
[c] Success condition.
[d] $.42 = 2 \times .3 \times .7$, or strength of approach motivation.
[e] $.21 = 2 \times .3 \times .7 - (1 \times .7 \times .3)$, or strength of approach-avoidance motivation.

The data indicated that subjects in whom $M_S > M_{AF}$ persisted significantly longer and performed the task faster in the Failure than Success condition. These data provide strong evidence in favor of the model which includes an inertial motivational component among the determinants of behavior.

However, contradictory results were obtained for subjects in whom $M_{AF} > M_S$. These individuals performed with significantly greater intensity and exhibited a tendency to persist longer in the repeated success than in the repeated failure condition. Neither Atkinson's 1957 version of the model nor the model including the inertial component were confirmed for this subject population. As indicated previously, the 1957 model predicted no difference in performance between the two conditions, and the inertial approach model specified more intense performance after failure than success for all subjects.

The results of the study raised two questions. First, was there other evidence which supported the observed pattern of results? And second, what were the implications of the data for the achievement-related conception? If the data were reliable, how could the theory be modified further to account for the behavior of subjects classified as low in resultant achievement motivation?

B. Reliability of the Results

Weiner's (1965b) study revealed an interaction between individual differences in resultant achievement motivation and the subsequent effects of success and failure experiences. A survey of the experimental literature in this area has revealed that failure generally dampens the subsequent performance of subjects who would be considered low in resultant achievement motivation, while success seems to enhance the performance of these individuals. Conversely, prior failure appears to facilitate the future performance of subjects high in resultant achievement motivation, while these individuals exhibit performance decrements after success experiences. The interaction reported by Weiner appears to be a reliable finding.

Evidence for this interaction has been obtained with a multiplicity of behavioral indices. Lucas (1952) found that subjects high in anxiety display decrements in their memory of consonant syllables following induced failure; subjects low in anxiety, however, increase their retention scores after failure experiences. Zeller (1951), employing a paired-associates task, demonstrated that subjects who would be considered high in anxiety exhibit impaired learning ability after being given false norms which indicate that they failed at a task. These subjects display increments in speed of learning after receiving feedback that they had succeeded on the previous task.

Studies employing intensity of performance as the dependent variable rather than retention or learning also provide empirical support for the proposed interaction. Analysis of the performance at a block design and digit-symbol substitution task led Mandler and Sarason (1952) to conclude that "the optimal condition for a low anxiety group is one in which subjects are given a failure report" (p. 173). Katchmer, Ross, and Andrews (1958) found that the performance of highly anxious subjects on a digit-symbol task decreases following reported failure, but performance of a group low in anxiety increases in that condition. Experiments with schizophrenic subjects, who are thought to be highly anxious, reveal the same general findings. Rodnick and Garmezy (1957) report great decrements in the level of performance of schizophrenic patients following censure, and Olsen (1958) found that success enhances the performance of schizophrenic patients more than does failure.

Recent studies utilizing two other behavioral indices have produced a similar pattern of results. Weiner (1965a) found that subjects low in M_s tend to resume previously interrupted tasks following an interpolated success experience, while subjects high in M_s tend to "relax" after an intervening success. And Mischel and Staub (1965) provide evidence that subjects with a low generalized expectancy for success are especially willing to delay gratification following success feedback as compared to a condition in which there is prior failure.

C. THEORETICAL IMPLICATIONS

The experiments manipulating success and failure have important implications for the models of achievement-oriented behavior. Atkinson's 1957 model specifies the conditions in which subjects high or low in resultant achievement motivation should exhibit increments or decrements in performance level. Individuals high in resultant achievement motivation should perform with greater vigor following success at a task which initially is perceived as difficult ($P_s < .50$), and after failure at a task perceived as easy ($P_s > .50$). Individuals low in resultant achievement motivation should display increments in their level of performance following success at a task perceived as easy, and after failure at a difficult task. These conclusions follow logically from the main derivations of the model, which are that subjects high in resultant achievement motivation are most attracted to tasks of intermediate difficulty, while individuals low in resultant achievement motivation are most attracted to (least inhibited by) tasks which are very easy or very difficult ($P_s \rightarrow 1$ or 0). Because of these restrictions Atkinson's 1957 model can account for the obtained interactions only if the initial P_s at the tasks conforms to the requirements imposed by the theory. This, however, is unlikely; the initial probabilities at the tasks discussed above were not specified. Hence, these results are congruent with the conclusion that the 1957 model for achievement motivation appears to be incomplete.

The modification of the model presented by Atkinson (1964) and Atkinson and Cartwright helps to overcome some of the inconsistencies between the theory and the data. The inclusion of an inertial motivational component enables Atkinson to account for evidence that subjects in whom $M_S > M_{AF}$ exhibit increments in performance following failure in situations where the initial P_s is unspecified, and perform with greater intensity following failure when the initial $P_s = .30$ than after success when the initial $P_s = .70$. However, neither of the models can account for the repeated finding that subjects relatively high in anxiety show decrements in performance after failure. To incorporate this result within the present theoretical framework, this writer (Weiner, 1965b) has suggested that both the tendency to approach a goal and the tendency to avoid the threat of failure persist following failure. That is, the inertial tendency is conceptualized as a *resultant* tendency consisting of both approach and avoidance components.[4] Among subjects high in resultant achievement motivation, greater approach than avoidance motivation is aroused when undertaking an achievement-related task. Consequently, the persisting motivation following failure will have instigating properties. These subjects are expected to exhibit increments in level of performance following failure, and to perform better following failure than after success. Conversely, for subjects low in resultant achievement motivation, greater avoidance than approach achievement-related motivation is aroused by achievement tasks. The persisting achievement motivation following failure therefore is inhibitory; these subjects are expected to show decrements in level of performance following failure, and to perform better after success than after failure (see Table I, resultant inertial model). This interpretation of the inertial tendency can account for the obtained interaction between individual differences in achievement and anxiety and success and failure experiences.

Table II summarizes a number of the implications of including a resultant inertial tendency among the determinants of achievement-related behavior. The table shows that among subjects high in resultant achieve-

---

[4]Atkinson does not include the avoidance component in his equation, although the final strength of motivation in his model is a summation of the tendency aroused by the immediate stimulus plus the strength of an inertial component.

TABLE II
THE MAGNITUDE OF ACHIEVEMENT MOTIVATION RELATED TO
INDIVIDUAL DIFFERENCES AND SOURCES OF MOTIVATION

Motive classification	Source of motivation	Strength of achievement motivation	
		Maximal	Minimal
High $(M_S > M_{AF})$	Environmental	$P_s = .50$	$P_s = 1$ or 0
	Inertial	$T_{G_i} > 0$	$T_{G_i} = 0$
Low $(M_{AF} > M_S)$		Least inhibitory	Most inhibitory
	Environmental	$P_s = 1$ or 0	$P_s = .50$
	Inertial	$T_{G_i} = 0$	$T_{G_i} < 0$

ment motivation, motivation is maximized when $P_s = .50$ and the resultant inertial tendency (here also represented as T_{G_i}) > 0. Among these subjects motivation is minimal when $P_s \rightarrow 1$ or 0 and $T_{G_i} = 0$. For subjects low in resultant achievement motivation, achievement-related acts are most inhibited when $P_s = .50$ and $T_{G_i} < 0$ (the inertial component for these subjects is negative). Subjects low in resultant achievement motivation are most likely to engage in achievement-oriented behavior when $P_s \rightarrow 1$ or 0 and $T_{Gi} = 0$.

The following derivations follow from a more detailed analysis of Table II. The difference in performance between individuals high or low in resultant achievement motivation should be maximized when there is intermittent failure at a task, i.e., when $P_s = .50$ and $| T_{Gi} | > 0$. That is the condition in which resultant achievement motivation is maximal for high achieving individuals and most inhibitory among individuals low in resultant achievement motivation. The two motive groups should display a smaller difference in performance at a task in which they receive continual failure. In that condition $P_s \rightarrow 0$ and $| T_{Gi} |$ again is greater than zero. Hence, only the inertial source of motivation maximizes the difference in the tendencies to perform the task.[5] Finally, the groups should differ least when receiving continued success at a task. Given repeated success, $P_s \rightarrow 1$ and $T_{Gi} = 0$. This condition minimizes the tendency to perform achievement-related tasks for individuals high in resultant achievement motivation, and minimizes the tendency not to undertake tasks for individuals low in resultant achievement motivation. The difference in aroused achievement motivation between the groups therefore is minimal. In the

[5]Failure when $P_s = .50$ theoretically increases motivation more on the subsequent trials than failure when $P_s = 0$ or 1. In the experiments to date the number of failures and the P_s at the task have not been manipulated independently. The relative importance of the number of failures as opposed to the P_s at the time of failure has not been determined.

three respective conditions the situational and inertial, only inertial, and neither the situational nor inertial sources of motivation maximize the differential magnitude of achievement motivation between the two motive groups.

Weiner and Rosenbaum (1965) found this expected rank order difference in performance between groups which differed in level of achievement motivation. In their study, subjects received 21 free-choice trials in which they could perform an achievement-related activity or an alternative activity for which achievement was not a source of motivation. The P_s at the achievement task varied between conditions. Subjects solved approximately 20%, 50%, or 75% of the puzzles. As anticipated, the greatest difference in choice behavior between the high and low resultant achievement motivation groups occurred when the P_s at the achievement task approached .50. In that condition subjects high in resultant achievement motivation chose significantly more achievement-related tasks than subjects low in resultant achievement motivation. A substantially smaller difference in choice was found in the $P_s = .20$ condition; the least difference in behavior between the motive groups was exhibited when the P_s at the achievement-related task approximated .75.

IV. Experiment I

The following studies provide further tests of the theoretical analysis presented in Table II. In the first study subjects are placed in a free-choice situation in which they can choose to perform either of two achievement-related tasks. There are two experimental conditions. In both conditions the P_s of one of the achievement tasks approaches .50 (Intermediate or I task). In one of the conditions the P_s of the alternative achievement task approaches .25 (Failure or F task). In the other condition the P_s of the alternative task approaches .75 (Success or S task). Therefore, in one condition subjects receive an I and an F task (IF condition); in the other condition they receive an I and an S task (IS condition). Table II indicates that subjects low in resultant achievement motivation should prefer the S task when given a choice between an I task at which failure is sometimes experienced, and an S task at which success is the more frequent experience. The inertial and environmental sources of motivation are less inhibitory toward undertaking the S than the I task among these subjects.[6] Conversely, in this condition subjects high in re-

---

[6] The predictions require the inertial tendency to be partially specific toward a task. Evidence presented by Ovsiankina concerning the resumption of incomplete tasks strongly suggests that persisting motivation is not general across all achievement tasks. This writer assumes that the persisting motivation is governed by the laws of stimulus generalization. That is, the tendency has both specific and general directional properties.

sultant achievement motivation should prefer the I task. Among these subjects both the inertial and environmental sources of motivation are greater toward the undertaking of the I than the S task. Therefore, the difference in choice behavior between the high and low achievement groups should be maximal in this IS condition. The $M_S > M_{AF}$ group should select the I task more frequently than the $M_{AF} > M_s$ group.

On the other hand, when given a choice between the I task and an F task at which failure acutally is experienced, the groups should exhibit greatly reduced differential task preference. The alternative failed task is relatively aversive to the group low in resultant achievement motivation, and relatively attractive to the subjects high in resultant achievement motivation. This is because the persisting motivation following failure increases the probability of selection for the high achievement group, while decreasing or inhibiting choice for the low achievement motivation subjects. Consequently, both groups in the IF condition are in a situation of heightened conflict; each of the two alternatives relatively attract and relatively inhibit choice. Because of this conflict the differences in choice behavior should be modulated.

In this investigation, as in prior studies (Weiner, 1965b; Weiner & Rosenbaum, 1965), the P_s at an achievement-related activity is symmetrical around the level of intermediate difficulty (.25 and .75). Atkinson's 1957 model, which does not include any inertial component, predicts that there would be no difference in choice behavior between the IS and IF conditions. In both conditions subjects high in resultant achievement motivation would be expected to prefer the I task more than subjects low in resultant achievement motivation.

A. SUBJECTS

Subjects were 102 male students enrolled in the introductory psychology course at the University of California, Los Angeles. The experiment was administered to the entire group in one 2-hour experimental session. During the first experimental hour the subjects were given a TAT, picture series 2, 48, 1, 7, 11, and 24 (Atkinson, 1958a), under neutral conditions (McClelland, Atkinson, Clark, & Lowell, 1953). The TAQ was administered after the TAT. This self-report measure of situationally aroused anxiety is essentially uncorrelated with scores on the TAT (Atkinson, 1964).

The TAT protocols were scored for n Achievement by a reliable scorer according to the method of content analysis described in Atkinson (1958a). Following the procedure outlined by Atkinson (1964), scores on the TAT and TAQ were transformed into Z scores and an index of resultant achievement motivation was obtained by subtracting the Z score on the TAQ from the Z score on the TAT. As in the previous investigations in this series (Weiner, 1965b; Weiner & Rosenbaum, 1965), subjects scoring in the upper and lower 25% of the combined distribution were classified into the high (H) and low (L) achievement motivation groups.

B. PROCEDURE AND MATERIALS

The procedure closely followed a previous method (Weiner & Rosenbaum, 1965). During the second experimental hour an empty open box 2 inches high and 4 inches square was given to the subjects, along with an envelope containing the experimental materials. The envelope contained two booklets and practice material. One booklet was comprised of thirty triangle-shaped designs mimeographed on slips of paper three inches square. The other booklet was comprised of thirty square-shaped designs printed on identically sized paper. Each puzzle was separated by a blank 3 × 3 slip of paper. The designs were variations of puzzles used previously by Birch (1964), Feather (1961), and Weiner and Rosenbaum (1965). They are closed line drawings, and the task is to trace over all the lines on the design without lifting the pencil from the paper or retracing a line. It is possible to construct soluble and insoluble puzzles which cannot be discriminated by naive subjects (see Birch, 1964).

The conditions of administration during the second experimental hour correspond to those described as achievement-oriented (McClelland *et al.*, 1953). The experimenter initially said:

> The next activity is a test, and it is called the Perceptual Reasoning Test. Some of you may have seen this type of design on the college entrance exam which you have taken. On the first page of the practice material place your name, grade point average, and high school class standing.

After describing the nature of the task, the subjects had two untimed practice trials with hexagon-shaped puzzles. To create a free-choice situation the experimenter then said:

> When I say to begin, tear off the blank sheet of paper in front of a puzzle and place that blank sheet in the box. Then begin working. You will have one minute to complete the puzzle. At the end of that period I will call time. If you have successfully finished the puzzle, put a plus in the upper right hand corner on the page of the puzzle. If you have failed to solve it, put a minus in the corner. After that I will say tear off the puzzle and place it in the box. You will then be viewing two blank sheets of paper and the cycle will start over again. Putting the puzzles in the box enables us to collect the material easily at the end of the hour.
>
> Many different kinds of booklets have been passed out. It is unlikely that the per-

son next to you has the same booklets as you. Also, the puzzles within a booklet
vary in their level of difficulty. You might find some very easy, and others very
hard. So just try your best on all the puzzles. Because we are collecting norms on
many different booklets, we placed two different booklets on your desk. It makes
no difference to us from which booklet you choose your puzzles. You can spend all
the time on one booklet, or switch around whenever you feel like it. So you can do
puzzles from either booklet, or switch back and forth whenever you like. Of course
there will not be time to do all the puzzles in both booklets. Remember not to go on
to other puzzles if you finish before the time limit, and do not go back to puzzles
already placed in the box.

Subjects then had 25 free-choice trials. To create the S, F, and I conditions the percentage of soluble puzzles varied in the booklets. The S
booklet contained five blocks of six puzzles; one puzzle in each block was
insoluble. This puzzle was randomly placed in the sequence. In the F
condition five out of every six puzzles were insoluble; in the I condition
one-half of the puzzles were insoluble. The puzzles in the I condition
were arranged so that there were not more than three consecutive insoluble puzzles. Subjects placed a plus or minus sign on the puzzle to emphasize the success or failure feedback. This also allowed the experimenter to
calculate the perceived percentage of success trials. This computation is
necessary because subjects sometimes fail soluble puzzles and "solve"
insoluble puzzles. The percentage of perceived successful puzzles constitutes the P_s.

In the IS and IF conditions the I puzzles were triangle-shaped; the S
and F puzzles were square-shaped. At the end of the 25 trials the boxes
were collected with the order of choices preserved. It has been shown
previously that this procedure successfully disguises the nature of the
choice experiment (Weiner & Rosenbaum, 1965).

C. RESULTS

Analysis of the percentage of perceived reinforcements indicates that in
the IS condition 74% of the S puzzles and 51% of the I puzzles were perceived as solved. In the IF condition, 26% of the F designs and 51% of
the I puzzles were perceived as solved. There were no significant differences in percentage of puzzles solved between any of the motive groups
within either condition. Therefore, the required experimental conditions
were established by the booklets. The percentage of perceived correct I
puzzles is identical in the two conditions, and the percentage of perceived
correct puzzles in the S and F booklets happens to be perfectly symmetrical around the level of intermediate difficulty.

Table III gives the percentage choice of the I puzzles in the two conditions for subjects in the two motive groups. Across both groups there was

TABLE III
PERCENTAGE CHOICE OF INTERMEDIATE PUZZLES

Condition	N	$M_S > M_{AF}$	N	$M_{AF} > M_S$
		Motive classification		
IF[a]	11	71%	16	71%
IS[b]	15	38%	10	22%

[a]Intermediate *vs.* Failure.
[b]Intermediate *vs.* Success.

a strong tendency to choose from the booklet which contained the greater percentage of soluble puzzles, i.e., the I booklet in the IF condition and the S booklet in the IS condition, $F(1,96) = 36.81$, $p < .001$. Within the IF condition there was virtual equality in choice between the groups. In the IS condition, subjects in whom $M_S > M_{AF}$ tended to choose more I puzzles than subjects in whom $M_{AF} > M_S$, $t = 1.78$, $df = 23$, $p < .10$.

An analysis also was performed with subjects classified as high or low in level of anxiety on the basis of their score on the TAQ (see Fig. 1). There were no significant differences in choice between the motive groups in the IF condition. It is important to note, however, that subjects high in anxiety chose more I puzzles in the IF condition than subjects low in anxiety.

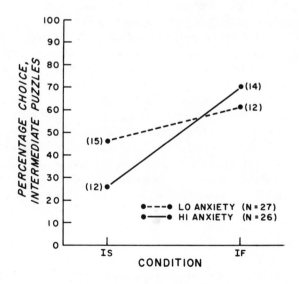

FIG. 1. Percentage choice of the task of intermediate difficulty in the two experimental conditions when subjects are classified according to level of anxiety (TAQ score).

In the IS condition subjects classified as low in anxiety chose significantly more I puzzles than subjects high in anxiety, $t = 1.97$, $df = 25$, $p < .05$.

D. Discussion

The results of the study show that there is an asymmetry between the effects of repeated success and repeated failure at a task. Although the S and F tasks were symmetrical around the level of intermediate difficulty, their behavioral consequents differed. This was evidenced by the difference in choice behavior between the IS and IF conditions between the groups which differed in level of resultant achievement motivation or level of anxiety. The results again suggest that Atkinson's 1957 model should be expanded to include a resultant inertial component among the determinants of behavior. As previously indicated, the 1957 model predicted no difference in choice behavior between the IS and IF conditions.

Two additional comments about the present experiment are necessary. Table III and Fig. 1 indicate that both motive groups prefer the booklet in which they attain the greater number of success experiences. Previously, Weiner and Rosenbaum found that success operates as a positive reinforcer in this experimental situation. The dramatic effects of success cannot be explained with the present conceptual scheme. It might be postulated that success satisfies other, nonachievement-related sources of motivation (e.g., social approval). However, extrinsic sources of motivation also might be expected to persist following failure. The main effect due to success makes comparisons within a motive group and between conditions questionable, but it does not invalidate the predicted differences between motive groups within a condition. Second, in this study motive differences based only on the TAQ were a better predictor of choice between the extreme groups than when the TAT and TAQ were jointly employed to establish the motive groups. Atkinson and Litwin (1960) previously had demonstrated that using the TAT in conjunction with the TAQ resulted in better predictions of choice behavior than use of only one of these two measures. The lack of consistency of the TAT as a predictor (see Zubin, Eron, & Schumer, 1965) clearly indicates that further development of this instrument is necessary. This point will be briefly discussed later in the paper.

V. Experiment II

Atkinson's 1957 model has proved extremely heuristic and has been able to explain a vast amount of data within the domain of achievement-oriented behavior. The main empirical finding guided by the model has been the differential preference for tasks of intermediate difficulty exhibited when high and low resultant achievement motivation subjects are constrained within an achievement-related context. In these investigations the subjects generally are given a task to perform from two or more possible alternatives. The tasks are virtually identical except for their level of difficulty, e.g., "Make five (ten) words out of these letters." An index of P_s at the task is calculated, and selection is related to difficulty of the task and motive classification of the subjects. The subjects in the studies do not choose between tasks at which they actually have experienced varying degrees of success or failure. The inertial source of motivation to undertake the alternatives does not differentially influence selection. Therefore, the difference in choice behavior between the motive groups primarily is a function of differences in the environmental source of achievement motivation. These conditions are represented as a special case within the framework of the model which includes a resultant inertial component: the case where T_{Gi} is a constant added to all motivational tendencies. Given T_{Gi} a constant, the model which includes the resultant inertial component reduces to Atkinson's 1957 model, and would make the same predictions as that model.

Feather (1961, 1963a) employed Atkinson's 1957 model to explain persistence of behavior in a situation where repeated failures were given. As previously discussed, Feather predicted that there would be an interaction between the initial P_s at the task and individual differences in motive classification. The model which includes a resultant inertial tendency leads to the same predictions as those made by Feather, but the conceptual representation differs. As Feather states, following failure the P_s in the .70 condition changes toward the level of intermediate difficulty, while the P_s in the .05 condition goes further away from the .50 level. In addition, however, greater motivation is aroused when $P_s = .70$ than when $P_s = .05$, and in both conditions there is nonattainment of the goal. The persisting unsatisfied motivation, therefore, is greater in the $P_s = .70$ condition than in the $P_s = .05$ condition. Both the environmental and inertial sources of motivation are operating to maximize the differences in persistence between the two conditions. Among subjects low in resultant achievement motivation, the analysis is reversed. For these subjects the inhibition attributable to the immediate stimulus situation is greater following failure at the easy than difficult task, as Feather indicated. However, the persisting resultant inertial tendency also is more inhibitory following failure at the relatively easy task than after failure at the task perceived as very difficult. When $P_s = .70$, greater avoidance of achievement tasks is aroused, and persists, than in the condition where $P_s = .05$. Therefore, persistence is expected to be greater following failure at the difficult than at the easy task for subjects low in resultant achievement motivation.

The analysis employed by Feather and the alternative inertial motivational conception are given in Table IV. For ease of presentation, it is again assumed that $M_s = 2$ and $M_{AF} = 1$ when $M_S > M_{AF}$, and vice versa when $M_{AF} > M_S$. It is also assumed that the change in P_s following failure is $\frac{1}{2}(1 - P_s)$ when the initial $P_s = .70$, and $\frac{1}{2}(P_s)$ when the initial $P_s = .05.$[7] The inertial tendency is assumed to be zero on Trial 1. The table presents the strength of resultant achievement motivation for the first and second trials; analysis of the remaining trials would take the identical form.

Table IV shows that in both models the absolute increase in the tendency to persist at the activity in progress is greater for high achieving individuals when the initial P_s is .70 than when the initial P_s is .05. For subjects low in resultant achievement motivation, the $P_s = .70$ condition leads to the greater increase in avoidance of the activity in progress in both models. The implication of the conceptual analysis presented in Table IV is that Feather's results primarily may be due to the failure manipulation per se (T_{G_i}), rather than to the change in P_s which occurs as a consequence of failure.

In Experiment II, Feather's study is altered to provide evidence concerning the effects of inertial motivation in his investigation. The experiment follows the same general procedure as Experiment I. Subjects classified high or low in resultant achievement motivation are placed in a free-choice situation in which they can perform either of two activities. One task is the achievement-related puzzle booklet described previously; the alternate activity is a nonachievement-related picture-judgment task. Three conditions are employed by varying the initial P_s at the achievement task and the subsequent success and failure experiences. In one condition subjects are given continual success at the achievement task when the initial $P_s = .30$. In a second condition continual success is experienced when the initial $P_s = .95$. The difference between the initial probabilities in these two conditions $(.95 - .30)$ is equal to the difference between the initial probabilities in Feather's experiment $(.70-.05)$. The predictions derived from Atkinson's 1957 model, as well as the model including the inertial tendency, would be similar to those of Feather. Subjects in whom $M_S > M_{AF}$ are expected to choose more achievement-related puzzles when the initial $P_s = .30$, while subjects low in resultant achievement motivation should select more puzzles when the initial $P_s = .95$. These predictions follow from the models because the P_s respectively

[7]These assumptions are made to keep the P_s from falling below the .50 level following the initial failure when $P_s = .70$, and to allow P_s to remain greater than zero following failure when $P_s = .05$.

TABLE IV

ANALYSIS OF FEATHER'S EXPERIMENT ACCORDING TO TWO MODELS FOR ACHIEVEMENT-ORIENTED BEHAVIOR

Model	Trial	Condition	Motive classification	
			$M_S > M_{AF}$	$M_{AF} > M_S$
1957 (no inertial component)	One	$P_s = .70$	$2 \times .7 \times .3 - (1 \times .3 \times .7) = .21^a$	$1 \times .7 \times .3 - (2 \times .3 \times .7) = -.21$
	Two	$P_s = .70$	$2 \times .55 \times .45 - (1 \times .45 \times .55) = .25^b$	$1 \times .55 \times .45 - (2 \times .45 \times .55) = -.25$
	One	$P_s = .05$	$2 \times .05 \times .95 - (1 \times .95 \times .05) = .05$	$1 \times .05 \times .95 - (2 \times .95 \times .05) = -.05$
	Two	$P_s = .05$	$2 \times .02 \times .98 - (1 \times .98 \times .02) = .02$	$1 \times .02 \times .98 - (2 \times .98 \times .02) = -.02$
Resultant inertial component	One	$P_s = .70$	$2 \times .7 \times .3 - (1 \times .3 \times .7) = .21$	$1 \times .7 \times .3 - (2 \times .3 \times .7) = -.21$
	Two	$P_s = .70$	$2 \times .55 \times .45 - (1 \times .45 \times .55) + .21 = .46$	$1 \times .55 \times .45 - (2 \times .45 \times .55) - .21 = -.46$
	One	$P_s = .05$	$2 \times .05 \times .95 - (1 \times .95 \times .05) = .05$	$1 \times .05 \times .95 - (2 \times .95 \times .05) = -.05$
	Two	$P_s = .05$	$2 \times .02 \times .98 - (1 \times .98 \times .02) + .05 = .07$	$1 \times .02 \times .98 - (2 \times .98 \times .02) - .05 = -.07$

[a] Strength of resultant achievement motivation.
[b] All numbers rounded to two decimal points.

is shifting toward and away from the level of intermediate difficulty in the two conditions.

In the third condition subjects receive continual failure when the initial $P_s = .05$. In the second and third conditions the probabilities are symmetrical around .50 (.95 and .05). These conditions essentially repeat those used previously by Weiner (1965b). Subjects in whom $M_S > M_{AF}$ are expected to choose more achievement-related puzzles than subjects in whom $M_{AF} > M_S$ in the repeated failure, but not repeated success, condition.

Comparing Condition One ($P_s = .30$ and success) with Condition Two ($P_s = .95$ and success) in this investigation will demonstrate the effect of situational determinants of behavior; the effect of inertial sources of motivation is controlled because continual success is experienced. Comparing Condition Two ($P_s = .95$ and success) with Condition Three ($P_s = .05$ and failure) will show the effect of the inertial determinants of behavior; the influence of situational sources of motivation is controlled because the P_s is symmetrical around the level of intermediate difficulty.

A. PROCEDURE AND MATERIALS

The general procedure was similar to that in Experiment I, and follows a methodology employed previously by Weiner and Rosenbaum. The motive classification of 220 male students was determined in the usual manner (see Experiment I). The TAT picture series was 2,8,4,48 (see Atkinson, 1958a). Then envelopes containing the experimental materials were randomly distributed throughout the room. The envelopes included two booklets. One booklet was comprised of the puzzle designs described previously; the other booklet contained 26 TAT pictures included in Murray's (1943) original series. The pictures were the same dimensions as the puzzles.

The subjects were told that they would be performing two different activities during the hour. They first were instructed to take the picture series out of the envelope. Attached to the booklet were the following instructions:

> The booklet which you have in front of you contains a series of pictures. Each picture can be described by the following five statements:
> a. It will be found on a movie marquee.
> b. It will be found at an art institute.
> c. It is a scene from a play.
> d. It is a photograph from a magazine or book.
> e. None of the alternatives describe the picture.
> For each picture, read the five statements and decide which statement best describes the picture, which is second best, third, fourth, and fifth. Mark the letter in the appropriate column.

Because of the preceding TAT administration, this task appeared relevant to the experiment.

The pictures were separated by blank 3 × 3 sheets of paper, and the entire series was stapled together. The general procedure was to tear off the blank paper covering a picture, place the paper in the box, and answer the questions for the displayed picture. One minute was allowed for each picture. Prior to the start of this activity the subjects were told that there were no correct or incorrect answers to emphasize the nonachievement-related character of the task.

After four 1-minute trials the subjects were asked to discontinue the picture-judging task and to take the remaining booklet from the envelope. The description of the achievement puzzles and general directions were the same as in Experiment I. Three conditions were created by varying the solubility of the puzzles and the norms which accompanied them. Norms were conveyed by the following statement attached to the puzzle booklet:

> The puzzles in this booklet are about equal in their level of difficulty. The norms which we have collected from male college students at UCLA indicate that each puzzle has been successfully solved by 95% (30%; 05%) of the students. So the puzzles are easy (relatively difficult; difficult).

In the $P_s = .30$ and .95 conditions all the puzzles were soluble; in the $P_s = .05$ condition all the puzzles were insoluble.

To create a free-choice situation the experimenter said:

> On this task, and on the picture-rating task which you were just doing, we are especially concerned about getting good and valid norms; norms when you are interested and involved in what you are doing. From past experience we realize that people differ in what they like to do, and we get better norms when you are working on what you like doing. Since each of the pictures takes one minute, and so does each puzzle, during any time period you can do either a puzzle or a picture. When I say to begin, tear off the blank paper in front of a picture and do that, or tear off the paper in front of a puzzle and do that. You may do whichever of the tasks that you prefer. You can spend all the remaining time doing puzzles, all of it doing pictures, or just shift back and forth whenever you like. The main point is that you can do whichever you prefer and shift around as you like. Of course, you will not have time to do all of the pictures and all of the puzzles. Now get ready for the first time period. Decide which of the tasks you want to do, tear off the paper covering the task and place it in the box, and begin working.

The subjects received 20 free-choice trials. After dismissing the subjects, the tasks in the box were collected with the order of choices preserved.

B. Results

In the Success conditions 92.3% of the puzzles were perceived as completed; in the Failure condition 89.2% of the puzzles were perceived as failed. There were no significant differences in the percentage of solved puzzles between the motive groups within a condition, or between the two Success conditions.

Figure 2 portrays the percentage choice of the puzzle task over the 20 trials. The figure clearly indicates that less puzzles were chosen in the Failure than Success conditions. An analysis of variance reveals a main effect attributable to the experimental conditions, $F\ (2, 113) = 11.8$, $p <$ .01. Comparing choice within the Success conditions reveals that subjects in whom $M_S > M_{AF}$ select more puzzles when the initial $P_s = .30$, while subjects in whom $M_{AF} > M_S$ choose more puzzles when the initial $P_s = .95$. However, the differences within a motive group between conditions, or between motive groups within a condition, do not reach statistical significance. (Within the motive groups in both Success conditions more than 50% of the subjects chose all puzzles. There is a ceiling effect and restricted range in these conditions.)

Separately comparing the results of the .95 Success condition and the

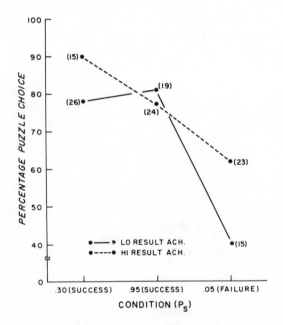

FIG. 2.   Percentage choice of the achievement task in the three experimental conditions.

.05 Failure condition revealed that within the Failure condition, subjects in whom $M_S > M_{AF}$ select significantly more of the puzzles than low resultant achievement motivation subjects ($p < .02$, Fisher Exact Test). As previously stated, in the .95 Success condition subjects in whom $M_{AF} > M_S$ chose more puzzles than subjects in whom $M_S > M_{AF}$; this difference does not approach statistical significance.

Analysis employing only the TAQ for motive classification reveals the same general pattern of results. However, the differences between the behavior of the motive groups generally are not as marked.

C. DISCUSSION

The general pattern of results in the Success conditions replicates Feather's findings and demonstrates the effects of environmental (P_s) determinants of behavior. Comparison of the .95 Success condition with the .05 Failure condition revealed that the direction of the results replicated Weiner's previous findings concerning the influence of inertial motivation. Both situational and inertial sources of motivation need to be included among the determinants of behavior.

Comparison of the .95 and .30 Success conditions indicated that none of the obtained differences within or between motive groups was statistically significant. The analysis in Table IV suggested that Feather's prior results may have been caused primarily by the persisting inertial tendency, rather than the shifting of the P_s level. Therefore, it was expected that the observed differences in behavior between the .95 and .30 Success condition would be less than the differences obtained by Feather between the .70 and .05 Failure conditions. However, because of the ceiling effect in this experiment, it is not justifiable to conclude that Feather's results are predominantly attributable to the inertial motivational component. Another study is needed which permits a better test of this hypothesis.

In the present experiment subjects in whom $M_S > M_{AF}$ chose more puzzles in the .95 Success condition than in the .05 Failure condition. This is contrary to the prediction of the resultant inertial model. As previously stated, success is a potent reinforcer in this experimental situation. Given this uncontrolled source of motivation, the more relevant behavioral observation in this experiment is that the high and low motive groups significantly differ in their selections in the .05 Failure condition, but not in the .95 Success condition. That is, again the comparisons most essential to the hypotheses are between motive groups and within conditions.

In this experiment, as contrasted with Experiment I, the TAT was as effective a predictor as the TAQ. The pictures employed to assess motive strength in Experiment II were highly cued for achievement. Saugstad

(1966) has argued that "the more meaningful a material is in relation to some motivational condition, the greater the probability will be that the reactions to the material are affected by this condition" (p. 80). Wallace (1966) also reasons that the usefulness of a projective measure decreases as the picture cues become more ambiguous. Clearly, one dimension which needs to be systematically studied in evaluating the effectiveness of the TAT as an assessment instrument is the degree of structure of the picture cues. The results of the two experiments presented here suggest that "the closer the approximation of the role-playing situation to the predictive situation, the greater . . . the accuracy of the predictions" (Wallace, 1966, p. 136). Further analysis of this study will be included in the general discussion which follows.

VI. General Issues

A. INTERACTION BETWEEN INDIVIDUAL DIFFERENCES AND SUCCESS AND FAILURE

The resultant inertial model specifies that there will be an interaction between the relative strengths of the approach and avoidance tendencies and the effects of attainment or nonattainment of a goal. This interaction might be general across other motives. It is intuitively reasonable to expect individuals considered to be "shy" (low in need for affiliation and high in fear of rejection?) to engage in more affiliative behavior following interpersonal acceptance than rejection. Conversely, it is hypothesized that individuals high in need for affiliation and low in fear of rejection will engage in more activities instrumental to the attainment of an affiliative goal after rejection than after interpersonal acceptance. Similarly, it is hypothesized that individuals considered to be highly aggressive (high in aggressive needs and low in aggressive inhibition) will act more aggressively after thwarting than following aggressive expression. That is, among these subjects relative "catharsis" will be exhibited. On the other hand, it is hypothesized that subjects low in overt aggression will initiate more aggressive actions following aggressive expression than after a punishment which interrupts the behavioral sequence. A study by Feshbach (1956) provides partial support for these hypotheses. Feshbach found that "boys initially low in aggression will tend to show an increase in aggressive behavior subsequent to a series of permissive free play experiences" (p. 459). However, the indulgent play periods did not reduce the subsequent aggressive behavior of children initially high in aggression, thus providing no support for the catharsis hypothesis. In general, in the area of aggression conflicting behaviors following successful aggressive expression have been reported (see Feshbach, 1964). The conflicting data may in part be caused by differences in the relative approach and avoidance dispositions of the subject populations.

B. IMPLICATIONS FOR CLASSROOM PERFORMANCE

The accumulated empirical knowledge in the area of achievement motivation has resulted in theoretical advancements which have important implications for classroom performance (see Weiner, 1967).

1. Programmed Instruction

Generally, learning programs are created with 100% reinforcement schedules. This pattern of reinforcements has motivational consequences. In a repeated success situation, $P_s = 1$ and $T_{Gi} = 0$. This constellation of factors theoretically maximizes the tendency to engage in achievement-orientated behavior for subjects low in resultant achievement motivation. However, for subjects in whom $M_s > M_{AF}$, this particular schedule minimizes achievement motivation. To maximize achievement striving for these subjects, success (and failure) should be experienced on one-half of the trials (see Table II and accompanying discussion). The data presented in this paper suggest that failure can be a positive "reinforcer" i.e., enhance subsequent response probability.

2. Ability Grouping

A dominant trend in education is to place students of equal ability in the same classroom. An overlooked aspect of ability grouping is that it may change the student's perception of his relative capabilities, or his P_s. Atkinson and O'Connor (1963) found that children in whom $M_s > M_{AF}$ exhibit better performance in a homogeneous than heterogeneous class. In addition, highly anxious students express less satisfaction in the homogeneous than heterogeneous class. It is presumed that in groupings of equal ability P_s and P_f approach an intermediate level.

3. Grades

Goldberg (1965) recently has reported that grades in the classroom do not affect the subsequent level of performance. However, in that study individual differences in achievement or anxiety were not measured. The model for achievement-related behavior indicates that success and failure experiences interact with these individual differences to influence future performance. To maximize performance of students relatively low in resultant achievement motivation, positive feedback or encouragement should be employed. On the other hand, to maximize the performance of students high in resultant achievement motivation, some negative feedback should be used. These derivations conform to intuitions and observations in the classroom that individuals anxious about their performance often benefit from a positive experience, while students quite confident about their ability often are motivated by temporary failure experiences.

Extremely few studies undertaken in educational settings have employed individual difference measures in conjunction with experimental manipulations. In one such study, Thompson and Hunnicutt (1944) found that "extroverts" perform better when "blamed," while "introverts" exhibit improved classroom performance following "praise." Eysenck (1957) has argued that introversion is positively related to level of anxiety. Hence, the findings of Thompson and Hunnicutt tend to support the hypotheses outlined above.

VII. Relation to Other Theories of Motivation

A. LEWINIAN THEORY

1. Tension

The inclusion of inertial motivation among the determinants of behavior was guided by Lewin's assumptions concerning the persistence of a system in a state of tension. Atkinson and Cartwright (1964) state: "It should be noted, of course, that Lewin was greatly interested in the persistence of motivation. In his scheme, the conception of tension accounts for persistence. In ours, the postulate of inertia in reference to motivation (an aroused tendency) accomplishes the same objective. Only further conceptual analysis, together with empirical research, can decide between these two approaches" (p. 587).

There are existing data which suggest that the persistence of force (aroused motivation) is a more adequate conception than the persistence of tension. Ovsiankina (1928) reports that the tendency to resume previously incompleted tasks is a function of the distance from the goal at the time of interruption. In general, greater resumption occurs the nearer to the goal at the time of interruption. Similarly, Haner and Brown (1955) report that the subsequent vigor of a response increases as a function of closeness to the goal at the time of thwarting. In Lewin's theory, force, not tension, varies as a function of the psychological distance from the goal. The observations that resumption and response intensity are affected by psychological distance from the goal at the time of a prior thwarting provides some evidence that force, rather than tension, persists following nonattainment of a goal.

2. Substitution

Lewin's conception of a system in a state of tension logically led into the investigation of substitution. In a previous paper this writer (Weiner, 1966, p. 342) has commented upon the inadequacies of the present inertial conception in handling the problems of substitution:

> The theory presented by Atkinson and Cartwright focuses upon the consequences of nonattainment of a goal, while the effects of goal attainment on subsequent performance are not stressed. If it were postulated that success reduces the magnitude of the persisting goal-oriented tendencies, then the model could incorporate data indicating that goal attainment has substitute value (Henle, 1944; Lissner, 1933; Mahler, 1933). Yet this conception is insufficient, for success has instigative as well as substitutive properties. As a general hypothesis, it is suggested that following goal attainment there is a decrement in the magnitude of both the persisting tendency to approach success and the persisting tendency to avoid threat of failure. The diminution in the strength of these tendencies is proportionate to the strength of motivation sustaining the original activity. When $M_S > M_{AF}$, the decrement in the magnitude of the persisting approach motivation is greater than the reduction in the magnitude of the persisting avoidance motivation. Consequently, these individuals should exhibit decrements in level of performance following success. When $M_{AF} > M_S$, the decrement in the strength of the persisting avoidance tendency is greater than the reduction in the strength of the persisting approach tendency. These individuals should exhibit increments in level of performance following success. This conception accounts for the differential reactions which subjects high or low in resultant achievement motivation exhibit following success experiences.

While the conception proposed above can account for much of the empirical data, there is suggestive evidence that subjects in whom $M_{AF} > M_S$ perform *absolutely* better than subjects in whom $M_S > M_{AF}$ after success experiences. None of the models for achievement-oriented behavior can explain this (yet inconclusive) fact.

3. The Zeigarnik Effect

Perhaps the most cited experiment guided by Lewin's conception is the finding by Zeigarnik (1927) of greater recall of incompleted than completed tasks (the Zeigarnik Effect). There was an unexpected reversal of these results when studies of task recall were conducted in America. Investigators such as Rosenzweig (1943) found greater recall of completed than incompleted tasks in ego-involving situations. He attributed this pattern of results to repressive forces which interfere with the retention of failure experiences.

Atkinson (1953) in part resolved the apparent contradiction between the findings of Zeigarnik and Rosenzweig. He found that subjects high in M_S recall more incompleted than completed tasks in achievement-oriented settings, while subjects low in M_S recall more completed than incompleted tasks. Analysis of the subject population used by Rosenzweig revealed that they were likely to be classified as highly anxious, while this was not the case with Zeigarnik's subjects.

Caron and Wallach (1957) have reinterpreted Atkinson's findings and contended the differential recall in Zeigarnik paradigms is due to inequalities in learning, rather than differential memory. Following their suggestion, it is hypothesized that the differences in learning are mediated by differential covert repetition of the material. Subjects highly anxious about failure tend to avoid failed tasks, while subjects high in achievement motivation are attracted to tasks they have failed. Hence, they might repeatedly think about the incompleted activity. This differential practice would result in disparities in original learning.

Weiner, Johnson, and Mehrabian (1968) replicated Atkinson's results in an examination setting. They found that high achievement-oriented subjects tend to recall missed exam items, while subjects low in resultant achievement motivation recall relatively more of the questions which they answered correctly. It was contended that subjects motivated to succeed more frequently attempt to solve the incompleted items, and therefore display greater retention of those questions. This persistent behavior also could be responsible for the contrasting academic performance which is at times displayed by the two motive groups (McClelland *et al.*, 1953).

B. HULLIAN THEORY

1. Paired-Associates Learning

Atkinson (1964) proposed that the model for achievement-oriented behavior be viewed as an alternative to the Drive × Habit conception of Hull (1943) and Spence (1956). Among the studies most cited in support of the Drive × Habit position are experiments conducted by Spence and his colleagues (Spence, Farber, & McFann, 1956; Spence, Taylor, & Ketchel, 1956; Taylor & Chapman, 1955) related to paired-associates learning. These investigators demonstrated that subjects high in anxiety (Drive) perform better than subjects low in anxiety on easy paired-associate tasks. Conversely, on difficult paired-associate lists, highly anxious subjects perform worse than subjects low in anxiety. Spence (1958) argues convincingly that these data confirm predictions derived from the Drive × Habit theory.

The results of the studies by Spence *et al.* are consistent with the theoretical formulation discussed in this paper. Weiner (1966, p. 340) reasons that:

> It is likely that the rapid learning of the easy list indicates to the subject that he is succeeding. That is, on the basis of the frequent number of correct responses he may evaluate his performance positively. On the difficult list the subject may perceive his performance as a failure. That is, because of the many incorrect responses he may evaluate his performance negatively. Thus the findings of Spence *et al.* can be included among the research which has demonstrated interactions between individual differences in level of anxiety and the effects of success and failure on subsequent performance.

To compare the adequacy of the two theoretical explanations, Weiner (1966, p. 340) states:

> . . . the inherent relation between the easy task-success experience and difficult task-failure experience was experimentally severed. Subjects learning an easy list of paired associates were told that they were performing poorly relative to others. In this manner the easy task was paired with a failure experience. Subjects learning a difficult paired-associates task were told that they were doing well relative to others, thus pairing the difficult task with a success experience. If the differential reactions to success and failure experiences are the essential determinants of behavior in this situation, then on the easy task highly anxious subjects experiencing failure should perform *worse* than subjects low in anxiety experiencing failure. On the difficult task, highly anxious subjects experiencing success should perform *better* than subjects low in anxiety experiencing success. The experimental design consequently provides a definitive test of the alternative explanation of the Spence *et al.* data.

The results of the investigation revealed that subjects in whom $M_S > M_{AF}$ (or classified low in anxiety) performed better at the easy task at which failure was experienced than subjects in whom $M_{AF} > M_S$ (or classified high in anxiety). On the other hand, on the difficult task at which success was experienced, subjects high in anxiety performed better than subjects low in anxiety. These results were contradictory to the predictions of Drive theory, and replicated findings revealing an interaction between individual differences and the effects of success and failure. Weiner (1966, p. 342) concluded that:

> These results strongly suggest that it is erroneous to cite prior research in this area as validating evidence for Drive theory. The important determinants of behavior in this situation are the cognitive and motivational consequences resulting from success or failure at the task, rather than the individual's drive level interacting with the structure of the task per se.

Of course, the analysis provided by the achievement model would not be able to explain data from other studies (e.g., eyelid conditioning) which are supportive of Drive theory. However, it does present an alternative frame of reference to view some of the empirical findings.

2. Frustration as a Drive

Data from diverse areas of psychology provide evidence that behavioral tendencies increase following nonattainment of an expected reward. For example, Skinner (1938) reports that following nonreinforcement after a 100% reinforcement schedule response strength temporarily increases. The current nonassociative explanation of increased responding after a nonrewarded trial was advanced by Amsel (1958). Amsel postulates that when fractional anticipatory goal responses (r_g-s_g) are not followed by a reward, frustration is elicited. Frustration is postulated to have drive and associative properties. The drive properties of frustration were demonstrated in a study conducted by Amsel and Rousell (1952). These investigators showed that an instrumental hunger response increases in strength following frustration.

The inertial motivational conception also leads to the prediction of increased response strength following nonattainment of a goal, for the aroused hunger tendency is postulated to persist on the next trial. In a single stimulus situation nonattainment of a reward increases the strength of the inertial tendency, but decreases the expectation that the response will be followed by the goal stimulus. This implies that following an unspecified number of nonrewarded trials the response will no longer be exhibited. That is, extinction will occur.

In both the achievement-related conception and the Drive × Habit theory two components in the models are affected by one operation. Nonattainment of a goal (failure) decreases the associative strength of approach relative to avoidance expectancies, but increases motivational effects (inertia). In single stimulus situations, the observed increment in behavior on trials immediately following nonreward indicates that the increment in drive (inertia) is greater than the relative decrement in the associative approach component. The eventual extinction of the response implies that the relative decrement in the expectancy offsets the increments in the inertial or drive components. Neither Drive nor Achievement theory explicitly states the relative changes in the strengths of the associative and drive components. Therefore, it is not possible for either conception to specify the exact trial at which decrements in performance will be exhibited.

There is one interesting difference in the predictions derived from the conception proposed by Amsel and the theory presented here. Amsel postulates that the amount of frustration following a nonrewarded trial is monotonically related to the expectation of the reward. However, in achievement-related situations, motivation is most aroused at tasks of intermediate difficulty. Hence, maximum inertial effects are anticipated following failure at a task which has an intermediate expectation of success. There should be a curvilinear relationship between expectancy and the motivational effects of frustration, according to the achievement model.

C. ATTRIBUTION THEORY

The reader undoubtedly has noted that the achievement models discussed here have been greatly influenced by physical conceptions, and are relatively mechanistic in orientation. Achievement motivation, however, also may be conceptualized within a more cognitive framework. Current work in our laboratory has focused upon the attributions (causal inferences) which mediate between the components in the achievement model and subsequent behavior (Weiner, Frieze, Kukla, Reed, Rest, & Rosenbaum, 1969; Weiner and Kukla, in press). These studies have attempted to unite the growing literature concerned with "locus of control" (see deCharms, 1968; Rotter, 1966) with the accumulated knowledge about achievement motivation. The data we have gathered thus far indicates that, given a successful outcome, males in whom $M_S > M_{AF}$ are more likely to attribute the cause of an event to internal (self) sources (ability and effort) than males in whom $M_{AF} > M_S$. On the other hand, males in whom $M_{AF} > M_S$ are more prone to attribute success to task ease (an external factor) than the high achievement-oriented male subjects. Because individuals in whom $M_S > M_{AF}$ tend to attribute success to themselves, they also should experience greater pride given goal attainment (Rotter, 1966). The inequality in the reward value of success between the two motive groups may account for the differential approach behavior which they exhibit. Conversely, it appears that subjects in whom $M_{AF} > M_S$ are more likely than the $M_S > M_{AF}$ subjects to attribute failure internally to a lack of ability. Thus, they may be more likely to avoid subsequent achievement-related tasks.

The environmental and inertial determinants in the model also can be conceptualized in attributional language. Evidence reported in Weiner and Kukla (in press) demonstrates that internal ascription for success is positively and linearly related to task difficulty (operationally defined as the percentage of others able to complete the task). It may be argued that greater pride (I_s) is experienced following success at a difficult task because the causal ascription is more internal than following success at an easy task (also see Heider, 1958). In a similar manner, the internal attribution for failure decreases as a task is perceived as more difficult. It is therefore suggested that less shame ($-I_f$) is experienced after a failure at a difficult task because the attribution for the outcome is more likely to be external than following failure at an easy task. In sum, attributional processes may aid in explaining the postulated (and observed) inverse relationship between task probability and the incentive value of success and failure.

As indicated previously, it appears that subjects in whom $M_{AF} > M_S$ tend to attribute failure to a lack of ability. This intimates that they should not persist in the face of failure (inertial avoidance motivation), for ability is a stable attribute. Therefore, these individuals should anticipate that future outcomes will be identical with those exhibited on past trials. On the other hand, when subjects in whom $M_S > M_{AF}$ attribute failure internally, they tend to perceive the outcome as caused by a lack of effort, rather than a shortcoming in ability. Their displayed performance increments following failure (inertial approach motivation) might be mediated by a cognition such as: "I just did not try hard enough last time." Inasmuch as effort is an unstable variable under personal control, these individuals can expect to improve on subsequent occasions, and thus persist in spite of prior failures. In sum, attributional processes related to the perception of ability *vs.* effort as the cause of failure might aid in the explanation of the performance interaction following nonattainment of a goal which is displayed by the two motive groups. (See Weiner *et al.*, 1969, for a more detailed discussion of these issues.)

VIII. Theoretical Considerations

A. WEIGHTING THE COMPONENTS

The model as presently formulated adds the inertial tendency to the environmental source of motivation to determine the final strength of motivation. In the model the inertial tendency can infinitely grow in strength, while environmental motivation varies between 0 and .25. This would indicate that generally inertial sources of motivation are weighted more heavily than situational determinants of behavior. With significant deprivation only minimal environmental support is needed for action, as evidenced in "vacuum behavior" or consummatory responses when under great hunger. But in most situations behavior is veridical, i.e., greatly influenced by the situational context. The model needs differential weights on the two motivational components to redress the imbalance, and give more importance to the stimulus or environmental determinants of behavior.

It also is likely that the motive groups differentially weight the inertial and environmental components. High achieving individuals are considered to be "realistic." That is, they might weight the environmental source more heavily than inertial motivation. On the other hand, pervasive avoidance behavior among highly anxious subjects perhaps indicates that the inertial component exerts a more profound influence on their behavior than the immediate environment. The present conception may be applicable in the understanding of aberrant patterns of behavior exhibited by highly anxious individuals.

B. Mathematical Relationship between the Components

Atkinson and Cartwright postulate that the inertial tendency is added to the environmental determinants of behavior. A multiplicative relationship might better capture the existing data. The analysis presented in Table II, and evidence supporting that analysis, indicates that when $M_S > M_{AF}$ motivation is maximal when $P_s = .50$ and $T_{G_i} > 0$. Further, achievement behavior in that condition appears to exceed that when $P_s \rightarrow 0$ and T_{G_i} is maximal. If this is true, then the two components perhaps should be related multiplicatively. A multiplicative relationship would suggest that behavior must be supported by an environmental source of motivation. In addition, such a relationship also would suggest that all behavior is determined in part by some past deprivation. This would be congruent with current psychoanalytic thought which specifies that all behavior is a function of id (drive) and ego (structural) determinants (see Rapaport, 1959).

Berkowitz (1964) presents a very similar conception in his analysis of aggression. He reasons that "anger arousal . . . does not necessarily give rise to an ongoing aggressive sequence. Appropriate cues . . . must also be present if the aggressive responses are to be made. . . . However, if the aggressive sequence is set into operation, but completion is prevented, internal tension is induced which is channelled into whatever response happens to be underway at the time" (p. 113).

The additive vs. multiplicative issue is amenable to experimental test. If inertial motivation is additive in the model, then following failure experiences the differential preference (or avoidance) of tasks of intermediate difficulty should be diminished. The inertial motivation added equally to tasks which differ only in level of difficulty decreases the ratio of the differences between the available choices. On the other hand, if the environmental and inertial components are related multiplicatively, then the differential task preference (or avoidance) should not lessen following failure experiences.[8]

IX. Summary

It is contended that a theory of achievement motivation formulated by Atkinson in 1957 be amended to include an additional determinant of behavior. The 1957 model is considered incomplete because it is "stimulus-bound." That is, the model cannot account for events such as the recall and resumption of incompleted tasks which occur in the absence of the instigating, external stimulus. The extended model outlined here contains a component which captures the idea that resultant (approach minus avoidance) motivation, once aroused, persists until the goal is attained. Therefore, the immediate determinants of behavior include past unsatisfied motivation ("inertial" tendencies) as well as the motivation aroused by the immediate stimulus situation.

The resultant inertial model for achievement-oriented behavior specifies that, among individuals high in resultant achievement motivation, the persisting motivation following past deprivation (failure) will facilitate subsequent performance. Conversely, among individuals low in resultant achievement motivation, the persisting motivation following failure is expected to be inhibitory and decrease subsequent performance. The model, therefore, predicts an interaction between the effects of nonattainment of a goal and individual difference in resultant achievement motivation.

In addition to reviewing prior data which support the above derivations, two previously unpublished studies are described in detail. In Experiment I, subjects classified according to strength of achievement motivation repeatedly select to perform one of two achievement-related tasks. In one condition choice is between a task intermediate in difficulty and a task which is continually failed (IF condition). In a second condition the choice is between the intermediate difficulty task and a task at which repeated success is experienced (IS condition). Atkinson's 1957 model led to the prediction that choice differences between the motive groups would be identical in the two conditions. On the other hand, the resultant inertial model predicted that there would be a different selection ratio between the motive groups in the IS, but not IF, condition. The latter prediction was confirmed.

[8]This discussion assumed that a model for conflict resolution would be based upon a ratio between the alternatives. If a model for the resolution of conflict is based upon the absolute difference between competing tendencies, rather than their ratio, then the differential preference for tasks of intermediate difficulty following failure should again be more pronounced if the inertial and environmental components are multiplicatively related.

In a second experiment, subjects had a continual free choice between an achievement-related puzzle task and an alternative activity for which achievement was not a source of motivation. There were three experimental conditions. The subjects either received repeated success at a task presented as very easy [probability of success (P_s) = .95]; repeated success at a task whose initial P_s = .30; or repeated failure at a task presented as very difficult $(P_s$ = .05). Comparing choice behavior between the two Success conditions demonstrated the motivational effects of the immediate stimulus situation; past deprivations were controlled because in both conditions there were minimal failure experiences. Comparing choice behavior between the .95 Success condition and the .05 Failure condition revealed the motivational effects of unsatisfied or inertial tendencies; the effects of the immediate stimulus situation were controlled because the P_s in the two conditions was symmetrical around the .50 level. (There is evidence indicating that in achievement-oriented situations approach and avoidance motivations aroused by the immediate stimulus are maximal when P_s = .50, and change symmetrically as P_s approaches 1 or 0.) The results of the study again supported the theory offered in the paper; both environmental and inertial sources of motivation had to be acknowledged to predict choice behavior.

The model suggested here has much in common with the Lewinian and Hull-Spence conceptions of behavior. However, the model differs from these approaches in important respects. Like Lewin's theory, data shedding light on persisting motivation (task resumption, substitution) are important sources of empirical support. However, the resultant inertial model specifies the persistence of force (aroused motivation) rather than the persistence of tension. Force, but not tension, is directional and varies as a function of distance from the goal. Data favoring the former interpretation are discussed. Like the Hull-Spence conception, the model is able to predict behavior obtained in specific verbal-learning situations and results of experiments investigating "frustrative drive." It is suggested that the achievement-related model is more adept at explaining some of these data than the Drive × Habit theory. Finally, the model also was related to attribution theory.

References

Amsel, A. The role of frustrative non-reward in a noncontinuous reward situation. *Psychological Bulletin*, 1958, 55, 102–119.

Amsel, A., & Rousell, J. Motivational properties of frustration: I. Effect on a running response of the addition of frustration to the motivational complex. *Journal of Experimental Psychology*, 1952, 43, 363–368.

Aronson, E. A need for achievement as measured by graphic expression. In J. W. Atkinson (Ed.), *Motives in fantasy, action, and society*. Princeton, N.J.: Van Nostrand, 1958. Pp. 249–265.

Atkinson, J. W. The achievement motive and recall of interrupted and completed tasks. *Journal of Experimental Psychology*, 1953, 46, 381–390.

Atkinson, J. W. Explorations using imaginative thought to assess the strength of human motives. In M. R. Jones (Ed.), *Nebraska symposium on motivation*. Lincoln: University of Nebraska Press, 1954. Pp. 56–112.

Atkinson, J. W. Motivational determinants of risk-taking behavior. *Psychological Review*, 1957, 64, 359–372.

Atkinson, J. W. (Ed.) *Motives in fantasy, action, and society*. Princeton, N.J.: Van Nostrand, 1958. (a)

Atkinson, J. W. Towards experimental analysis of human motivation in terms of motives, expectancies, and incentives. In J. W. Atkinson (Ed.), *Motives in fantasy, action, and society*. Princeton, N.J.: Van Nostrand, 1958. Pp. 288–305. (b)

Atkinson, J. W. *An introduction to motivation*. Princeton, N.J.: Van Nostrand, 1964.

Atkinson, J. W., Bastian, J. R., Earl, R. W., & Litwin, G. H. The achievement motive, goal setting, and probability preferences. *Journal of Abnormal and Social Psychology*, 1960, 60, 27–36.

Atkinson, J. W., & Cartwright, D. Some neglected variables in contemporary conceptions of decision and performance. *Psychological Reports*, 1964, 14, 575–590.

Atkinson, J. W., & Litwin, G. H. Achievement motive and test anxiety conceived as motive to approach success and motive to avoid failure. *Journal of Abnormal and Social Psychology*, 1960, 60, 52–63.

Atkinson, J. W., & O'Connor, P. Effects of ability grouping in schools related to individual differences in achievement-related motivation. Final Report Office of Education Cooperative Research Program, Project 1283. Available in microfilm from Photoduplication Center, Library of Congress, Washington, D.C., 1963.

Berkowitz, L. Aggressive cues in aggressive behavior and hostility catharsis. *Psychological Review*, 1964, 71, 104–122.

Birch, D. Incentive value of success and instrumental approach behavior. *Journal of Experimental Psychology*, 1964, 68, 121–139.

Caron, A. J., & Wallach, M. A. Recall of interrupted tasks under stress: A phenomenon of memory or learning? *Journal of Abnormal and Social Psychology*, 1957, 55, 372–381.

deCharms, R. *Personal causation*. Academic Press: New York, 1968.

Eysenck, H. J. *The dynamics of anxiety and hysteria*. New York: Praeger, 1957.

Feather, N. T. The relationship of persistence at a task to expectation of success and achievement related motives. *Journal of Abnormal and Social Psychology*, 1961, 63, 552–561.

Feather, N. T. Persistence at a difficult task with alternative task of intermediate difficulty. *Journal of Abnormal and Social Psychology*, 1963, 66, 231–238. (a)

Feather, N. T. Mower's revised two-factor theory and the motive-expectancy-value model. *Psychological Review*, 1963, 70, 500–515. (b)

Feather, N. T., & Saville, M. R. Effects of amount of prior success and failure on expectations of success and subsequent task performance. *Journal of Personality and Social Psychology*, 1967, 5, 226–232.

Feshbach, S. The catharsis hypothesis and some consequences of interaction with aggressive and neutral play objects. *Journal of Personality*, 1956, 24, 449–462.

Feshbach, S. The function of aggression and the regulation of aggressive drive. *Psychological Review*, 1964, 71, 257–272.

French, E. G. Motivation as a variable in work-partner selection. *Journal of Abnormal and Social Psychology*, 1956, 53, 96–99.

French, E. G. Development of a measure of complex motivation. In J. W. Atkinson (Ed.), *Motives in fantasy, action, and society*. Princeton, N.J.: Van Nostrand, 1958. Pp. 242–248.

French, E. G., & Thomas, F. H. The relation of achievement motivation to problem-solving effectiveness. *Journal of Abnormal and Social Psychology*, 1958, **56**, 46–48.

Freud, S. (1915) Instincts and their vicissitudes. In *Collected papers*. Vol. IV. London: Hogarth, 1949.

Goldberg, L. Grades as motivants. *Psychology in the Schools*, 1965, **II**, 17–24.

Green, D. R. Volunteering and the recall of interrupted tasks. *Journal of Abnormal and Social Psychology*, 1963, **66**, 397–401.

Haner, C. F., & Brown, P. A. Clarification of the instigation to action concept in the frustration-aggression hypothesis. *Journal of Abnormal and Social Psychology*, 1955, **51**, 204–206.

Hebb, D. O. *The organization of behavior*. New York: Wiley, 1949.

Heckhausen, H. Achievement motive research: Current problems and some contributions toward a general theory of motivation. In D. Levine (Ed.), *Nebraska symposium on motivation*. Lincoln: University of Nebraska Press, 1969 (in press).

Heider, F. *The psychology of interpersonal relations*. New York: Wiley, 1958.

Henle, M. The influence of valence on substitution. *Journal of Psychology*, 1944, **17**, 11–19.

Hull, C. L. *Principles of behavior*. New York: Appleton-Century-Crofts, 1943.

Isaacson, R. L. Relation between achievement, test anxiety, and curricular choices. *Journal of Abnormal and Social Psychology*, 1964, **4**, 447–452.

Katchmar, L. T., Ross, S., & Andrews, T. G. Effects of stress and anxiety on performance of a complex verbal-coding task. *Journal of Experimental Psychology*, 1958, **55**, 559–563.

Lewin, K. *A dynamic theory of personality*. New York: McGraw-Hill, 1935.

Lissner, K. Die Entspannung von Bedurfnissen durch ersatzhandlungen. *Psychologische Forschung* 1933, **18**, 218–250.

Lucas, J. D. The interactive effects of anxiety, failure and interserial duplication. *American Journal of Psychology*, 1952, **55**, 59–66.

McClelland, D. C. Risk taking in children with high and low need for achievement. In J. W. Atkinson (Ed.), *Motives in fantasy, action, and society*. Princeton, N.J.: Van Nostrand, 1958. Pp. 306–321.

McClelland, D. C., Atkinson, J. W., Clark, R. A, & Lowell, E. L. *The achievement motive*. New York: Appleton-Century-Crofts, 1953.

McKeachie, W. J. Motivation, teaching methods, and college learning. In M. R. Jones (Ed.), *Nebraska symposium on motivation*. Lincoln: University of Nebraska Press, 1961. Pp. 111–142.

Mahler, W. Ersatzhandlunger verschiedener realitatsgrades. *Psychologische Forschung* 1933, **18**, 27–89.

Mahone, C. H. Fear of failure and unrealistic vocational aspiration. *Journal of Abnormal and Social Psychology*, 1960, **60**, 253–261.

Mandler, G., & Sarason, S. B. A study of anxiety and learning. *Journal of Abnormal and Social Psychology*, 1952, **47**, 166–173.

Mischel, W., & Staub, E. Effects of expectancy on working and waiting for larger rewards. *Journal of Personality and Social Psychology*, 1965, **2**, 625–633.

Morris, J. Propensity for risk taking as a determinant of vocational choice: An extension of the theory of achievement motivation. *Journal of Personality and Social Psychology*, 1966, **3**, 328–335.

Moulton, R. W. Effects of success and failure in level of aspiration as related to achievement motives. *Journal of Personality and Social Psychology*, 1965, **1**, 399–406.

Murray, H. A. *Thematic apperception test manual.* Cambridge, Mass.: Harvard University Press, 1943.

O'Connor, P. An achievement risk preference scale: A preliminary report. *American Psychologist,* 1962, 17, 317 (Abstract).

Olsen, G. W. Failure and the subsequent performance of schizophrenics. *Journal of Abnormal and Social Psychology,* 1958, 57, 310-314.

Ovsiankina, M. Die wiederaufnahme unterbrochener Handlungen. *Psychologische Forschung,* 1928, 11, 302-379.

Peak, H. Psychological structure and psychological activity. *Psychological Review,* 1958, 65, 325-347.

Rapaport, D. The structure of psychoanalytic theory. In S. Koch (Ed.), *Psychology: A study of a science.* Vol. 3. New York: McGraw-Hill, 1959. Pp. 55-167.

Raynor, J. O., & Smith, C. P. Achievement-related motives and risk-taking in games of skill and chance. *Journal of Personality,* 1966, 34, 176-198.

Rodnick, E. H., & Garmezy, N. An experimental approach to the study of motivation in schizophrenia. In M. R. Jones (Ed.), *Nebraska symposium on motivation.* Lincoln: University of Nebraska Press, 1957. Pp. 109-184.

Rosenzweig, S. An experimental study of "repression" with specific reference to need-persistive and ego-defensive reactions to frustration. *Journal of Experimental Psychology,* 1943, 32, 64-74.

Rotter, J. B. Generalized expectancies for internal versus external control of reinforcement. *Psychological Monographs,* 1966, 80.

Ryan, E. D., & Lakie, W. L. Competitive and noncompetitive performance in relation to achievement motive and manifest anxiety. *Journal of Personality and Social Psychology,* 1965, 1, 342-345.

Saugstad, P. Effect of food deprivation on perception-cognition. *Psychological Bulletin,* 1966, 65, 80-90.

Skinner, B. F. *The behavior of organisms: An experimental analysis.* New York: Appleton-Century-Crofts, 1938.

Spence, K. W. *Behavior theory and conditioning.* New Haven, Conn.: Yale University Press, 1956.

Spence, K. W. A theory of emotionally based drive (D) and its relation to performance in simple learning situations. *American Psychologist,* 1958, 13, 129-139.

Spence, K. W., Farber, I. E., & McFann, H. H. The relation of anxiety (drive) level to performance in competitional and noncompetitional paired-associates learning. *Journal of Experimental Psychology,* 1956, 62, 296-305.

Spence, K. W., Taylor, J. A., & Ketchel, R. Anxiety (drive) level and degree of competition in paired-associates learning. *Journal of Experimental Psychology,* 1956, 62, 306-310.

Taylor, J. A., & Chapman, J. P. Paired-associates learning as related to anxiety. *American Journal of Psychology,* 1955, 68, 671.

Thompson, G. G., & Hunnicutt, C. W. The effect of repeated praise or blame on the work achievements of "introverts" and "extroverts." *Journal of Educational Psychology,* 1944, 35, 257-266.

Vaught, G. M., & Newman, S. E. The effects of anxiety on motor-steadiness in competitive and noncompetitive conditions. *Psychonomic Science,* 1966, 2, 519-520.

Wallace, J. An abilities conception of personality: Some implications for personality measurement. *American Psychologist,* 1966, 21, 132-138.

Weiner, B. Need achievement and the resumption of incompleted tasks. *Journal of Abnormal and Social Psychology,* 1965, 1, 165-168. (a)

Weiner, B. The effects of unsatisfied achievement motivation on persistence and subsequent performance. *Journal of Personality,* 1965, 33, 428-442. (b)

Weiner, B. The role of success and failure in the learning of easy and complex tasks. *Journal of Personality and Social Psychology*, 1966, 3, 339-343.

Weiner, B. Current conceptions of achievement motivation and their implications for research and performance in the classroom. *Psychology in the Schools*, 1967, 4, 164-171.

Weiner, B., Frieze, I., Kukla, A., Reed, L., Rest, S., and Rosenbaum, R. M. An attributional (cognitive) model of motivation. Unpublished manuscript, 1969.

Weiner, B., Johnson, P. B., & Mehrabian, A. Achievement motivation and the recall of exam questions. *Journal of Educational Psychology*, 1968, 59, 181-185.

Weiner, B., and Kukla, A. An attributional analysis of achievement motivation. *Journal of Personality and Social Psychology* (in press).

Weiner, B., & Rosenbaum, R. M. Determinants of choice between achievement and non-achievement-related tasks. *Journal of Experimental Research in Personality*, 1965, 1, 114-122.

Zeigarnik, B. Über das Behalten von erledigten und unerledigten Handlungen. *Psychologische Forschung*, 1927, 9, 1-85.

Zeller, A. F. An experimental analogue of repression: III. The effect of induced failure and success on memory measured by recall. *Journal of Experimental Psychology*, 1951, 42, 32-38.

Zubin, J., Eron, L. D., & Schumer, F. *An experimental approach to projective techniques.* New York: Wiley, 1965.

SOCIAL BEHAVIORISM, HUMAN MOTIVATION, AND THE CONDITIONING THERAPIES

Arthur W. Staats

DEPARTMENT OF PSYCHOLOGY, UNIVERSITY OF HAWAII,
HONOLULU, HAWAII

I. Introduction

In recent times interest in learning applications to clinical psychology has increased sharply. In contrast to the opposition generally evident only 5–10 years ago clinical psychologists in growing numbers have begun applying learning principles and procedures to specific problems of behavior. These contemporary developments, however, have in general constituted primarily piecemeal empirical operations with little theoretical content of any kind. It is suggested that the major reason for this is that the traditional learning theories require revision and development before they can serve very well as a theory of human behavior (personality). As a consequence of the inadequacies of the basic learning theories and their associated general methodologies (philosophies), the clinical applications, while an improvement over other treatments in many cases, in addition to being atheoretical have been circumscribed, have not exploited the potentialities of a learning approach, and have other inadequacies that will be more fully described.

In various areas of the study of personality theory and its clinical and social extensions, there is the need for the development of an improved learning theory. The present paper will indicate some of the lines to follow in filling the need. Most basically, it will be suggested that the interrelations of classical and instrumental conditioning must be elaborated, and the principles of learning extended through the use of observations and concepts of the clinic as well as those of the social and behavioral sciences. Moreover, detailed stimulus-response analyses must be made of various complex human repertoires. In this way theoretical structures for dealing with complex human behavior may be developed. The present concern is also to elaborate more fully a learning approach to a conception of human motivation, as part of a theory of personality, and to indicate how the conceptualization can serve as a theoretical framework within which to treat better some of the techniques and findings of behavior therapy and behavior modification.

First, however, it is illuminating to consider briefly some of the characteristics of other learning approaches to personality theory and clinical psychology. Early interest in the extension of learning theory to clinical problems was shown by Dollard and Miller (1950) and Mowrer (1950). While both endeavors, especially the former, were very productive and very influential in later developments, they shared a common defect. The full power of a learning conception of human behavior was not realized; rather the learning principles were applied as an adjunct to a psychoanalytic theory of behavior. The full break was not made—the break where the basic personality theory is a learning theory and the naturalistic observations and concepts of the clinic are used to develop further the basic theory. Furthermore, conditioning procedures tended not to be employed in treatment, instead, traditional psychotherapeutic methods were suggested. It should be noted, however, that in the present view these early theoretical efforts were correct in realizing that the laboratory principles of learning by themselves do not constitute a theory of personality (human behavior).

Even more recently learning approaches have been applied to clinical problems in another way. That is, learning principles and conditioning procedures have been applied to specific behavioral problems or treatment in a straightforward empirical manner. Most investigators in this development have made no attempt to establish a general learning theory of personality and of problems of human behavior. The concern has been with treating specific overt problems of human adjustment. Actually this straightforward empirical learning approach has had two aspects, each of which developed independently. One has been called behavior therapy and the other behavior modification.

Investigators in the area of behavior therapy have drawn their primary learning theory foundation from Hull (1943). The part of behavior therapy to be discussed herein will involve the use of classical conditioning procedures. It should be noted, however, that behavior therapy has dealt with instrumental conditioning as well. Perhaps because of the lack of distinction of the two types of conditioning principles in the basic learning theory, behavior therapy has generally not distinguished classical and instrumental conditioning procedures. Theorizing in the area of behavior therapy has been largely restricted to manipulating some of Hull's intervening variables in deriving principles to treat various specific behavior disorders. While empirical results of behavior therapy have been compiled in several sources (Eysenck, 1960; Franks, 1964; Ullman & Krasner, 1965), there has been an almost total lack of elucidation of a learning theory of personality. Eysenck, for example, one of the originators of modern behavior therapy and a very positive influence in the spread of this approach has had a constitutional theory of personality (Eysenck, 1952, 1957, 1960), and has been critical of the present author's learning conception of human behavior for ignoring biological interpretations (Eysenck, 1965).

Similarly, the work to apply instrumental conditioning principles and procedures to behavior problems, in its contemporary form called behavior modification, has remained almost entirely on an unsophisticated empirical level. The first straightforward application of instrumental conditioning principles to abnormal behavior (Staats, 1957) dealt with simple behaviors. Behavior modification studies which followed this approach (see Ayllon and Michael, 1959) have continued in this pattern — within the context of an operant conditioning methodology and a Skinnerian philosophy of psychology. Contemporary work has remained restricted to this mold, when it is no longer necessary to do so, and is only beginning to move again toward more advanced developments in a learning conception of complex human behavior. Adoption of Skinner's atheoretical experimental analysis of behavior philosophy has had the effect of limiting applications of the *various* learning concepts and *various* experimental findings. The functional-analysis, operant conditioning approach has also led to such misguided efforts as creating a huge Skinner box for research with a single person under total environmental control. Less dramatic, but with a more devastating effect has been the impetus toward a narrow, specific view and a disregard of the observations, concepts, and findings available from naturalistic observations and from nonlaboratory clinical, social, and behavioral sciences.[1]

In essence, thus, the presently popular operant conditioning approach and also that of behavior therapy, while containing principles and procedures that are crucial parts of a learning theory of personality and of clinical psychology, have been largely restricted to dealing with separate instances of relatively simple behaviors. Learning principles alone do not constitute a theory of human behavior — normal and abnormal, child and adult, individual and group — of the type that must underlie a comprehensive human behavior theory and its treatment procedures. It is suggested that while learning principles must be basic in the theoretical structure —

[1]This criticism is not to be taken as a criticism of the use of the simple conditioning principles and procedures. The author began his own learning applications in the early 1950's with simple behaviors, and has continued to contribute to the extension of instrumental conditioning principles to the understanding and treatment of human behavior problems. For example, the author developed the first token-reinforcer system in 1959 in working with children with learning problems. He communicated the efficacy of the reinforcement system to Jack Michael at the University of Houston. Michael and Lee Meyerson began to work with mentally retarded children employing a similar token-reinforcer system. In addition, Patricia Corke and Samuel Toombs, students of Michael, set up a remedial classroom which was also based upon a token system. Montrose Wolf, who as a graduate student had contributed to several later studies employing the author's token-reinforcer system (Staats, Staats, Schutz, & Wolf, 1962; Staats, Minke, Finley, Wolf, & Brooks, 1964; Staats, Finley, Minke, & Wolf, 1964), went to the University of Washington and introduced the token-reinforcer system and behavior modification research design. On the basis of such personal dissemination, along with the publication of token-reinforcer studies, including the author's (see also Staats, 1968; Staats and Butterfield, 1965; Staats and Staats, 1962, 1963), behavior modification work then began to employ the token-reinforcer system widely as did a number of later education and special education studies. It may be added that the token-reinforcer system, and later developments such as the token economy (Ayllon and Azrin, 1969), are very effective in making it possible to clinically treat with instrumental learning procedures many human problems — and there is great potential for further development as the author has indicated (Staats, 1968; Staats and Staats, 1963). However, learning theory has much greater potential than that which resides solely in the use of the simple principle of reinforcement. The simplicity characteristic of the first behavior modification developments, and most contemporary efforts, should not be taken to be immutable characteristics of the learning approach. They are rather characteristics of development, rather than maturity, as the following discussion will show.

not a secondary consideration—they must be employed to develop a general theory of human behavior. This general personality theory is the structure into which the learning clinical psychology must be fitted. Then the methods and rationale of clinical treatment will be derived from the structure. While the theory must be based upon laboratory principles, not accepting other personality theories as a superstructure, the laboratory principles themselves do not constitute the whole theory. The theory must be a human learning theory involving (a) selection of a consistent set of 'heavyweight' learning principles from among the confusion of experimental and theoretical products available, the selection of the principles being determined by the events to which the theory is to be applied. That is, it is in considering human behavior that the perspective for the selection of learning principles and for elaborating their interrelationships is gained. (b) Theoretical efforts must also be expended to integrate the principles in the basic theoretical set, and to elaborate their interrelationships, using a terminological convention that reflects the interrelationships (see Staats, 1966, 1968a, and following discussions). (c) It is necessary to extend the set of learning principles to comprehensive S-R considerations of various areas of complex human behavior. In this task it is the author's strategy that the observations and concepts of the behavioral and social sciences, including those of the clinic, must be incorporated into the approach (see Staats, 1964a, 1968a,b; Staats & Staats, 1963). Although not all of these naturalistic concepts may prove productive or acceptable by operational definition, it is in these areas of study that the most systematic observation of human behavior has occurred. In these three tasks of developing and elaborating the personality theory, the traditional learning theories and their associated philosophies of psychology will not suffice.

The author has called his general approach *social behaviorism* to characterize the emphasis on constructing the basic learning theory explicitly to serve as a foundation for the study of personality (see Staats, 1968a,b), as well as the emphasis on joining the learning theory to the observations and concepts of the social and behavioral sciences as well as those of clinical psychology (Staats, 1964a, 1968a,b, in press; Staats & Staats, 1963).

Having sketched these general points, the present paper will outline a conception of human motivation that exemplifies the points of the approach. After presentation of the theoretical structure, an area of investigation within the field of clinical psychology (aspects of behavior therapy and behavior modification) will be incorporated into the analysis—with mutual enhancement of the clinical areas and the theory, and with implications for further development.

II. Integrated Learning Principles[2]

As the author has indicated (Staats, 1966, 1968a) the field of learning has been separatistic. It has been dominated by theoretical conflict between the traditional viewpoints. This has led to the expenditure of major efforts in developing and maintaining separate experimental methods, separate general (philosophical) methodologies, and separate terminologies, even when the empirical referents involved the same principles. The separation has extended even to the empirical level where investigators have tended to work either with classical or instrumental conditioning. This has been followed on the human level where, for example, until recently, behavior therapy and behavior modification were quite separated.[3]

The various results of the already mentioned separation cannot be dealt with here. However, it is relevant to indicate that theoretical orientations prevalent in learning have prevented us from realizing the various interrelationships between classical and instrumental conditioning. To begin, Hull (1943) did not differentiate between the basic principles of classical and instrumental conditioning. Perhaps because of this Hull *did* indicate the relationship of conditioned stimulus value and conditioned reinforcement value. Later approaches, although distinguishing the principles better, in other respects produced an even less effective basic approach to human learning. Thus, Skinnerian theory is nominally a two-factor (classical–instrumental) learning approach. However, he has over emphasized the separation of the principles and has given a separate terminology to the principles, where quite separate symbols are used for classical and operant conditioning. This has helped prevent the recognition of the interrelationships of the principles (Staats, 1964b, 1966, 1968a). In his system operant conditioning has been by far the focus of study and has been given overriding significance. Thus, operant conditioning theory has almost entirely neglected classical conditioning in basic research as well as

---

[2]Parts of Sections II and III have appeared in substantially the same form in Staats, A. W. Social behaviorism and human motivation: Principles of the *A-R-D* system. In *Psychological Foundations of Attitudes*, A. G. Greenwald, T. C. Brock, and T. M. Ostrom (Eds.). New York: Academic Press, 1968.

[3]In formulating an integrated learning theory of human behavior the author saw in the 1950's the possibilities for the unification of the American behavior modification (instrumental conditioning) and the British behavior therapy (classical conditioning) applications in clinical treatment. It was possible to establish the needed bridge between the two in discussions with H. J. Eysenck and S. Rachman during the author's visit to Maudsley Hospital, Eysenck's Center for early behavior therapy development, during the fall semester of 1961.

in extensions to complex human behavior. In operation, then, Skinner's approach has been a one-factor learning theory, especially in the realm of complex human behavior — a crucial weakness.

Moreover, Skinner's rejection of the theoretical endeavors of Hull and others, although correct in part in the context of that period, has had the effect of generally suppressing theoretical endeavors in learning. This has prevented elaboration on a theoretical level of the basic learning principles and their interrelationships. Skinner's approach has also rejected detailed stimulus-response theorizing, a crucial drawback which, again, has retarded detailed theoretical analysis of complex human behavior. Because Skinner has not had a clear view of what theory is, his philosophy of science has prevented his followers from developing along theoretical lines. The present article cannot deal generally with these topics, however, they will be reflected in the analysis to follow.

In beginning the present analysis and in demonstrating the approach, it is necessary to outline the basic principles to be employed, and their interrelationships, in a notational system which reflects those interrelationships. First, it may be said that many stimuli have both classical *and* instrumental functions. That is, for example, there are stimuli that can function as a ^{UC}S when paired appropriately with a ^{C}S. These stimuli will elicit responses which will be conditioned to the ^{C}S. In addition, however, the same stimulus that functions as a ^{UC}S may also function as an unconditioned reinforcing stimulus or a $^{UC\text{-}R}S$. That is, the same stimulus presented after an instrumental response will result in the response becoming stronger on *future* occasions, or remaining strong if it is already in good strength.

There are many such stimuli. Food will serve as a ^{UC}S and elicit the salivary response, among other emotional responses. Food will also serve as a $^{UC\text{-}R}S$, and will strengthen instrumental behaviors when presented in a response-contingent manner. Although this is readily apparent, its implications have not been seen, perhaps because of our separatistic traditional theoretical terminology which symbolizes an unconditioned stimulus as ^{UC}S and a primary reinforcer as S^{R}. Furthermore, in textbooks and lectures the principles are presented separately so the interrelationship is obscured.

This defect in traditional learning theories becomes even more important when the topic of learned or secondary (conditioned) reinforcement is considered (as well as discriminative stimulus control). This topic may *only* clearly be considered when it is realized that stimuli may have multiple functions in classical and instrumental conditioning. That is, it was suggested that food as a stimulus functions as a ^{UC}S and as a reinforcing stimulus $^{UC \cdot R}S$. It may also be suggested that a new stimulus when paired with such a stimulus in a classical conditioning procedure actually acquires both functions. That is, the new stimulus will become a conditioned stimulus and elicit (at least in part) the emotional responses that the unconditioned stimulus elicits. In addition, however, as a consequence of this conditioning the new stimulus will become a conditioned reinforcing stimulus, or $^{C \cdot R}S$. Hull (1943) also suggested that the secondary reinforcing value of a stimulus was due to the fact that it had come to elicit a conditioned response. (It should be realized that the pairing operation may actually occur in many situations. In operant discriminative training, for example, food is paired with a discriminative stimulus. Thus, the discriminative stimulus ^{D}S should come as part of this training to be a $^{C \cdot R}S$. Operant conditioning in general may be said to involve the classical conditioning of reinforcement value since any time a $^{UC \cdot R}S$ (or $^{C \cdot R}S$) is presented the emotional responses it elicits will be conditioned to any other stimuli that are present.)

It may be noted that it would be expected that higher-order conditioning could also be involved in the formation of conditioned reinforcers. That is, when a conditioned reinforcing stimulus, $^{C \cdot R}S$, is paired with a new stimulus, the latter will also become a ^{C}S as well as a $^{C \cdot R}S$. This by no means completes the integrated learning analysis. However, it does present several concepts that are of importance to a learning theory of attitudes and human motivation. An additional elaboration of the interaction between classical and instrumental conditioning will be made later. More complete accounts of the author's integrated analysis are given in Staats (1961, 1964a, 1966, 1968a) and Staats and Staats (1963). Recent accounts also are beginning to deal with some of the interrelationships between classical and instrumental conditioning (see Rescorla & Solomon, 1967; Trapold & Winokur, 1967) in a manner which supports relevant parts of the theoretical formulation.

III. Integrated Learning Principles and Human Motivation Theory

The author has already described parts of a learning analysis of the attitudinal system (Staats, 1964a, 1968a,b; Staats & Staats, 1963) which will be systematized and extended here. It should be noted that because of traditional categorization schemes and the multiple functions of "motivational stimuli," such stimuli are referred to by different terms such as *emotions, values, instincts, needs, drives, motives, goals, cathexes, reinforcers, urges, utility* (economics), *fetishes, evaluative word meaning, and so on,* in addition to the term *attitudes. The distinctions set up by demarcating such terms and areas of study constitute artificial barriers to the comprehensive study of human behavior. The present analysis is thus thought to apply to these various terms. It is suggested that the study of attitudes — formation, change, and function — in its broad context is the study of human motivation.*

Generally, the naturalistic observations and conceptions of these various aspects of human "motivation stimuli" are not couched in terms of empirical principles that are precisely stated and "causative" in the sense that variables are indicated by which to *affect* (or manipulate) human behavior. The laboratory-established principles of learning, on the other hand, are relatively precise, detailed, and "causative." When the two are combined, based upon the empirical principles, the result is a theory concerned with significant, functional, human behavior, but with the potential for making empirical predictions and producing control of (solutions to) human problems. The present section will present a conception of the human motivational system which will describe the three functions of motivational stimuli: (a) the attitude or emotional (classical conditioning), (b) the reinforcing, and (c) the discriminative controlling functions which such stimuli acquire. The human motivation system may be referred to as the attitude-reinforcer-discriminative (A-R-D) system, thus naming the triple functions of the stimuli included in the system. The first two functions will be treated at length initially and the third later.

A. The Formation and Change of the Attitude-Reinforcer-Discriminative System

Many of the theories of the social and behavioral sciences which are based upon naturalistic evidence have recognized that attitudinal stimuli are subject to variation within an individual and between individuals. This has been true even when the concept is of a biological sort, such as Freud's; that is, in his view an investment of body energy is made in the object, giving the object its motivational characteristics. However, while such psychodynamic theories have recognized that objects can change in their motivational functions for a person (in psychoanalytic terms the investment of energy (cathexis) can shift from object to object, increase and decrease, and so on) the means by which these changes (or the effects) occur are not clearly stated in terms of empirical principles. It is suggested that naturalistic observations of long- and short-term shifts in individual and group "motivational stimuli," and the like, may be handled in greater detail by the employment of a learning analysis. Moreover, as will be described in part, when the learning analysis is employed it suggests means by which human behavior can be predicted, measured, and modified.

The important principle for discussing the *formation* of the individual's

A-R-D system is that of classical conditioning, not operant conditioning. That is, as has been described there are stimuli that naturally have functions as unconditioned stimuli (^{UC}S). Food, water, air, sexual stimulation, warmth, and so on, elicit upon presentation positive "emotional" responses (when the organism has been deprived of them). On the other hand intense tactile, auditory, visual, and chemical stimuli, elicit negative "emotional" responses. When these various stimuli are paired with neutral stimuli, eliciting their particular emotional response, the emotional response is classically conditioned to the neutral stimulus. When a stimulus has come to elicit an emotional response it may be defined as an attitudinal stimulus. This is an important quality that some stimuli can have or acquire, that is, the function of eliciting an emotional or attitudinal response. When a stimulus has acquired this quality, it can be transferred to new stimuli with which it is paired in the process of higher-order conditioning.

Thus, it is suggested that the individual's A-R-D system is founded upon the stimuli that originally elicit emotional (attitudinal) responses in him on an unlearned basis, and elaborated by extensive first-order and higher-order classical conditioning. The individual's conditioning history in this respect is infinitely complex and extends over his life history—ample opportunity for a fantastically large number of conditioning trials and all the uniqueness we see in the human attitudinal system. It is also important to note that the A-R-D system differs not only from person to person, but also from small group to small group: by social class, by nation, and by culture. And, finally, language plays a central role in the classical conditioning formation of individual and group differences in the A-R-D system (see Staats, 1964b, 1968a,b), as the author has demonstrated in a series of studies.

It should be pointed out that in the naturalistic situation the fact that a classical conditioning process is involved in the establishment of an attitudinal response to a stimulus may be obscured. The presentation of the original attitude stimulus, the $^{UC \cdot R}S$, may be contingent upon some instrumental response, producing instrumental conditioning. The process may thus appear simply as an instrumental conditioning situation even when the more important result is to make a stimulus present in the situation a new conditioned stimulus and consequently a new conditioned reinforcing stimulus ($^{C \cdot R}S$). An example from everyday life may be seen when the parent applies reinforcing verbal stimuli (that elicit positive emotional responses) contingent upon the cooperative play behavior of two siblings. This would have the effect of strengthening the motor response. In addition, however, the positive attitudinal response elicited in each case by the "social" approval would be conditioned to the other sibling as a social stimulus. In both laboratory and naturalistic (and clinical) situations the investigator may be misled by the appearance of an instrumental conditioning procedure and fail to realize that a classical conditioning process is just as essentially involved.

It may be added that the principles of classical conditioning are empirical and are known in great detail. As a theory they improve markedly upon the naturalistic concepts of the formation and alteration of attitude stimuli. And, as will be shown, by drawing upon the observations of the clinic and other social and behavioral sciences it is possible to invest the classical conditioning analysis with greater significance. Moreover, a great deal of information about individual and group behavior is given when the nature of the individual's or the group's attitudinal system is known. The principles involved in this case are those of instrumental conditioning, and the account thus begins to deal with the *function* of attitude stimuli.

B. The Reinforcing Function of the A-R-D System

Traditionally, the study of attitudes has concentrated upon attitude formation and change and the measurement of attitudes. The principles involved in the function of attitudes have been assumed, or based upon naturalistic expectations rather than experimentally derived principles. It is suggested, however, that systematic study must be made of the instrumental function of attitude-eliciting stimuli.

In outlining this approach, a short description of the manner in which the attitudinal system determines one's instrumental behaviors will first be given, beginning with an example from the animal laboratory. Let us say that we have two rats of the same biology. One of them, *rat A*, we subject to training in which a buzzer is presented many times, each time paired with food, in what constitutes classical conditioning trials in an instrumental situation (see Zimmerman, 1957). *Rat B* receives experience with the buzzer, but not paired with food. It would be expected that the buzzer would become a positive attitudinal stimulus for *rat A*, but not for *rat B*. Now let us individually place each animal into the *same* instrumental learning situation involving a lever which when pressed results in the brief sound of the buzzer. We will see that *rat A* will be an enthusiastic learner; he will come to press the bar actively, but *rat B* will not. The *difference* between animals, however, would rest solely upon the fact that for one organism the stimulus has acquired a reinforcer function — would be an attitudinal and thus motivational stimulus — while for the other it has not.

Using the same analysis, we can see how different behaviors will be formed in children with different A-R-D systems in situations important to child adjustment. Some children are raised in such a manner that some stimuli will elicit attitude responses in them while other children lack the necessary conditioning experience. It has been widely recognized (see, for example, Rosen, 1956; Maccoby & Gibbs, 1954) that differences in the "value" of various events is affected by social class and familial training circumstances. Middle-class children ordinarily are rewarded many times for learning new skills of various kinds. The products (stimuli) resulting from learning new skills (achievements) should thus come to elicit positive attitudes and consequently serve as conditioned reinforcers. It may be added that through similar conditioning experiences the approval of adult "authority" figures can also come to be a strong positive reinforcer for some children.

With these givens it is not difficult to see how child learning, for example, classroom learning and adjustment, may be affected by the A-R-D system. The approval of the teacher and other students and the products of one's own developing skill are among the most important sources of reinforcement for 'student' behaviors in the traditional classroom. In a manner analogous to our two animals, let us say that two children with differing A-R-D systems are placed in the classroom. For one child, *child A*, the teacher's approval and the child's own achievements are reinforcing; for the other, *child B*, these stimuli are not reinforcing. Let us say that they receive the same treatment in the class. Whenever they pay attention to materials the teacher presents and respond in the manner directed they receive the teacher's approval, and their instrumental behaviors produce stimuli that evidence their skill (achievements). Under such a circumstance, *child A*'s attentional and working behaviors will be maintained in good strength and as a result he will continue to develop new skills. *Child B*'s behavior, on the other hand, will not be maintained. His attentional and working behaviors will wane, and other competitive behaviors that are strengthened by stimuli that *are* effective reinforcers will become relatively dominant.

Child A will be seen as interested, motivated, hardworking, and *bright*. Ultimately, he will also measure as very able and bright on class, achievement, and intelligence tests. *Child B* will be seen as disinterested and dull, and possibly as a behavior problem if problem behaviors are reinforced. Later he will also measure this way and this evidence may be used to support the contention that the child's behavioral failure was due to some personal defect. It may be suggested that many problems of school adjustment which are important for psychology involve deficient or defective A-R-D systems (see Staats & Butterfield, 1965). It may be stated generally that 'normal' behavior will only emerge from a situation which has a fixed set of stimuli supposed to have A-R-D qualities only when those stimuli actually *do* have those qualities. When 'normal' behavior does not emerge from the situation we have to scrutinize the A-R-D system of the individual *and the A-R-D system in effect in the situation.*

Many other examples may be given that involve behaviors important to human adjustment. Let us take two adult males one of whom has come to find other males to be strong sex reinforcers because of his conditioning history; that is, males elicit positive sexual attitudes in him. For this individual females do not have as strong sexual reinforcing properties. Let us say, also, that the other adult male in this example has an A-R-D system that is just the reverse. These two individuals, placed in the same life situations, will be likely to develop two quite opposite sets of sexual behaviors. Behaviors (and mannerisms) that are successful in attracting and gaining contact with males will be strengthened in the first case. Behaviors that are successful in attracting and gaining contact with females will be strengthened in the second. The same analysis would also hold for other aberrations in sexual behavior. The person for whom children elicit sexual attitudinal responses and have sexual reinforcing value is likely to develop behaviors that are strengthened by sexual contact with children. The person for whom pain and violence are positive sexual reinforcers will be likely to develop instrumental behaviors that culminate in such events.

In addition, certain aspects of neurotic and psychotic behaviors can be considered in terms of abnormalities in the individual's A-R-D system, for example, neurasthenia or simple schizophrenia. (Later discussions will elaborate these points.) Fetishes may also be considered to involve cases where because of the individual's conditioning history an object has come to have strong sex reinforcing value for an individual to an extent that is unusual in comparison to other individuals. It should be noted that these are only examples. Many other abnormal behaviors can be considered in terms of an abnormal A-R-D system and the instrumental conditioning that is consequently effected.

It is important to add also by illustration that the A-R-D system can also suffer impairments because stimuli have come through conditioning to elicit negative attitudinal responses and act as negative reinforcers thus resulting in behavior disorders. In the area of sex behavior, for example, aberrant behaviors will be produced if the stimuli that must become positive attitudinal stimuli and sex reinforcers are instead, through conditioning, made into negative reinforcers. When this occurs, of course, behavior that takes the individual away from the stimuli will be strengthened. This will make it impossible for the individual to acquire the instrumental behaviors necessary to obtain the reinforcement that otherwise would be available.

This is the same principle that is involved in phobias, irrational fears, anxieties, and so on. That is, while the presence of a phobia (where a stimulus inappropriately elicits a negative attitudinal response) may be of importance in and of itself because of the unpleasant quality of negative emotional responses, or because of an effect upon health, it is important to note that the effect upon the individual's adjustive instrumental behaviors may be of even greater importance. For example, a strong negative attitude to being outdoors will result in the behavior of staying inside. When one is *forced* (by one's classical conditioning history and instrumental behavior principles) to remain indoors various types of social interactions are ruled out, one's occupational success may be ruled out, sexual reinforcement may suffer, and so on. The individual's poor life adjustment in which lessened positive reinforcement and increased negative reinforcement occurs may result in further unfortunate development of the A-R-D system and thus additional problems.

It should also be indicated that groups of people can differ from each other in their A-R-D systems. Following the above analysis this would result in different types of behavior coming to be dominant in the group. That is, for example, if a group has a reinforcement system in which success in competition is a strong positive reinforcer, then this will serve to make behaviors that culminate in such success dominant in that culture. If success in competition is less positive, or even negative, then fewer examples of such instrumental behaviors will develop. Much description in sociology and anthropology can be considered in terms of differences in the A-R-D system between groups, subgroups, cultures, and so on. Many times it is important to the treatment of social problems to describe the A-R-D system of subgroups in our own society. Through this type of description, an understanding of the causes of undesirable behaviors may be gained, and possibilities of prevention and treatment may be suggested by the analysis. Thus, many of the aspects of problem behaviors of the children we now call culturally deprived arise from social conditions that prevent the development of an A-R-D system that is appropriate for the conditions to which they are subjected. This has, of course, been true for American Negroes in various ways. For example, when the social situation prevents the positive attitudinal stimuli of 'success' from being paired with the stimuli of hard work, acquiring skills, intellectual achievement, educational status, and so on, these latter *stimuli* will not acquire positive attitudinal, and thus, reinforcement value. In addition, when a group within the larger group has been discriminated against in various aversive ways, this will also constitute negative attitudinal conditioning for the individuals involved. By verbal means, involving the principles of classical conditioning of meaning and attitudes (see Staats, 1966, 1964b, 1968a; Staats & Staats, 1958), this conditioning can be passed to other individuals. When there is a consistent aversive experience of a subgroup culture presented by members of the larger group, the reinforcement system of the subgroup will come to include strong negative attitudes toward members of the larger group. This will affect the extent to which members of the larger group can serve as positive social reinforcers of the behavior of members of the subgroup. For example, the member of the subgroup who interacts with a member of the larger group in a learning situation, such as the case where the member of the larger group is a supervisor, therapist, or a teacher, will respond 'atypically' if the member of the larger group elicits negative attitudinal responses and, as will be described, thus controls avoidance and oppositional behaviors.

The applications of the learning theory of human attitudes to problems of human behavior, and to a general conception of human behavior, cannot be exhausted in this paper. The preceding discussion attempts only to indicate some of the potentialities, and, by the examples chosen, to indicate that the realm of attitude study is concerned with various types of human behavior—from theoretical to applied areas—even though the behaviors are not traditionally included in the study of attitudes. In order to spell out some of the additional implications of the concept of the A-R-D system, the straightforward learning principles require additional elaboration, which will be the concern of the next sections.

C. The Hierarchical Nature of the A-R-D System and Its Functions

Additional conceptions within psychology and the other social and behavioral sciences can be employed in the further development of the learning theory of attitudes (human motivation). Maslow (1954), as one example, has suggested that one's needs (or in the present terms one's attitudes and reinforcers) are ordered in terms of strength. When the strongest 'needs' are satisfied, then the next strongest becomes prepotent, and so on. Another example of a social science principle which lends itself to a hierarchical conception concerns the law of diminishing (marginal or extra) utility, from economics (Samuelson, 1958, p. 430). This states that "the more the individual has of some given commodity [in the present terms, a reinforcer], the *less* satisfaction (or utility) he would obtain from an additional unit of it (Ulmer, 1959, p. 319)."

The present concept of the A-R-D system may be elaborated by characterizing the system's 'hierarchical' nature, and by outlining some of the laboratory principles that would be expected to be involved, again utilizing naturalistic observations and conceptions. To begin, it may be suggested that the A-R-D system is a system because the elements in the system have modes of 'interaction,' one of which is involved in the hierarchical nature of the system. At any moment in time the various stimuli in the individual's system would be expected to have *relative* reinforcing intensity. Relative, as well as absolute, strength would have an important effect upon the individual's or group's behavior.

Let us say, for example, that two individuals have a stimulus in each of their 'reinforcer systems' that has precisely the same reinforcing value, *reinforcer A*. Let us also say, however, that for one individual there are no stronger reinforcers in his system while for the other individual there is another stimulus, *reinforcer B*, that is an even stronger reinforcer. Now let the individuals be placed in a situation in which both reinforcers are available, but one reinforcer is presented contingent upon one instrumental behavior, and the other reinforcer is presented contingent upon an incompatible behavior. Under these circumstances the two individuals will develop different behaviors. The individual with the reinforcer system in which *reinforcer B* is the most 'dominant' reinforcer will develop most dominantly the behavior that is followed by that reinforcer. The other individual with the system in which *reinforcer A* is relatively stronger will develop predominantly the other behavior. It is thus suggested that it is not only the absolute value of reinforcers that determines individual and group differences in behavior, but also the relative values of the various reinforcers in the A-R-D system.

One corollary should be added here. It appears that there are subsystems within the major system. That is, there are classes of reinforcers that are related. Take sex reinforcers for example. It may be suggested that there are many different individual sex reinforcers which constitute a class, and probably there are subclasses within the class. Certainly, food reinforcers constitute another class of the A-R-D system (with subclasses also). When one is deprived of food, as an example, it would be expected that the whole class would be increased in reinforcing value. If the strongest food reinforcer in the hierarchy is not available, then the next strongest would be the dominant available reinforcer. The model would suggest that a relatively weak member of a class of reinforcers could be raised into a position of relative dominance in the total system through deprivation of stronger members of its class. A man deprived of potable fluids might be more affected by some brackish water than by a usually stronger reinforcer in some other class of reinforcers such as sexual reinforcers, food reinforcers, social approval reinforcers, and so on.

Several other specifications may be indicated here in elaborating the conception. The relative strengths of the reinforcers in the system may be changed by first-order or higher-order classical conditioning experiences. This conditioning may be of the usual variety, or it may involve incompatible conditioning; that is, a stimulus that has come to elicit one attitudinal response will no longer do so (or not to the same extent) when an incompatible emotional response is conditioned to the stimulus. This has been called counterconditioning. In addition, the relative strengths of reinforcers in an indi·vidual motivational system may be changed by extinction procedures. These two processes may require a number of conditioning (or extinction) trials in any case, and thus may develop slowly. Also, once a stimulus has come to elicit an attitudinal response thus being a reinforcer, it will remain so unless further conditioning or extinction procedures produce a change.

D. Deprivation and Satiation and the A-R-D System

In addition to these enduring and slowly acquired processes of change in the relative (and absolute) strength of reinforcers in the motivational system, there are also operations that can change the system more rapidly, usually with a less permanent effect. That is, deprivation operations also increase the reinforcing strength of a positive reinforcing stimulus in an absolute sense. Satiation, on the other hand, decreases the strength of a reinforcing stimulus. In both cases the operation can be expected to change also the relative dominance of reinforcers in the system. When the condition of deprivation or satiation is returned to the starting point, however, the reinforcers will regain their former relative position—the changes produced directly follow the deprivation-satiation variations.

The manner in which groups and individuals can vary in behavior because different stimuli are effective in their A-R-D systems has already been discussed. A few examples will be given here where the relative (hierarchical) ordering of the A-R-D system is affected by deprivationsatiation variations, producing variations in behavior. As an example, adult social reinforcement may occur in small portions for the housewife with several small children. As a result of this deprivation this class of social stimuli may increase in reinforcement value to a far greater extent than is the case with her husband. He, being satiated on social reinforcers because of his work situation, finds spending evenings at home more reinforcing; she finds social events more reinforcing. As another example, deprivation of sex reinforcers would be expected to increase the reinforcing value of this class of stimuli, at the expense of other reinforcers in the individual's system. For the adolescent under this type of deprivation other reinforcers may be relatively weak and the behavior maintained by those reinforcers—study, reading, family activities—may weaken.

Deprivation-satiation also causes attitudinal differences in social groups. While experiencing less deprivation for sex reinforcers, the lower economic classes on the other hand suffer much more deprivation of material reinforcers such as money, fine clothes, cars, and so on, as well as more deprivation of social reinforcers such as prestige, social approval, and so on. Juvenile delinquency and criminality have been considered by the author in terms of a partial statement of this principle (Staats & Staats, 1963), and this and other aspects of the present approach recently have been employed in another analysis of criminal behavior (Burgess & Akers, 1966).

It is important to indicate that deprivation may also affect the A-R-D system, and thus behavior, in another way that does not emerge from consideration of laboratory learning principles. For example, when a prisoner is deprived of contact with the opposite sex, the general class of sex reinforcers will increase in relative strength. As a consequence, reinforcers of lesser value in the class, but which are more accessible, such as homosexual contact, will be relatively stronger and may instrumentally condition behavior that would be unlikely to occur without the deprivation. It should be emphasized that in this way each instance of a homosexual act constitutes a whole series of classical conditioning trials since a sexual act extends over a considerable length of time. The homosexual conditioning experience would be expected to increase the sexual attitudinal value of the class of social stimulus involved – members of the same sex – thus further altering the structure of the A-R-D system on a more permanent basis.

E. RULES OF APPLICATION OF REINFORCERS AND THE A-R-D SYSTEM

It was said in introducing the present paper that the straightforward statement of learning principles does not constitute a theory of human behavior, even when the principles have been demonstrated with simple human behaviors. It is necessary to extend the basic principles into the realms of human behavior of interest to the behavioral and social sciences. In doing this the naturalistic observations and the concepts they have yielded must exert a prominent influence in the theory construction task. New principles not suggested in the laboratory may be expected to emerge from extending the laboratory principles in the analysis of the complex circumstances of human life. Examples of this have already been presented in the preceding analyses, but it will help to elaborate this methodological suggestion by more pointed examples of the ways that basic principles alone are inadequate. As one illustration, the *relationship* between the basic principles may not be seen in the laboratory because one is concerned about *isolating* the principles and studying them independently. The *relationship* of the principles, on the other hand, may be very important when dealing with complex human behavior. The relationship between the attitudinal-reinforcing value of a stimulus and its discriminative stimulus value, yet to be discussed, is such an example.

It is also the case that effects which are difficult to produce in the laboratory because of limited numbers of conditioning trials, and the like, may take place readily and importantly in real life where conditioning opportunities may be unlimited. The principle of higher-order conditioning is such an example. Furthermore, certain conditions or principles may be an irrelevant part of laboratory manipulation and yet be very significant when the principles or conditions are extended on a theoretical—empirical level to the study of man. The hierarchical nature of the reinforcement system and the principles involved, for example, unlike the case on the human level, are not crucial in the animal laboratory. The present section will be concerned with describing another such case relevant to the present theory.

To begin, in the laboratory there is a certain 'rule' in existence when the principle of reinforcement is studied. The rule involves what behavior the investigator elects to reinforce and in what manner (e.g., schedule of reinforcement). In the rat he will reinforce bar pressing behavior, or running down a runway, or turning in one direction in a T maze; in the pigeon he will reinforce pecking a key, or a key of a certain color, and so on. The behavior is selected for various practical reasons relevant to laboratory work: to be specifiable objectively, naturally occurring, simple enough to be treated as a unit, of limited duration enabling repeated trials, and so on.

This aspect of the principle of reinforcement, which only has practical importance in the basic study, involves some of the most significant matters in the study of human organization. *Independently of what* attitudinal stimuli serve as reinforcers for a particular group or culture, there can be differences between groups in the rules by which the reinforcers are applied. The ways that groups differ in this respect, the ways that these differences develop and change, and the effects that are produced on human behavior may be seen as primary topics of study for scientific and professional areas concerned with man. A few examples indicating the importance of the rules of applying reinforcers will be made.

As one illustration, in our society some of the stimuli that have a good deal of reinforcing value are titles, positions, status roles, social and personal attention, acclaim and respect, money, fine clothes, expensive cars and houses, and various honors and awards. In our society, there are also rules (not necessarily formal or explicit) for the application of these stimuli. That is, they (or tokens which can be exchanged for them) are delivered contingent upon some kinds of behavior but not upon others. Thus, large amounts of these stimuli are delivered contingent upon exceptionally skilled baseball, football, acting, dancing, or comic behaviors, among others. Relatively small amounts are delivered contingent upon the behaviors of skilled manual work, studying, unskilled manual work, nursing, and many others.

These characteristics of our reinforcing system and its rules of application, to continue with the example, have an effect upon the manner in which behavior in our society is shaped. Consider, thus, a boy who has two classes of skilled behaviors, one a set of intellectual skills consisting of knowledge and well-developed study and scholarly work habits, and the other consisting of some form of fine athletic prowess. Let us say that either behavior could be developed to 'championship' caliber. Now, in a situation in which the societal rule is that the larger amount of reinforcement is made contingent upon the one behavior, this behavior will be strengthened, and as must be the case, at the expense of the other to the extent that the behaviors are incompatible. *It is very important to note that the rules of application of A-R-D stimuli in the family, class, or societal group may be "abnormal," and thus produce "abnormal" behavior.*

When groups are compared, it would also be expected that the reinforcer system and its rules of application will determine the types of behaviors that are dominant. A society that has a differing set of reinforcers and rules will evidence different behavior over the group of people exposed to that set of conditions. A society, for example, whose reinforcers are made contingent upon scholarly behaviors to a larger extent than another society will create stronger behaviors of that type, in a greater number of people, than will the other society. In general, many of the different cultural, national, class, and familial behaviors that have been observed in sociology, anthropology, clinical and social psychology, and other behavioral sciences, can be considered to involve this aspect of human motivation—the A-R-D system and its *rules of application.*

It should be indicated that sometimes the rule specifies a particular *behavior-social stimulus-reinforcement* relationship. Thus, sexual behavior and sexual reinforcement occur in all societies. However, the rules regulate the type of behavior and the type of social stimulus. Thus, in our culture, sexual behavior will be reinforced but only in certain situations with certain people. People such as siblings, parents, children, same sex partners, unwilling partners, and so on are excluded. We also have many examples of cultures and subcultures with markedly different rules, for example, the ancient Greek, Roman, Hawaiian, and Egyptian cultures, homosexual groups, marital "switching" clubs, and so on.

It may be added that there are also rules for the application of negative reinforcers as well as positive and these can differ for families, subcultures, and cultures. For example, a family has rules by which certain behaviors are punished. A group or a society also does. Many rules concerning the application of negative reinforcers when the behavior or social stimulus involved is inappropriate are made explicit in the form of legal or religious laws. Certain *behavior-social stimulus-reinforcement* relationships are relatively likely to be heavily controlled by laws, as occurs in the area of sex. These rules concerning negative and positive reinforcers may also be called mores or values or norms in the social sciences.

The experimental, social, or clinical psychologist who is interested in human behavior must go to the social and behavioral sciences and their naturalistic observations of man for information concerning these important matters. It may be suggested, however, that the concepts and the principles of the basic science serve as the theory within which to understand and extend the naturalistic observations and concepts. Thus, the theory of human behavior does not emerge from the basic laboratory principles *themselves* (as some philosophies of psychology would imply, for example, Skinner's "experimental analysis of behavior" methodology), nor from the naturalistic observations themselves.

F. THE CONTROLLING (GOAL) FUNCTION OF THE A-R-D SYSTEM

There is another aspect of a learning theory of attitudes and human motivation that also involves a principle that does not emerge from the laboratory, but which has antecedents in the naturalistic observations and concepts of clinical psychology and other social sciences. The author has in part described this principle elsewhere (Staats, 1964a, 1968a,b; Staats & Staats, 1963). The analysis requires an integration of the principles of classical conditioning, conditioned reinforcement, and discriminative stimulus control. The analysis provides the principles with which to treat the *D* (discriminative) aspect of the A-R-D system.

The laboratory study of the principle of reinforcement has been largely concerned with the reinforcing effect of reinforcing stimuli. It should be noted that the effect of a reinforcing stimulus occurs when it is presented *after* some response, *and the effect involves strengthening future occurrences of that behavior.* The reinforcing function of a stimulus is not defined by the ability of the stimulus to control (or bring on) instrumental behavior. The traditional learning theories did not explicitly make the point. Consequently, many investigators have not understood this definition clearly or followed it in their research with humans. Thus it is not uncommon to see a study in which the reinforcing value of a stimulus is increased by the experimental manipulation; but the effect is measured by the increase in the instrumental behavior the stimulus *elicits*, not by an increase in its reinforcing function. Although the stimulus has never been presented as a reinforcer, contingent upon the behavior studied, the effect is erroneously discussed as if it was due to the reinforcing action of the stimulus. Bandura, Ross, and Ross, (1963), for example, make this theoretical error in an otherwise valuable paper.

This is an easy confusion, however, for there has not been an appreciation by laboratory investigators of how conditioned stimulus and reinforcing value are inextricably intertwined with discriminative stimulus value when studying or treating complex human behavior. Clinical and social theories, on the other hand, while at times recognizing the multiple functions of motivational stimuli, have not clearly defined the functions or indicated the operating principles. Newcomb (1950, p. 80) and Klineberg (1954, p. 76), as examples, discuss motives as including states of *drive*, as well as *directing* behavior toward some goal. Norms and values play the same role in sociology referring to control of behavior and to satisfaction, and these functions are ordinarily not clearly distinguished (Johnson, 1960, p. 50). Freud, as another example, posited that an instinct has both an aim and a particular behavior for attaining the object that satisfies the aim and reduces the tension of the instinct.

In the laboratory, on the other hand, the several functions of stimuli have been clearly seen, but the relationship has not been adequately stipulated. (Hull suggested that the concept of motivation or drive had both an "energizing" and "guiding" function, with the concept of anticipatory goal response also relevant, but the learning theory was not developed to serve as a basis for a theory of human motivation, or human behavior in general, and the theory serves poorly in this role. Skinner has not treated the interacting function of stimuli.)

Actually, the analysis of the "rewarding" and "goal" functions of reinforcing stimuli is complex. It may be reduced for a summary account, however. To begin, the sensory stimuli of an object or event that also has a reinforcing quality are likely to come to control behaviors that approach or avoid the stimuli. As an example, when a child sees a food stimulus, if he crawls toward the stimulus this response is followed by obtaining the stimulus, which is a reinforcement. This process fulfills the requirements for making a stimulus a discriminative stimulus; that is, a stimulus in the presence of which a response is reinforced will come to control the response.

This brief analysis must be expanded in human behavior in several directions. First, the child will learn a large class of "striving" behaviors that will come under the discriminative control of such reinforcing stimuli, for example, crawling toward, walking toward, running toward, climbing over and around obstacles, reaching and grabbing for, fighting and struggling for, asking, begging and crying for, working for, wheedling for, arguing for, flattering for, being ingratiating for, being respectful for, as well as competing for in various ways.

In addition, the child's class of striving behaviors will come under the discriminative control of a large number of different reinforcing stimuli on the basis of his experience with those, or similar, stimuli. Thus, in the child's conditioning history a wide variety of stimulus objects that are reinforcers will come to control responses that result in obtaining those objects.

Furthermore, through various mediated generalization mechanisms, stimulus objects with which the individual has *previously had no direct conditioning experience* will have the goal (discriminative) value immediately. This may take place through language, as one example. That is, after the word "food" has come to be a conditioned reinforcer (through classical conditioning) and also a discriminative stimulus for striving behavior, a new stimulus that is labeled by the word food will thereby immediately gain discriminative control. It may also be suggested, although the complete mediated generalization analysis will not be given here, that any stimulus that elicits a positive emotional or attitudinal response (any reinforcing stimulus) will also have to that extent discriminative stimulus value, the first time the stimulus is contacted. The principle is again that of mediated generalization (see Staats, 1968a, for a more complete analysis).

(It should be noted that although a stimulus will tend to control a wide number of striving responses, whether or not a response occurs will also be a function of other controlling stimuli that are present in the situation. For example, although a reinforcing stimulus may control "reaching for" and "asking for" behavior, the latter will be more likely to occur when there is another person present. As another example, a stimulus object that is labeled food will not control striving for behavior if it elicits a negative emotional response because of its visual characteristics.)

At any rate, it is suggested that the strength of the discriminative stimulus value will vary, in part, as a function of manipulation of the reinforcing value of the stimulus. Thus, the discriminative value of the stimulus will increase or decrease according to *classical conditioning variables* as well as a *deprivation-satiation* conditions.

The preceding analysis was made only for positive reinforcing stimuli. However, an analogous analysis can be made for negative reinforcing stimuli. Because of their effects on behavior negative reinforcing stimuli come to control "striving away from" or "striving against" behaviors, which would include a broad class of responses ranging from running away from through fighting, avoiding, arguing with, insulting, voting against, rating negatively, and so on.

It should be noted that in contrast to the laboratory situation, it is usually the discriminative control of instrumental behaviors that social and behavioral science investigators use to index motivational stimuli. The social psychologist, clinician, sociologist, or anthropologist, for example, ordinarily observes what people strive for (verbally or otherwise) when he studies attitudes or motivation. This is why he has so generally introduced the concept of goal directed behavior (while correct in certain respects is usually also teleological), and frequently has glossed over the principles of classical conditioning and reinforcement. The social theorist, or clinical theorist, does not see whether the receipt of a stimulus elicits an emotional response or whether it strengthens *future* occurrences of an instrumental behavior. In fact it would ordinarily be impossible to do so in view of the complexity of many human behaviors studied or treated, the infrequency of their occurrence, the internal nature of the emotional responses, and so on. It is probably for this reason that the principles of the laboratory worker and those of the social scientist were not readily brought into a productive relationship in this important realm of study. More will be said of the effects of the discriminative functions of the A-R-D system in personality and abnormal behavior in the following sections.

G. DEFICITS AND INAPPROPRIACIES IN THE A-R-D SYSTEM

This section is intended to describe several additional characteristics of the A-R-D system which are implied in some of the preceding discussions but which should be specified and elaborated.

It has already been suggested herein that the individual's A-R-D system is formed on the basis of the classical conditioning of emotional responses in primary and higher-order conditioning. While the laboratory animal's conditioning history may run into a few hundred or a few thousand conditioning trials, it is important to note that for humans the classical conditioning history is infinitely greater. In considering this one should remember that unconditioned stimuli such as eating a dinner, engaging in the sex act, and so on actually involve numerous conditioning trials over an extended period of time. Any conditioned stimulus presented for an instant during that extended period will receive a conditioning trial. Moreover, any stimulus present during the whole interval will receive many, many conditioning trials. The same thing is true with respect to higher-order conditioning. There are opportunities for an infinite number of classical conditioning trials here which will result in development of the individual's A-R-D system. This can be seen easily on the verbal level, since one's language will contain many, many, words which elicit positive or negative emotional responses. These words may then serve to make other stimuli into emotion eliciting stimuli when the words are paired with these stimuli (see Staats, 1968a). Even in one day such conditioning trials are legion.

The large number of conditioning possibilities, and the opportunity for an infinite variation in one's personal conditioning history, insure that there will be no precise similarity in A-R-D systems between individuals. The universals we look for in human behavior must be universals in behavior principles, not universals in the A-R-D system or the behaviors influenced by the system.

On the other hand, the similar conditions provided for individuals and groups in conditioning histories would be expected to result in similarities, if not identities. Thus, it would be expected that families would ordinarily provide similar conditioning histories for their members in contrast to the conditioning existing between families. One would thus expect variation in A-R-D systems that would take place between families. The same would be true of many groups: peer groups, social classes, fraternities, social institutions like education, professions, clubs, readers of particular periodicals, newspapers, books, and so on. The experiences obtained from contact with each social grouping should result in conditioning which affects the formations of the A-R-D system. This is not to say that members of a grouping may not receive an atypical attitude conditioning history for that group. There are many circumstances under which this can occur.

The theory of the A-R-D system must be spelled out in greater detail in the context of its formation, its measurement, its effects upon social interaction, its relevance for additional topics of personality, and so on. (See Staats, 1968b, for additional specifications and implications in these areas.) One of the important areas of specification must be that of the abnormal development of the A-R-D system and the consequent effects upon the individual's emotional responses and overt, instrumental, behaviors. The section to follow will indicate some additional principles in these areas. First, however, it may serve to stress briefly again the three effects which an abnormal A-R-D system will have.

First, a conditioning history that is abnormal will affect abnormal emotional responses to stimuli with which the individual is confronted. Second, abnormal conditioning will result in abnormalities in the stimuli which will reinforce the individual. Third, abnormal conditioning will result in abnormalities in the stimuli for which the individual will strive for or against. Regardless of the type of abnormality in the A-R-D system, it should be remembered that there may be three effects. There will be an abnormal presence or absence of emotional responding to stimuli; this will make the stimuli abnormal in reinforcing power which will affect the individual's behavior, and the abnormal emotional value of the stimuli will abnormally control the individual's striving behavior.

1. Deficits in the A-R-D System

Examples of abnormal behavior have already been given in previous sections. The present discussion is meant only to indicate the general ways in which A-R-D systems may be abnormal — which needs additional specification. The present author (Staats & Staats, 1963) has suggested that many aspects of abnormal behavior can be considered in terms of deficits in behavior, or in terms of behaviors acquired which are inappropriate for the individual. It is important to make the general statement here that the A-R-D system also differs in these two dimensions. That is, the general principles are that abnormalities in conditioning history can provide individuals with an A-R-D system that has *deficits* such that stimuli which should elicit positive or negative attitudes do not do so; or the A-R-D system may be inappropriate such that stimuli which should not elicit an attitude response (either positive or negative) have come to elicit such a response.

The effect of either a deficit or inappropriacy in the A-R-D system may be shown in any one of the three functions of A-R-D stimuli. Thus, for example, one could consider deficits simply in terms of the fact that stimuli do not elicit emotional responses in an individual when they do in others. Thus, an individual attending a symphony concert for whom the music elicits no positive emotional responses misses the pleasure of most concert-goers. A person for whom a joke elicits no positive emotional response is in the same situation. A person who is not horrified by some horrible situation is considered callous or brutal.

In the reinforcing value characteristic of the A-R-D system, one has only to refer to the accounts of abnormal psychology textbooks to obtain abundant descriptions of individuals (and types) whose central difficulty is that stimuli which should be reinforcing to them, if they are to display certain behaviors, are not reinforcing. Take the case of the young neurasthenic housewife. She "has no energy" to do her housework. She is listless, depressed, and unable to apply herself to the tasks her life situation presents. She may become worried that something must be wrong with her and may seek medical or psychological help. The primary problem is frequently that there are inadequate sources of reinforcement to maintain the behaviors requisite for performing her new tasks as a housewife. As a young girl she may have had a conditioning history in which social events and social interaction of all sorts, attending school, studying for exams, recreational activities, and so on have come to be powerful reinforcers.

However, staying alone in a house and doing housework may not be reinforcing at all. The problem is not that the young housewife does not have the requisite motor skills. These could have been well acquired. However, without positive reinforcement for the behaviors, they will not occur. It will be observed, however, that when adequate reinforcers are available to the young woman, the listlessness will drop out, and active, energetic, behavior will be exhibited. Thus, a visit from a friend, a social event, and so on, will strengthen her behavior and show it is not a matter of a deficit in the instrumental behaviors that is involved, but a deficit A-R-D system for her life situation. (A more complete analysis of such a case would require greater specification of the A-R-D system and its manner of origin. In addition, the manner in which the individual will avoid social disapproval for the neurasthenic behavior through rationalizations and physical complaints, and so on, will also be important in the complete description of such difficulties.)

The behavior of schizophrenics many times involves deficits in the A-R-D system. The description of schizophrenics as indifferent, lacking interests, ambition, and so on refers to a lacking A-R-D system. Cases of antisocial personality may also be considered in terms of deficits in the A-R-D system. For example, it is frequently said that the psychopath cannot anticipate negative consequences, cannot profit from warnings, displays verbal remorse seemingly but without later behavior being affected, and so on. One of the things involved here would seem to be deficits in the verbal aspect of the individual's A-R-D system. That is, as has been mentioned, one of the prominent aspects of the A-R-D system is that the individual should acquire a very large repertoire of words which elicit either positive or negative emotional responses in him (see Staats, 1968a). Words such as *dangerous* must come to elicit a negative emotional response, serve as a negative reinforcer, and moreover serve to control appropriate avoidant behaviors or the individual's behavior will not be properly controlled. As another example, aberrant sexual behavior may also be considered in terms of the A-R-D system. That is, usual sexual behavior will only take place if usual sexual stimuli have become reinforcing for the individual.

It is not possible here but to characterize briefly the principle that deficits in the A-R-D system will lead to behaviors described as abnormal. The author has given additional examples (see Staats & Staats, 1963, pp. 483–488); however, a complete account of the role played by the A-R-D system in abnormal behavior is necessary. Actually what is needed is an abnormal psychology textbook in which the descriptions of abnormal behavior are analyzed in terms of learning principles. This discussion, however, along with the author's other analyses, do provide a method and examples of what would constitute a general learning conception of abnormal psychology.[4]

2. Inappropriate Aspects of the A-R-D System

Sometimes the way in which the A-R-D system deviates from normal is not in its deficits but in the fact that stimuli that should not elicit attitudes do so. Again, the abnormal behavior produced may reside in any one of the three functions of A-R-D stimuli. Thus, as has been suggested, stimuli may elicit intense emotional responses in the individual which are injurious to the individual's health or happiness. Psychosomatic illnesses may in part be considered in these terms.

In addition, it has been suggested that when a stimulus inappropriately elicits an attitudinal response, it will serve inappropriately to strengthen or weaken an instrumental behavior that results in obtaining or avoiding the stimulus. Thus, the phobic emotional response to being out of doors is important because the individual learns to avoid the stimulus by the inappropriate behavior of remaining indoors.

Another effect of the inappropriate A-R-D system is that inappropriate striving for or striving against behavior will be elicited. The man who finds winning inordinately positive emotionally will strive for this state to an inordinate degree, perhaps to the detriment of his health or his social adjustment. The person for whom social stimuli elicit anxiety responses inappropriately will strive to avoid them, perhaps physically, or by some chemical means such as alcohol.

3. Interactions of Deficit and Inappropriate Aspects of the A-R-D System

It has already been indicated that there are interactions that take place in the A-R-D system as a result of deprivation circumstances. Thus, it was suggested that if the individual is deprived of the presence of a loved person it is likely that he will develop new individuals who come to elicit emotional responses in him and thus assume a more dominant role in the A-R-D system. As another example, it was suggested that a prisoner is more likely to develop homosexual reinforcers in his A-R-D system than he would be in society where he has access to heterosexual contact and is not under deprivation.

There is also a type of interaction that may take place between deficits

[4]It is interesting to note that Bandura (1968) has utilized the author's outline of a learning analysis of behavior disorders and treatment (see Staats and Staats, 1963) in a chapter dealing with this topic. Ullman and Krasner (1969) also have more extensively followed this method of making learning analyses of the clinical descriptions of behavioral abnormalities in their new textbook.

in the A-R-D system and inappropriate aspects of the A-R-D system where a defect in one may lead to a defect in the other. That is, the person who simply has not learned appropriate heterosexual emotional responses is likely to learn to respond inappropriately to other potential sex reinforcers. Conversely, the individual who has already learned an inappropriate emotional sexual response to persons of the same sex is not likely to have experiences that would classically condition him to positive emotional responses to persons of the opposite sex. Actually, the mechanism by which these interactions take place involve the effects of the A-R-D system upon instrumental behavior, and vice versa, and the principles of these types of interaction should be described.

H. Interactions of the A-R-D System and Instrumental Behavior Repertoires

The primary thrust of this analysis has been to show that the nature of the individual's A-R-D system will heavily determine the type of instrumental behaviors he will display; thus, the A-R-D system is a determinant of what is called personality. It should be indicated, however, that there are additional interactions between the A-R-D system and the individual's instrumental behaviors and, moreover, the relationship between the two may go back and forth, each affecting the other and in turn being further affected by the changes it has produced in the other.

Thus, the individual who has deficits in behavior may not as a consequence gain positive reinforcement, the receipt of which in contiguity with other stimuli would produce additional development of his A-R-D system. For example, the male with deficits in social behavior may not be able to interact with normal women and thereby experience the sexual reinforcement necessary to develop his learned 'sexual' A-R-D system. As another example, certain deficits in behavior (e.g., the lack of intellectual or social skills) are punished socially, and the punishment may help produce an inappropriate 'social' A-R-D system.

On the other hand, the individual with unpleasant inappropriate behavior may be shunned as a result and thereby not obtain the social experiences necessary to prevent deficits in his A-R-D system.

It has already been indicated that deficits or inappropriacies in the A-R-D system can lead to deficits and inappropriacies in the individual's instrumental behavior. Thus, there are possibilities for elaborate sequences of interactions between the A-R-D system and the individual's instrumental behaviors.

An example may be helpful here, taken from a previously conducted case study (Staats & Butterfield, 1965). The case involved a culturally deprived juvenile delinquent who had severe deficits in such cognitive skills as reading. His case history suggested that the problem began in part because of an inadequate A-R-D system. In cases where the training is long term, such as school learning, adequate reinforcement must be available to maintain the attentional and work behaviors necessary for learning. However, the reinforcers present in the traditional schoolroom are inadequate for many children as occurred in the present case. Their attentional behaviors are not maintained, and they do not learn as a consequence.

In such a case there may be no learning disability involved. However, after a few years of school attendance where the conditions of learning are not appropriate for the child, he will not have acquired the behavioral repertoires acquired by more fortunate members of the class, whose previous experiences have established an adequate motivational system. Then, lack of skilled behavior is likely to be treated aversively. That is, in the present case, the child with a reading deficit (or other evidence of under-achievement) is likely to be gibed at and teased when he is still young and ignored, avoided, and looked down upon when he is older. Although the individuals doing this may not intend to be aversive, such actions constitute the presentation of aversive stimuli. Furthermore, this presentation of aversive stimuli by other "successful" children, and perhaps by teachers, would be expected to result in further learning, but learning of an undesirable nature. These children, teachers, academic materials, and the total school situation can in this way come to elicit negative attitudes in the child with the motivational and thus behavioral deficits.

This, in line with the present theory, sets the stage for further unfortunate developments. That is, as has been suggested, the attitudinal value of stimuli controls a whole class of striving for or against behaviors, depending upon whether the attitude is positive or negative. The behaviors in either class will depend upon the learning history of the individual. In the present case the juvenile delinquent had previously learned a large class of hostile-aggressive behaviors. Thus, when the school and its occupants became negative attitude stimuli, he responded with various undesirable behaviors. He baited teachers, cursed in school, scuffled and fought with other students, and so on. He was punished for this, which can be considered further classical conditioning that would intensify his negative attitudes toward school. The intensity of his conditioning may be seen in other undesirable behaviors of this child also. That is, he was apprehended for vandalizing a school. Again, this would be expected to lead to further punishment, to additional negative attitude conditioning, and to the elicitation of additional undesirable behavior.

It can be expected that in many cases vicious cycles of interaction can occur in which the defective A-R-D system leads to undesirable behaviors which lead to further defective developments in the A-R-D system, which again produce additional undesirable behaviors. The spiral can continue to aggravate the individual's adjustment in society until some type of incarceration is necessary, or until some therapeutic occurrence reverses the cycle. The author has described other cases which may be considered in such terms as paranoid psychosis (Staats & Staats, 1963, pp. 387–389) and neurasthenia (Staats & Staats, 1963, 485–486). The deterioration seen in many cases of psychosis may be in part described in these terms. It is thus suggested that the concepts and principles may be utilized in understanding additional cases of abnormal behavior.

It should be noted that this may also be extended to the consideration of exceptionally desirable personalities. That is, a child who goes to school with a well developed A-R-D system, for example, will more rapidly than usual acquire cognitive skills. As a consequence of better than usual performance he will gain positive social reinforcement in greater abundance. This positive classical conditioning helps develop the child's social A-R-D system as well as the child's A-R-D system relevant to cognitive learning in general and to school associated stimuli. After a spiraling cycle, the individual can acquire a very well-developed A-R-D system in these areas as very well-developed repertoires of instrumental cognitive skills.

The primary suggestion of this discussion is that we need a great deal of additional development of the concept of the A-R-D system which includes specification of the manner in which the system undergoes a continued development in interaction with other aspects of the individual's learned repertoires. This theoretical development will necessarily include observations and concepts from the other social and behavioral sciences, education, clinical psychology, and so on.

IV. Behavior Therapy and Behavior Modification and the A-R-D System

Human motivation has played a central role in personality theories, including those that apply to clinical problems. However, these theories have not had a specific, well-verified set of principles within which to couch their motivational concepts and their observations of human behavior. Basic learning theory, on the other hand, has had the principles. But basic learning theory has been concerned primarily with detailing the principles in experimentation and getting a particular systematic statement of the principles (theory) accepted. As a theory of human behavior, however, the basic principles require statement in a manner that is oriented specifically toward the task. Furthermore, it is necessary to relate the observations and concepts of the clinical and social sciences to the basic principles, as has been suggested.

The contemporary learning psychotherapies, although working with learning principles in the context of clinical problems, have tended to accept the viewpoint of the basic laboratory restricting themselves to the use of the traditional learning theories. Thus, as will be discussed further, learning psychotherapies have not had a concern with broad aspects of human motivation, but have been restricted to the application of learning techniques to specific and seemingly unrelated aspects of human behavior. This section will briefly place certain parts of the learning therapies within the structure of the human motivation theory that has been outlined. By doing so it will be possible to see the contributions the learning therapies can make to the development of personality theory, to understand better the general significance of the learning therapies, and also to see some of the aspects of the task which lies ahead in creating a better learning theory of human motivation (and human behavior or personality) as well as better methods of treating problems of human behavior.

A. BEHAVIOR THERAPY AS A PROCEDURE FOR CHANGING THE A-R-D SYSTEM

Before discussing behavior therapy within the context of human motivation it should be indicated that some aspects of this area of investigation and treatment are not related to the *several* aspects of the present discussions. For example, there are classical conditioning treatments that are concerned only with the way the individual "feels" (emotionally) about certain events; with the attitude aspect of the A-R-D system, not with the reinforcing and discriminative properties of those events. The fact that there are objects that elicit a fear response in the individual may, for this reason only, be important to his physical health and to his happiness. Many inappropriate emotional responses acquired or changed (treated) through conditioning may be of concern to the study of psychosomatic illnesses (see Dekker, Pelser, & Groen, 1956, for an example). Thus, certain stimulus objects and events may elicit asthmatic attacks in the individual, or other internal (emotional) responses such as irregular or rapid heart beat, inappropriate secretion of digestive (or other glandular) juices, and so on. Anxiety states, depressions, phobias, and other unusual "emotional" responses may be considered and treated in terms of classical conditioning—without being concerned with the manner in which instrumental behaviors are affected. These and other aspects of behavior therapy are placed in the present theoretical context. However, since they concern only the attitudinal part of the A-R-D system, they will not be dealt with in any detail here.

There is, however, another type of treatment in the field of behavior therapy which, while employing classical conditioning procedures, has not been primarily concerned with emotional responses but rather with instrumental responses. This type of behavior therapy, which has been of important concern, may be understood in greater detail by employing the theoretical structure already outlined. That is, it has been suggested that an individual's A-R-D system is a determinant of his instrumental behavior. It may be stated in summary form that when a necessary reinforcer is not in the individual's system there will be a deficit in the relevant aspect of the individual's adjustive instrumental repertoire. On the other hand, when there is a stimulus in the A-R-D system that should not have reinforcing value, or which has an inappropriate amount of reinforcing value (that is, is too high in the reinforcer hierarchy), then inappropriate instrumental behaviors will occur in the ways that have been described. The inappropriate reinforcer, either positive or negative, may promote the absence of appropriate behaviors as well as the surplus appearance of inappropriate behaviors. It is enlightening to consider part of behavior therapy as changing the individual's A-R-D system and through this inducing changes in his instrumental behavior repertoire.

Behavior therapy techniques have been employed in which the unconditioned stimulus (which is both a ^{UC}S and a $^{UC \cdot R}S$) is positive and elicits positive emotional responses as well as where the unconditioned stimulus is negative and elicits negative emotional responses. Usually the procedures can be seen as clear cut cases of classical conditioning. The unconditioned stimulus is paired with the stimulus which is intended to come to elicit the new emotional response, ordinarily called counterconditioning. It is important to note that both first-order and higher-order classical conditioning procedures are used but this important distinction is not made — part of the general lack of analysis.

Several case studies may be used to provide illustration of the present analysis. For example, in one case study (Lazarus, 1960), a child would not enter any vehicle (a case of phobia for automotive vehicles). The successful treatment consisted of pairing "vehicular" stimuli with positive unconditioned reinforcing stimuli (e.g., candy), and as a consequence the instrumental behavior of avoiding vehicles was lessened. This may be seen as a case where the class of stimuli, vehicles, had previously come to elicit a negative emotional response. This gave negative reinforcing value to the stimuli, and hence, the stimuli had discriminative stimulus value controlling striving away from responses. When, through classical conditioning, positive emotional responses were conditioned to the stimuli the discriminative stimulus value was changed in a positive direction and the child no longer so vigorously moved away from the vehicles. It should be noted that in this case (as in the other cases to be cited) the discriminative stimulus value was changed prior to getting the child to approach a car. Thus, instrumental conditioning (response contingent reinforcement) was not involved in the process described. Instrumental conditioning could only be conducted *after* the response of approaching the car had been made.

Another case of behavior therapy (Raymond, 1960) may be analyzed in the same terms. In this case study the aberrant behavior of an adult male involved contacting women's purses and baby carriages in a manner that was undesirable. This instrumental behavior had resulted in repeated arrests. Treatment consisted of pairing the "fetish stimuli" with an aversive unconditioned reinforcing stimulus in a classical conditioning procedure. The result was that the instrumental behavior no longer occurred. It is necessary again to account for the change in the instrumental behavior through the same analysis. It is suggested that the fetish stimuli had come to elicit sexual emotional responses in the individual and thus to have sexual reinforcing value which discriminatively controlled the undesirable instrumental behavior. The emotional conditioning changed the reinforcing value of the fetish stimuli (in this case in a negative direction), and hence, the discriminative stimulus value controlling the undesirable approach instrumental behaviors.

Behavior therapy treatment of alcoholism involves the same analysis. Through treatment the sight and smell of the alcoholic beverage becomes the conditioned stimulus which elicits a negative emotional response, rather than a positive emotional response. The stimulus of the beverage thereby comes to act as a *discriminative stimulus* which controls escape and avoidance instrumental responses.

Desensitization therapy may also be considered in the same terms. That is, the patient may be asked to list in order of intensity the various stimulus situations which elicit anxiety (negative emotional responses). Then the patient is presented with these situations, or asked to imagine them, while relaxing, beginning with the stimulus situation that elicits the least intense response. Since the phobic stimuli are conditioned stimuli that have come to elicit negative emotional responses through the individual's particular conditioning history, it would be expected that continued presentation of the offending stimuli would result in *extinction* of the inappropriate emotional responses. [If this type of therapy is thought of as counterconditioning, as has Davison (in press), then the instructions to relax may be considered as a learned ^{UC}S, and the process is thus a case of higher-order conditioning. It should be noted, also, that desensitization therapy requires further analysis since images are involved in many cases, not primary stimulus situations.]

To continue, however, the success of desensitization therapy lies in the extent to which the discriminative stimulus control of the stimuli changes. Thus, using an example of an agoraphobia, when the individual's A-R-D system is changed so that "out-of-door" stimuli no longer elicit a negative emotional response, the stimuli will no longer have discriminative stimulus value controlling escape behaviors which drive the individual inside.

In general, thus, while these behavior therapy procedures manipulate changes in the A-R-D system through the use of classical conditioning principles and procedures, it is the change in the *discriminative control of instrumental behaviors that indicates the success of the therapy.* It is emphasized that instrumental behavior can be changed by using classical conditioning procedures to change aspects of the A-R-D system. It is this analysis that has not been clearly set forth and which when extended to a general concern with the A-R-D system has a general significance for understanding and treating human behavior.

1. The Instrumental Conditioning Effect of Behavior Therapy

The instrumental behaviors that are ordinarily dealt with in such therapy as described above are actually already well learned. They are approach or avoidance behaviors that are very common. In cases where the instrumental behavior is not the individual's repertoire, however, a simple change in the individual's reinforcer system would not be expected to result in immediate improvement. The patient would still require a training program (formal or informal) where the instrumental behavior has to be learned. Thus, as an example, making same sex stimulus objects (men or women) come to elicit negative emotional responses would not cure the homosexual's problems of behavior if he did not have the appropriate heterosexual instrumental behaviors already in his repertoire. He would still have to acquire the very complex courting behaviors of various social, emotional, and cognitive kinds. As another example, changing the extent to which the general school situation elicits a fear response in the child will not successfully treat his school phobia if the fear response has arisen because of the receipt of negative reinforcing stimuli from his classmates because his cognitive repertoire is poor, because he is maladroit athletically, because he has an odd appearance, and so on. Although in some cases the school phobia is simply a problem of an inappropriate A-R-D system many other times this is complicated by inadequate social, cognitive, and sensory-motor instrumental repertoires of great complexity.

The extent to which one could rely on instrumental learning of complex behaviors simply through the change of the A-R-D system should be of concern in the diagnosis and treatment of any clinical problem. Such analyses would no doubt involve the complexity of the skill to be acquired, the duration of the treatment induced change in the reinforcer system, which is of importance if the training is to be long-term, and so on. Homosexual problems and alcoholism, as examples, do not seem to be successfully treated by changing the A-R-D system through conditioning. While this is not the place for a full discussion, it would seem that the complexity of the instrumental (and other) behaviors to be learned in these cases probably requires more than an ephemeral change in restricted aspects of the A-R-D system. In such cases, as will be further discussed, behavior therapy treatments could well be called symptomatic.

In addition to the straightforward conditioning of emotional responses, and the process just described of changing instrumental behaviors by changing emotional responses, other treatments of various kinds have been labeled behavior therapy without theoretical distinction (see Eysenck, 1960). In some cases the treatment has involved indirect instrumental conditioning, for example, the case of dermatitis caused by scratching maintained by social reinforcement, as reported by Walton (1960). These aspects of behavior therapy will not be of concern here, except as an example of the lack of theoretical clarification in the field.

In concluding this section, it may be said that the field of behavior therapy involving changing aspects of the A-R-D system has other limitations, which will be discussed further on. It may be suggested, however, that the findings already made indicate that a feasible manner for the change of instrumental behavior is through the change of aspects of the individual's A-R-D system. This has been shown in a number of studies and constitutes a very significant development.

B. Behavior Modification as Manipulation of Reinforcers in the Existing A-R-D System

Again, as in the preceding discussion, no attempt will be made to summarize the work in what has come to be called behavior modification. Rather the purpose will be to fit this type of work into the general theoretical framework to relate it better to behavior therapy and to indicate avenues for further development in learning therapies.

In contrast to behavior therapy, behavior modification studies have been self-consciously concerned with instrumental behaviors and direct instrumental conditioning procedures. As in the case of behavior therapy, the reinforcer system is centrally concerned. Moreover, it is actively manipulated. Unlike behavior therapy, however, the individual's A-R-D system is not changed or, at least, this possibility is not usually dealt with by investigators in this area. Thus, deficiencies in the individual's reinforcer system are usually left untouched. Rather, an artificial (but already effective) reinforcer subsystem is employed or natural reinforcers are manipulated according to changed rules to treat problems of instrumental behavior. This is done when the rules in force in the individual's life situation are inappropriate or the sources of reinforcement are inadequate or inappropriate. The behavior modification worker ordinarily has restricted his interest to instrumental conditioning principles and instrumental behaviors.

There are a number of studies that are of interest in this area, but only a few will be mentioned as examples. An early article that adumbrated the behavior modification treatment of psychotic symptoms (Staats, 1957) may be used as an introduction.[5] That is, it was suggested that (a) psychotic symptoms may be considered behaviors that are instrumentally conditioned, (b) reinforcers manipulated by hospital personnel inadvertently condition and maintain such symptoms, and (c) the symptoms could be treated by instrumental conditioning procedures, including extinction. Several of the earliest and best known studies of behavior modification were based upon this rationale and provided direct support of these suggestions. For example, Ayllon and Michael (1959) showed that psychotic behaviors were maintained by social reinforcement and could be manipulated through the use of instrumental conditioning procedures. Compulsive visits to the nurse's office were maintained by social reinforcement and when this source of reinforcement was removed the undesirable behavior extinguished. Psychotic talk was diminished by extinction and sensible talk was reinforced, with expected instrumental conditioning results. Compulsive magazine hoarding was reduced by

[5]The earliest behavior modification study, which contributed background to this 1957 article, was an informal treatment of a graduate student who had a deficit in confident, fluent speech. The author reasoned that the argumentative aversiveness which usually followed the student's statements of opinion suppressed confident, fluent speech according to the principles of instrumental punishment. The author then enlisted the aid of Jack Michael and his late wife Betty in successfully treating this problem by applying social attention and approval contingent on the speech. The results were dramatic enough to impress the several "behavior modifiers" involved and constituted background for the other later developments. The most important basis for the analysis in the article, however, was the author's general observation that much of the professional's interactions with patients in the neuropsychiatric setting ran counter to what would be derived from a learning approach. That is, the professional with a psychodynamic approach attends more to abnormal behaviors of the patient than he does to normal behaviors, because he considers the abnormal behavior to be a result of unresolved psychic conflicts, and thus the key to the individual's problems. The learning approach indicates, conversely, that social attention strengthens behaviors on which it is contingent and focuses upon conditions that will maximize desirable behaviors and minimize undesirable behaviors.

removing the social reinforcement that had been contingent upon hoarding and by satiation operations. That is, the ward was flooded with magazines.

More recently, there have been a number of extensions of the same principles to child behavior (for example, Staats, Staats, Schutz, & Wolf, 1962; Wolf, Risely, & Mees, 1964; Allen, Hart, Buell, Harris, & Wolf, 1964). Staats *et al.,* showed that single subjects could be subjected to experimental (reinforcement) treatment and then using each subject as his own control the conditions could be reversed to reliably demonstrate the effect of the reinforcement. Wolf, Risely, and Mees (1964) showed, among other things, that temper tantrums in an autistic child could be treated by making a mild punishing circumstance contingent upon the behavior and by withdrawing social reinforcement. The same child was trained to wear glasses through the use of food reinforcement and good-deprivation procedures. Allen *et al.,* (1964) showed that social interaction behavior with other children could be increased in an asocial child by making social reinforcement of teachers contingent upon the social interaction behavior. Similar procedures have been applied to the treatment of excessive crying (Hart, Allen, Buell, Harris, & Wolf, 1964) and to the treatment of regressed crawling (Harris, Johnston, Kelley, & Wolf, 1964), and so on.

Many other studies which deal with behavior problems through the manipulation of reinforcers in the alteration of instrumental behaviors have been described or summarized in books of readings by Krasner and Ullman (1965; Ullman & Krasner, 1965), and Staats (1964a). Although there are again a number of studies with different types of subjects and different behaviors, for the most part, the behaviors dealt with have been of a simple sort. Nevertheless, although the scope of behavior modification, and others that will be discussed, bear this limitation, it is clearly evident that many important human behaviors that are relevant to personal adjustment are acquired and changed through instrumental conditioning and that treatment procedures based upon the response contingent manipulation of reinforcers are of great value.

C. RELATIONSHIP OF BEHAVIOR THERAPY AND BEHAVIOR MODIFICATION

The previous discussions indicate the relationship of behavior therapy and behavior modification when considered within a theory of human motivation. Several additional points may be made in specifying the role of each and thus the relation of the two.

Behavior therapy is primarily concerned with changing aspects of the

A-R-D system through classical conditioning techniques. The manipulation concerns the first function of the A-R-D system.

The primary dependent variable, however, is a change in instrumental behavior. It is noteworthy that in this type of therapy the instrumental conditioning circumstances are not manipulated; rather, one depends upon the naturalistic conditions of reinforcement to remold the undesirable instrumental behavior in a manner that is in many cases not controlled in any way by the experimenter. As will be discussed, the assumption that the variables in the naturalistic situation will take over to produce the benign behavior change, after the A-R-D system has been altered, may or may not be met in any particular case.

Behavior modification, on the other hand, has as a primary concern instrumental conditioning principles, and ignores the classical conditioning effects that are part of its manipulations. Unlike behavior therapy, behavior modification directly deals with the instrumental behaviors. Moreover, the changes in the instrumental behaviors has been dealt with systematically and in a specified manner. However, as has been indicated, when a reinforcing stimulus is presented in an instrumental conditioning procedure, the stimulus elicits an emotional response which is classically conditioned to the other stimuli in the situation. Thus, classical conditioning of new reinforcing stimuli occurs in the instrumental conditioning (behavior modification) procedure, as will be illustrated later. Nevertheless, behavior modification work has not specified the changes it produces in the individual's A-R-D system, nor has it attempted to assess or manipulate such changes. At this point it will suffice to say that behavior modification has been as unsystematic about emotional conditioning (change in the A-R-D system) that is a by-product of its procedures, as behavior therapy has been about the instrumental conditioning aspect of its procedures.

It may be suggested that each type of learning treatment has made large contributions, but has also been inadequate by itself in the ways implied above. That is, instrumental behaviors of concern to clinical psychology must be dealt with in great detail. Even more pertinent to the present paper, the A-R-D system must be dealt with in greater scope and specificity. In addition, both behavior therapy and behavior modification must realize the complex outcomes of their oversimplified treatments, and this calls for detailed analyses of the stimulus-response components involved. These topics will be treated in the following section.

V. Limitations and Inadequacies in Present Learning Therapies

Methods of psychotherapy that deal with the undesirable behavior itself, rather than a supposed underlying cause (psychodynamic), have been called symptomatic. A thorough-going learning approach, however, considers that personality—the individual's complex social, emotional, cognitive, and what have you, behaviors—is learned. This admits of no hypothesized inner mental determinants, only stimuli and responses of various kinds and complexities of arrangement. To be labeled a symptomatic approach in terms of dealing with specifiable behavior, is not pejorative from a learning viewpoint.

However, there are several reasons for describing both contemporary behavior therapy and behavior modification as symptomatic, and in a pejorative sense. The limitations and inadequacies that make the learning therapies as they exist today symptomatic can be described under several headings which will be dealt with separately. The analyses will also illustrate the advantage of the present learning theory in considering the conditioning therapies. The heuristic value of the analysis will also be exemplified.

A. LIMITATIONS IN SCOPE

Behavior therapy that has been concerned with changing the emotional, and, thus, reinforcing value of stimuli, has been a symptomatic approach in several respects. First, behavior therapy has been very atomistic. Only specific stimuli are dealt with. There is no general recognition of the individual's A-R-D system, as a system, let alone consideration of the aspects of the cultural and subcultural variations in the A-R-D system as they affect individual and group behavior. Behavior therapy has restricted itself to the types of problems that its limited theory and procedures can handle. These have by and large been single emotional responses to single stimuli, or narrow classes of stimuli. Thus, most of the work of behavior therapy of this type has been with phobias. Fetishes have been dealt with but these are also quite simple disturbances in terms of the stimuli and responses involved. While sexual disorders have been dealt with in instances, success has depended upon the simplicity of the problem, as will be indicated below. The same is true of alcoholism. In this area behavior therapy (aversion therapy) is so restricted that it can only be considered an adjunct treatment both on practical and on theoretical levels.

We do not see in the work of behavior therapy the treatment of the more general problems that humans have. The theory and procedures of behavior therapy have not been developed to deal with cases where *many* aspects of the A-R-D system are involved, and where the behaviors that are affected are consequently quite complex. Thus, we do not have behavior therapy that deals with the "lack of motivation" that we see in such general problems as neurasthenia, schizophrenia, psychopathic personality, school underachievement, criminal behavior, cultural deprivation, mental retardation, and so on. Each of these types of problems when generally considered, concern widespread deficits and inappropriacies in the A-R-D system — and many times this is the original or focal problem.

In addition, of course, the bag of techniques of behavior therapy is quite restricted. First-order and higher-order classical conditioning procedures have been applied, but the lack of analysis of the procedures and the weak theoretical basis of the approach has restricted their general application. The author will deal with one of the primary faults of behavior therapy, promulgated by Eysenck (1960), in a later analysis: its lack of analysis, and rejection, of verbal psychotherapy. In addition, however, behavior therapy has not employed schedules of classical conditioning to produce resistance to extinction of the effects. Nor has behavior therapy employed deprivation-satiation operations (at least self-consciously), which become an apparent device once an analysis is made of behavior therapy in terms of altering the hierarchical reinforcer system. Furthermore, the rationale of behavior therapy has not included an understanding of the effects of treatment upon the discriminative stimulus value of the stimuli it manipulates, and so on.

Behavior modification studies suffer from the same types of weaknesses. Thus, with few exceptions behavior modification procedures have been restricted to work with simple responses. This has been the case, in part, because only simple manipulations of the A-R-D system have been attempted — with little attempt to change the individual's A-R-D system or the A-R-D system of the institution in which the problem behaviors are generated, such as school, work, prison, hospital, family, and so on. A prominent weakness has been in the lack of consideration of the wide range of problems that involve the A-R-D system and consequently the things that could be done to deal with such general problems. For the most part, thus, behavior modification studies have involved simple responses: crawling instead of walking, putting on and wearing glasses, the extinction of temper tantrums or the suppression of self-destructive behavior through punishment, getting a mute schizophrenic to talk who already has a language repertoire, reduction of visits to the nurse office or reduction in magazine hoarding through the removal of social reinforcement for these behaviors, and the like. Almost entirely, the literature of behavior modification consists of repeated demonstrations that abnormal behaviors follow the principles of instrumental conditioning. There is almost a total lack of detailed, explicit, long-term training programs that deal with general and widespread problems of behavior, programs involving general understanding, and manipulation, of an individual's A-R-D system.

We see the same simplicity when inspecting the manipulations of the A-R-D system that have been attempted. Thus, there are studies in which candy is used as the reinforcer system. There are studies where social reinforcement is manipulated, in extinction and in conditioning, and so on. Generally, however, the possibilities for large-scale manipulations of effective reinforcers for individuals and groups in treatment of behavior problems have not yet been exploited. As the author has indicated, although simple reinforcer manipulations will suffice if the behavior being treated is simple and the treatment is consequently of short duration, much more effective A-R-D system manipulations are necessary when the behavioral repertoires are complex and the training is of long duration. The author (Staats, 1964a, 1968a; Staats & Butterfield, 1965; Staats, Minke, Finley, Wolf, & Brooks, 1964; Staats & Staats, 1963; Staats et al., 1962) has discussed the possibility for overcoming some of the problems of the reinforcer system by the use of a token system. The token-reinforcer system involves presentation of conditioned reinforcers for the desired behavior, the reinforcing value of the tokens being maintained by pairing them with a variety of backup reinforcers which the individual selects. In this procedure instrumental learning behaviors may be maintained over long periods of time, while complex repertoires are acquired, since the limitless variety of reinforcers prevents satiation. Token systems of reinforcement, as already indicated, have been used in additional behavior modification studies (Ayllon, 1965; Birnbrauer, Wolf, Kidder, & Tague, 1965; Staats & Butterfield, 1965). As will be suggested in a following section, however, these applications do not begin to deal with the problems of behavior which arise because of defective individual and group reinforcer systems, nor do they exploit the possibilities inherent in the approach (see Staats, 1968a).

In general, the same types of limitations already mentioned in describing behavior therapy apply equally well to behavior modification. Schedules of reinforcement have been little used although one study (Staats, Finley, Minke, Wolf, and Brooks, 1964b) shows the potentiality of the utilization of the principles for the treatment of complex behavior problems. Deprivation-satiation operations have been little employed as a means of altering the reinforcer system, and then only in a limited fashion (see Ayllon & Michael, 1959). Such complexities as the interrelationship of reinforcement value and discriminative stimulus value have not been dealt with in behavior modification treatments or in behavior modification theoretical analysis, a topic relevant to the next section.

B. Limitations Imposed by Lack of Sophisticated
   Theoretical Analysis

When a detailed analysis is not made of the general problems of behavior of the patient, and when oversimplified methods of treatment are employed, it must be expected that unless the treatment restricts itself to simple behaviors there will be cases of failure. It is here that conditioning therapies have been most open to the charge of symptomatic treatment and the possibilities of symptom substitution. It is not possible to go into this topic fully, but several examples may be used to illustrate the point.

Let us take the behavior therapy case reported by Raymond (1960) that has already been summarized herein. The problem, in the theoretical terms employed herein, was that women's purses and baby carriages had strong sexual reinforcing value for the patient, and thus strong discriminative stimulus value which controlled his instrumental behaviors of "handling" the objects. The treatment, which was successful, changed the attitudinal and reinforcing value of the stimulus objects and thus their discriminative stimulus value. The effect upon the patient's behavior had several facets. He no longer approached the stimulus objects. He did not masturbate while thinking of the objects, and his sexual behaviors with his wife improved. When the treatment and its effects are analyzed more deeply, however, it may be seen how the success of the treatment depended upon certain factors which were not understood or controlled in the behavior therapy, and how, if these unassessed factors had been different, the treatment could well have resulted in symptom substitution.

A more complete analysis of the treatment would include the following. The treatment changed the attitude and thus reinforcing value of the fetish objects. This, however, resulted in short-term "motivational" changes in the patient's A-R-D system, as well as in long-term changes. That is, let us say, that the patient had a hierarchy of sexual reinforcing stimulus objects in his A-R-D system as would be expected. At the top of the hierarchy were the fetish objects. Somewhere lower in strength was the patient's wife. No doubt, as must be the case with people in general, other social stimuli (women, girls, men, boys) and other objects, and perhaps animals, would also have sex reinforcing value for the patient. It would be expected that lowering the reinforcement value for the class of fetish objects in the individual's sexual reinforcing system would have several effects. It would raise the reinforcement value of the other reinforcers in the system relative to the stimuli whose value was lowered. Moreover, especially if the stimulus involved was the strongest reinforcer in the system, when a dominant sex reinforcer is no longer available (because of absence or because the individual no longer finds it sexually reinforcing) the individual to that extent suffers deprivation. Deprivation has the effect of raising the value of all the positive sex reinforcers in the individual's system.

On both of these bases it would be expected that the patient in this example, after treatment, would find his wife a stronger sex reinforcer — *provided she was a strong positive reinforcer in his system in the first place.* That being the case, it would be expected that the likelihood of sexual interaction between the patient and his wife would be increased. Each successful instance of such sexual interaction would be expected to increase further the reinforcing value of the wife through positive classical conditioning, a lasting result.

When this analysis is made, however, it can be seen that the treatment could easily have gone awry. What, for example, would have been the predicted outcome if small girls were the second strongest class of sexual reinforcing stimuli in the patient's system? Removing the fetish objects as sex reinforcers would have raised the sexual reinforcing value of little girls in the patient's reinforcer system. It would then be more likely that the possibility of aberrant sex behaviors involving children would have arisen as a symptom substitution. If members of the same sex were sexual reinforcers for the patient, then homosexuality could well have been precipitated or increased in incidence. The message is clear. An unsophisticated analysis of the factors involved in the individual patient's behavior, in this case that of the individual's A-R-D system, could lead to unsuccessful treatment and possibly to the production of even less desirable behaviors in a process reminiscent of classical symptom substitution. It must be concluded that the behavior therapy treatment at issue was based upon unsophisticated theory and *unsophisticated assessment of the patient's reinforcer system* and was thus potentially hazardous.

Several other examples that could occur may be briefly mentioned to illustrate the points. Thus, it would be ineffective to look at the weak behavior of the neurasthenic by putting him in a bar pressing compartment and by instituting a reinforcement schedule to promote vigorous responding. Dealing with a simple instrumental behavior, the symptom, would be ineffective although many contemporary operant conditioners accept such a naïve "experimental analysis" approach. Similarly, the employment of reinforcers in a behavior modification situation to strengthen the neurasthenic's actual behaviors (the symptom) would also be ineffective, if the fault was the inappropriate nature of the individual's A-R-D system for the life situation in which the individual found himself. In such a case general changes in the individual's reinforcer system would have to occur, or general changes would have to be made in the available reinforcers as imposed by the individual's life situation. The instrumental behavior itself is not the problem; these behaviors are usually well learned already and when the neurasthenic is properly "motivated" will be exhibited in good strength.

As another example, it would be ineffective to condition a negative emotional response to alcohol if the reason for drinking was to reduce the anxiety (negative emotional) responses elicited by the social situations the patient is forced to face. The denial of the alcohol to the patient through behavior therapy, without dealing with the problems the patient has with the other aspects of his reinforcer system relative to his life situation could also backfire. The patient could turn to drugs as an escape from the aversive social experiences, or social withdrawal could occur, or he might run away from his life situation as amnesics do.

By the same token, it would be ineffective to remove a child's school phobia by positive classical conditioning (or desensitization) if going back to school means that the child will receive additional negative emotional conditioning in that situation. The types of cases that could be listed here to exemplify the symptomatic nature of behavior therapy and behavior modification, because of lack of detailed and sophisticated analysis and assessment, are indeed large in number.

It may be suggested that the present type of analysis offers an answer to the charge of Breger and McGaugh (1965). They asked, correctly so, in an article that included less well-founded criticisms, if a neurosis consists solely of specific symptoms, how do behavior therapists account for the *general* results of their *specific* treatments? Specific symptoms of behavior are treated, but other behaviors are also affected in learning therapies. The patient treated for his handbag and baby carriage fetish later had better sexual relations with his wife, for example. The production of general results from specific treatments is not difficult to understand when it is realized that the specific treatment effects a *system of related stimuli*, and when the analysis shows the various principles involved and the various events that are effected. Breger and McGaugh's criticism should have been directed at the lack of sophistication or oversimplification of conditioning therapies, rather than at learning approaches in general. There is nothing necessary in a learning approach that produces oversimplification or lack of theoretical analysis and sophisticated assessment, although the traditional learning approaches have exhibited these inadequacies.

Several additional examples should also be given that deal even more specifically with behavior modification and its shortcomings. When aspects of the A-R-D system are manipulated there are effects on other aspects of the system which may have unforeseen outcomes. A simple case may be seen in the use of edibles, such as candy, as reinforcement. This will have the effect of lessening the strength of food reinforcers in the individual's system, and of increasing the relative strength of other reinforcers. This principle can be involved in more crucial ways. It may be suggested, in a very analogous example, that one of the drawbacks to traditional psychotherapy can be that the social reinforcement provided by the therapist may satiate the individual for this class of reinforcers, making the patient less likely to "strive" for other social relationships. The author knows of a case in which the social withdrawal of a patient seemed to be enhanced through this process, and where improvement in this respect did not commence until psychotherapy terminated.

An additional limitation is the lack of recognition of the general *changes* in the reinforcer A-R-D system that can occur through behavior modification procedures. That is, as has been suggested, when a reinforcer is presented this results in conditioning the emotional response elicited by the reinforcer to the other stimuli in the situation. This could be a positive result, but negative by-products are quite possible. For example, although punishment might be used to weaken an undesirable behavior (as in the early work of Lovaas, *et al.*, 1964), it should also be noted that punishment is an unconditioned stimulus that elicits negative emotional responses. These responses will be conditioned to any stimulus present in the situation, including the therapist who administers the unconditioned negative reinforcer, the general stimulus situation, and so on. In a recent study, for example, an autistic child was shocked when he made a self-injurious behavior. During this training the therapists "talked to him, praised virtually all non-injurious responses, and generally behaved pleasantly" (Tate & Baroff, 1966). Although this case was reported to be generally successful, it should be noted that the procedures would be expected to make "pleasant behavior" of adults into a negative reinforcing stimulus, an undesirable outcome. It would have been more effective in terms of the broader learning of the child to pair the punishment with words that should become aversive such as "no" or "bad." It must be realized that negative classical conditioning occurs when using punishment to weaken an instrumental response in behavior modification procedures. And the converse is also true. In each case the A-R-D system may be affected in undesirable ways.

It is in the realm of the inadequacy of theoretical analysis that Skinner's learning theory and philosophy of psychology have had an unfortunate effect. In his overemphasis upon operant conditioning technology, the principle of reinforcement, and the philosophy of the nonanalytic experimental analysis of behavior, Skinner has had a detrimental effect upon the extension of learning theory to human behavior generally. His antitheory position and opposition to S-R analysis have reduced the followers of this position largely to exploring the manipulation of the principle of reinforcement with a new sample of simple behavior or with a new type of subject. Investigators can perform this type of research with knowledge only of the one principle of reinforcement. The unadorned principle of reinforcement is a crucial one in understanding human behavior. However, while at one point it is important to *demonstrate* the importance of the principle in the context of various behaviors, this is not a sufficient activity to yield a general conception of human behavior. It is not even sufficient for obtaining a profound understanding of specific repertoires of behavior, with the related ability to treat problems in that area of behavior. We must go past simple demonstrations in which different aspects of behavior are affected by reinforcement.

A sophisticated theory of learning and a sophisticated philosophy of psychology, and of science in general, offers a much more effective base for the investigation and treatment of specific aspects of human behavior as well as for establishing a general conception of personality. The potential of the learning approach will only be realized within such a sophisticated theory.

C. The "Ahistorical" Limitation

It has been suggested that conditioning therapies are not concerned with the history of the individual. Eysenck, for example, has been a strong advocate of an ahistorical approach, and has indicated that behavior therapy accepts the individual as he is. "All treatment of neurotic disorders is concerned with habits existing at *present;* their historical development is largely irrelevant" (Eysenck, 1960, p. 11). The oversimplification characteristic of contemporary learning therapies has already been suggested, and the ahistorical tenet is one of the prime examples. Thus, Eysenck's injunction was very appropriate and significant in the context of the psychoanalytic denial of the importance of the abnormal behavior itself—insisting rather upon the primordial role of unconscious psychodynamics. But it is necessary to consider the injunction as anachronistic in terms of a learning theory. That is, the whole foundation of a sophisticated learning conception of human behavior is that conditioning history is all important in accounting for complex human behavior (personality). Thus, the ahistorical injunction is an obstacle to progress.

It should be indicated that the interest in personal history which should be central to a learning theory has also been rejected in the oversimplification dictated to by the operant conditioning approach and its attendant philosophy of psychology (Skinner's functional analysis). Lovaas (1966) states the following, for example:

> The experimental laboratory design and the objective of isolating functional relations place restrictions on certain kinds of questions that the investigator may want to raise concerning abnormal behavior—for example, about the parent's role in the etiology of childhood schizophrenia. Answers to such questions, though often intriguing, entail so much confounding that they are meaningless in a functional analysis of abnormal behavior (pp. 111-112).

Since the ahistorical position represents a philosophical statement, one which could be expected to influence a variety of works of many investigators, it is worth spending a moment in correcting its errors and disadvantages.

First, the approach leads to a neglect of the naturalistic conditions that could be maintaining the abnormal behavior. Let us say, for example, that a patient utilizes aberrant sexual reinforcers because his wife's sexual behavior has resulted in her being very low in his reinforcing system as a sexual reinforcer. Behavior therapy (aversive conditioning) which would make one of his aberrant sexual reinforcers ineffective may have unfortunate consequences, as has been described. It would be more important in the correct treatment of this case to ascertain the wife's sexual behavior, and the effects upon the patient's reinforcement system, than to neglect this naturalistic history and to deal only with the aberrant sex reinforcer in the controlled conditioning procedures.

In general, thus, when one considers the complex learning determinants of human behavior it appears totally unreasonable to expect to be able to treat problems of human behavior in such a simple minded fashion, unless the behavior is indeed very simple and very isolated. In many cases it must certainly be necessary to concern oneself with the individual's conditioning history prior to treatment. Moreover, it would be necessary to be as fully conversant with the individual's present life circumstances and social, emotional, and cognitive repertoires in as sophisticated manner as possible prior to treatment. With children, for example, it would be necessary to know what the nature of the child's training was and is. Treatment could easily be reversed by the parents otherwise.

This has concerned individual *treatment*. It is even more important that learning approaches are considered for their research potential and ultimate use in a prophylactic manner (as well as for the opportunity of yielding a general theory of human behavior). That is, only by detailed S-R theoretical analyses and experimental investigation of the types of conditioning circumstances that lead to various abnormal behaviors will we be able to devise instructions to improve methods of child training, as well as provide bases for devising treatment procedures. Otherwise learning therapies are mere techniques. One of the crying needs of a learning approach to clinical psychology will involve analyses that will indicate how various complex behavior problems arise and are maintained in the naturalistic circumstance. Moreover, it may be suggested that a learning theory that integrates the principles of classical and instrumental conditioning forms a theoretical structure into which various problems of human behavior, and the manner in which they arise, can be analyzed in specific S-R terms in the necessary detail. Oversimplification, historical or otherwise, is not at all advantageous or inherent in a learning approach.

VI. Implications and Extensions

The foregoing by no means includes a complete analysis of human motivation and its implications for clinical treatment; rather, an approach and a method of analysis have been suggested. The most general suggestion is that learning therapies require a great deal of further development along theoretical (and empirical) lines to realize the potential of a learning approach. It is not possible to deal extensively with specific implications for further development. However, a few examples that have general significance may be briefly mentioned.

Some of the specific lines of development have been implicit in the foregoing criticisms. Thus, it has been suggested that behavior therapy has been limited in scope, largely restricted to dealing with simple, singular distortions in the individual's A-R-D system—such as occurs in fetishes, phobias, and so on. When the area of study and treatment is considered in terms of the present motivational theory many other more complex problems that concern general distortions in the reinforcer system can be seen. These examples suggest that we begin investigating the possibility of treating such general problems. We should, for example, consider theoretically and empirically the possibility of changing the reinforcer system in a child for whom the teacher's approval is not a positive reinforcer, for whom acquiring new skills is not reinforcing (who has a deficit in achievement motivation), and for whom school buildings, school books and materials, teachers, other "good" students, and so on have become stimuli that elicit strong negative emotional responses (which control 'striving against' behaviors). (It should be noted in this and the other examples that any particular problem may require treatment of other deficits and inappropriacies of behavior as well as general changes in the A-R-D system. These considerations, however, are topics for another paper.)

Let us, as another example, investigate the possibility of changing the A-R-D system of an individual who finds winning so exceedingly reinforcing that his behavior is aversive to others — as an example of a behavior that is important and problematical, but not of the dramatic nature of traditional abnormal behaviors. In addition, there are many problems of various kinds, not just sexual problems, that involve the fact that the individual's social reinforcement system is awry, sometimes because the wrong people elicit positive emotional (reinforcing) responses, sometimes because they elicit negative emotional responses. As has been suggested, the drinking problems of some alcoholics may involve escape from anxiety (negative emotional responses) elicited by people and social situations that the individual must confront. This is thus a general problem of the individual's A-R-D system which could not be treated by making an ephemeral change in the reinforcing value of alcohol.

It has already been suggested that some psychotics suffer centrally from general deficits and disturbances in their A-R-D systems. The author has briefly described a type of personal history that could produce a social reinforcer system in which people are so aversive that violent behavior could ensue (Staats & Staats, 1963, pp. 387–389). Even more widespread distortions and deficits would seem to be involved in most cases of simple schizophrenia. Research and treatment investigations should be made to study the possibility of general reconstructing the A-R-D systems of such cases. Only good could ensue from such treatment for many "backward" patients. The task would require building the individual's A-R-D system deliberately in various areas to include social reinforcers, achievement reinforcers, work reinforcers, sex reinforcers, play reinforcers, and so on. The same is true of autistic, retarded, and culturally deprived children, and criminals and neurotics of various kinds. These are not tasks to begin full force immediately, but goals to work toward in research and treatment.

There are many more examples in clinical psychology where first theoretical analyses of the problem in terms of the A-R-D system, and then the development of learning treatment procedures would seem to be very productive. This type of extension should also include analyses showing the relationship of the change in one reinforcer (or one class of reinforcers) to effects on the other reinforcers in the system in the various ways that have been described, for example, through the direct conditioning of emotional responses, through the effects of deprivation and satiation operations, and through the additional conditioning resulting from deprivation, and so on. Thus, as has been suggested, the A-R-D system must be considered to be a system, with changes in one aspect affecting other aspects. Other principles, such as schedules of reinforcement in classical conditioning and deprivation–satiation operations should be applied to treatment. Basic and clinical studies should also be conducted to study systematically the effects on instrumental behaviors that changes in the A-R-D system cause, rather than leaving this aspect of treatment to uncontrolled life circumstances. This would involve study of instrumental conditioning as well as study of the discriminative control of instrumental behaviors that reinforcing stimuli exert.

More general research on behavior modification is also needed to further the possibilities for manipulating reinforcers in the direct production of desirable instrumental behaviors. This enlargement of scope should be of several types. Thus, behavior modification research and treatment studies must come to include work that extends over a longer period and deals with more and more complex types of behavior. The author deals with this topic more extensively (Staats, 1968a,b). It may be said here, however, that the study must progress away from working with simple behaviors over short periods of time. Complex social, cognitive, and sensory-motor repertoires must be subjected to study and treatment.

As suggested, this means the development and test of A-R-D systems for work with individuals that are effective for long periods. It also means that various types of A-R-D systems for work with individuals of various "reinforcer system impairment" will have to be investigated. This should become a self-conscious field of study. A-R-D systems will have to be developed for different types of problems and different types of institutional treatment. In developing more effective, more economic, and more practical systems for treatment and study, the principles of learning will have to be employed more generally. This should include the application of schedules of reinforcement, deprivation-satiation operations, and the like.

In addition to this type of extension, behavior modification work should be enlarged to include investigations of the possibility of changing institutional reinforcement systems for groups of people as well as for individuals. This would amount to dealing with social change or social reorganization. That is, many problems that we have been attempting to handle by treating individuals are actually social problems, difficulties common to groups of individuals. They are clinical problems in that they involve the same theory, the same problems of behavior, and the same rationale for procedures of treatment; but the treatment should be group or institutional rather than individual. Take, for example, the case of the public school institution. The A-R-D system in effect in schools has been developed by people with a particular socioeconomic conditioning history to be effective with children who have the same history and thus have the same A-R-D system. However, many of the children who are subjected to the institutional A-R-D system have a different socioeconomic conditioning history, and their A-R-D systems are thus not appropriate to the institutional system. Under those circumstances these children do not develop desirable behaviors; many times they develop "abnormal" instrumental behaviors as well as additional inappropriacies in their A-R-D systems. We must begin to investigate the way that social problems of behavior can be treated by changing the reinforcer system of the institutions to which the children are subjected, in addition to the research to change the children. The author has previously suggested (Staats, 1968a; Staats & Staats, 1963) that a school has a large number of very attractive, unutilized reinforcers for many children who have motivational problems in school. That is, there are activities and facilities at schools – gyms, playing fields, playing equipment, auditoriums and movies, and so on – that are not used as reinforcers except in the grossest way. If these were incorporated into a token system of reinforcement and applied to individual learning responses, it would be possible to treat many individual and social problems of school adjustment. The author has experimented with the use of material reinforcers for working with various types of clinical and educational problems of learning in maladjusted children, ranging from schizoid children through retardates to culturally deprived youngsters, and the results indicate that many behavior problems in children can be treated in this manner (Staats, 1968a).

We must also investigate the possibility of changing institutional A-R-D systems in treating other types of individual and social problems. Thus, much could be done in other public institutions such as prisons, homes for the mentally retarded, homes for juvenile delinquents, adult education programs, mental hospitals, and so on. It may be expected that in some cases the "treatment" indicated may require social reorganization and change. First, of course, it will be necessary to begin studies which show positive effects of making such manipulations.

The foregoing should indicate that it is not possible to approach general problems of the individual's A-R-D system by working exclusively with either changes in the system (behavior therapy) or by manipulating reinforcers to utilize better the individual's system (behavior modification). It will be necessary to work out procedures to change individual and group A-R-D systems through conditioning (training) along with manipulation of existing systems. Let us take the example of a schizophrenic with severe disturbances in his A-R-D system. While an artificial system might be instituted that could be used to train him to various social, cognitive, and sensory – motor skills, it would also be necessary to provide him with training that would culminate in a personal A-R-D system that would enable him to function within the system which is in effect in everyday life. Unless the latter was accomplished, the patient's functioning would always be dependent upon the artificial system. Much theoretical thought and experimental work will be required to investigate these possibilities. As an example, this will have to involve the manner in which classical conditioning of emotional responses takes place in the instrumental conditioning (behavior modification) treatment.

A primary point of this statement is that we need theoretical analyses that combine the integrated principles of learning with the observations of clinical psychology and the social and behavioral sciences. These will be needed in many cases before the type of empirical work suggested here becomes possible. We must make specific analyses of various abnormal behaviors in terms of abnormalities in the A-R-D system. This must be done on a broad basis, including various diagnostic categories, and in detail including a description of the development of the "abnormal" A-R-D system. Suggestions have been made in the present paper and in other analyses of the author (Staats, 1964a, 1968a,b; Staats & Butterfield, 1965; Staats & Staats, 1963), but complete and detailed coverage is necessary. The descriptions of abnormal and clinical psychology provide much of the data which is necessary to begin such a project, as do the data of some of the other social and behavioral sciences. As part of this it is also necessary to begin to specify what an appropriate (normal) A-R-D system should consist of, and to indicate the conditions necessary to produce this basic feature of human learning. It is suggested that this constitutes a theoretical task of the highest level. Several additional elaborations of characteristics of the A-R-D system in understanding personality will be made in the next section.

VII. Conclusion

The present paper has been restricted to considerations relevant to the conception of the human attitude-reinforcer-discriminative (motivational) system. It is suggested that theoretical analyses of the present type will also have to be made for various instrumental behaviors: social behavior, work behavior, cognitive behavior, sensory-motor behavior, and so on. The author has attempted to indicate the possibilities for such a comprehensive learning theory of personality (Staats, 1964a, 1968a,b; Staats & Staats, 1963), but much further development is necessary as the present paper suggests.

The traditional learning theories have not generated this type of theory. That is, the simple statement of learning principles, even with the demonstration of the principles in the context of various human behaviors, is not enough. Moreover, it is suggested that learning therapies must be based upon general and comprehensive learning theories of human behavior. Otherwise they will remain on the level of treating isolated and specific (symptomatic) problems which may indeed be an improvement upon traditional treatments, at least in certain cases, but which do not exploit the various potentialities.

The learning therapies require incorporation into a more general theory of personality which deals in detail with various aspects of human behavior. To exploit more fully the potentialities of a learning approach, the basic principles must be elaborated for the purpose of serving as a human learning theory. This theoretical structure then requires extensions which incorporate the observations of clinical psychology and the other social and behavioral sciences, as well as the empirical concepts that have been derived from such observations. Detailed analyses of human behavior and its determinants must be made if one is to understand and deal with complex problems of human behavior. For example, it is inadequate to simply state and extend the principle of reinforcement to a specific abnormal behavior. (Unfortunately, the present day field of behavior modification has followed this path.) However, when the principle is elaborated in its relationship to other learning principles and treatments, and extended in detail to a consideration of the human motivational system and other aspects of the personality theory, it can then be included in a general theory into which a number of specific observations can be fitted and from which many implications can be derived. This structure then has the features of a classic theory.

Learning *theory* has been traditionally seen as concerned with the basic principles of learning with their systematic statement and derivation. It is suggested, however, that another role of learning is seen as a basic theory of human behavior. For a learning theory to serve this role it must be able to deal with functional human behaviors of importance to the behavioral and social sciences, including clinical psychology. It is for these reasons that the term *social behaviorism* is employed to characterize the present approach, for it is suggested that a central concern of the human learning theorist is in dealing with significant, complex, functional, human behavior.

One further point may be made herein concerning the traditional schism between basic and applied psychology, in this case between work in learning and the practice and theory of clinical psychology. It is suggested that the schism has been maintained on both sides: by the basic (or basically oriented) psychologist who rejects the observations and concepts of the clinic and the social sciences, and also by the clinical worker and social scientist who sees the findings of the laboratory as irrelevant or as antagonistic to his approach. Each in this monolithic manner is in error. It is suggested that the schism is breached, however, when the personality theory extends basic learning principles to consideration of complex human behavior and its problems, incorporating and using the rich observations of the clinic and social sciences, and systematically using and further defining the empirical concepts derived from these observations. Thus, although the present approach is a thoroughgoing S-R approach, founded on basic learning principles, it constitutes an avenue for a rapprochement with traditional social and clinical theories. In fact it suggests that neither learning theory (or learning procedures) nor traditional social and clinical theories are complete. They are at major points complementary. As the present paper has attempted to show, social and clinical observations and concepts must be included to fill out the bare empirical principles of learning to constitute a theory of human behavior and a practice of clinical psychology. The term *social behaviorism* can be employed to denote the contribution of both aspects of the approach. This integration, it should be noted, is not a strategem for professional and scientific harmony. It is a strategem for theory building, but has within it the seeds for producing that harmony.

Over 10 years ago — in the paper that outlined the general points underlying the early behavior modification studies — the author concluded with the appeal "(I)t is suggested that learning theory has reached a state where it has something to offer clinical theory *and practice*" (Staats, 1957, p. 269). This is well accepted today. It may be added at this point, however, that the vast potentialities in the extension of learning to clinical theory, research, and treatment are largely untapped. It is suggested that the personality and social theorist and the clinical theorist (and the practitioner) must be prepared to deal with the whole continuum of knowledge that has been touched upon herein. This ranges from detailed concern with the basic, integrated, learning principles and their systematic statement, through an intensive concern with the concepts and observations of the social and behavioral sciences. When this is done *social behaviorism* has the potential for dealing with the most significant aspects of human behavior: individual, group and cultural, child and adult, as well as normal and abnormal.

Acknowledgments

This manuscript was prepared under the support of Office of Naval Research Contract N00014-67-A-0387-0007 as Technical Report No. 2.

References

Allen, K. E., Hart, B., Buell, J. S., Harris, F. R., & Wolf, M. M. Effects of social reinforcement on regressed crawling of a nursery school child. *Journal of Educational Psychology*, 1964, 55, 35–41.

Ayllon, T. Conditioning procedures in the rehabilitation of psychotic patients. Paper presented to the First International Congress of Social Psychiatry, London, August, 1965.

Ayllon, T., & Azrin, N. *The token economy*. New York: Appleton-Century-Crofts, 1969.

Ayllon, T., & Michael, J. L. The psychiatric nurse as a behavioral engineer. *Journal of the Experimental Analysis of Behavior*, 1959, 2, 323–334.

Bandura, A., Ross, D., & Ross, S. A comparative test of the status envy, social power, and the secondary reinforcement theories of identification learning. *Journal of Abnormal and Social Psychology*, 1963, 67, 527–534.

Bandura, A. A social learning interpretation of psychological dysfunctions. In P. London and D. Rosenhan (Eds.), *Foundations of abnormal psychology*. New York: Holt, Rinehart & Winston, 1968.

Birnbrauer, J. S., Wolf, M. M., Kidder, J. D., & Tague, C. Classroom behavior of retarded pupils with token reinforcement. *Journal of Experimental Child Psychology*, 1965, 2, 219–235.

Breger, L., & McGaugh, J. L. Critique and reformulation of "learning-theory approaches to psychotherapy and neurosis." *Psychological Bulletin*, 1965, 63, 338–358.

Burgess, R. L., & Akers, R. L. A differential association-reinforcement theory of criminal behavior. *Social Problems*, 1966, 14, 128–147.

Davison, G. C. The elimination of a sadistic fantasy by a client-controlled counterconditioning: A case study. *Journal of Abnormal Psychology*, in press.

Dekker, E., Pelser, H. E., & Groen, J. Conditioning as a cause of asthmatic attacks: A laboratory study. *Journal of Psychosomatic Research*, 1956, 1, 58–67.

Dollard, J., & Miller, N. E. *Personality and psychotherapy*. New York: McGraw-Hill, 1950.

Eysenck, H. J. *The scientific study of personality*. London: Routledge, Kegan Paul, 1952.

Eysenck, H. J. *The dynamics of anxiety and hysteria*. London: Routledge, Kegan Paul, 1957.

Eysenck, H. J. *The structure of human personality*. New York: Macmillan, 1960.

Eysenck, H. J. Complex human behavior (a review). *Behaviour Research and Therapy*, 1965, 2, 241.

Franks, C. M. *Conditioning techniques in clinical practice and research*. New York: Springer, 1964.

Harris, F. R., Johnston, M. K., Kelley, C. S., & Wolf, M. M. Effects of positive social reinforcement on regressed crawling of a nursery school child. *Journal of Educational Psychology*, 1964, 55, 35–41.

Hart, B. M., Allen, K. E., Buell, J. S., Harris, F. R., & Wolf, M. M. Effects of social reinforcement on operant crying. *Journal of Experimental Child Psychology*, 1964, 1, 145–153.

Hull, C. L. *Principles of behavior*. New York: Appleton-Century, 1943.

Johnson, H. M. *Sociology: A systematic introduction*. New York: Harcourt, 1960.

Klineberg, O. *Social psychology*. New York: Holt, Rinehart & Winston, 1954.

Krasner, L., & Ullman, L. P. *Research in behavior modification*. New York: Holt, Rinehart & Winston, 1965.

Lazarus, A. A. The elimination of children's phobias by deconditioning. In H. J. Eysenck (Ed.), *Behavior therapy and the neuroses*. New York: Macmillan (Pergamon), 1960.

Lott, B. E., & Lott, A. J. The formation of positive attitudes toward group members. *Journal of Abnormal and Social Psychology*, 1960, **61**, 297–300.

Lovaas, O. I., Freitag, G., Kinder, M., Rubenstein, B., Schaeffer, B., & Simmons, J. Developing social behaviors in autistic children using electric shock. Papers presented at the meetings of the American Psychological Association, Los Angeles, September 1964.

Lovaas, O. I. A behavior therapy approach to the treatment of childhood schizophrenia. In J. P. Hill (Ed.), *Minnesota symposium on child psychology*. Vol. I. Minneapolis, Minn.: Univ. of Minnesota Press, 1966.

Maccoby, E. E., & Gibbs, P. K. Methods of child-rearing in two social classes. In W. E. Martin and C. B. Stendler (Eds.), *Readings in child development*. New York: Harcourt, 1954.

Maslow, A. H. *Motivation and personality*. New York: Harper, 1954.

Mowrer, O. H. *Learning theory and personality dynamics*. New York: Ronald Press, 1950.

Newcomb, T. M. *Social psychology*. New York: Holt, Rinehart & Winston, 1950.

Raymond, M. J. Case of fetishism treated by aversion therapy. In H. J. Eysenck (Ed.), *Behavior therapy and the neuroses*. New York: Macmillan (Pergamon), 1960.

Rescorla, R. A., & Solomon, R. L. Two-process learning theory: Relationships between Pavlovian conditioning and instrumental learning. *Psychological Review*, 1967, **74**, 151–182.

Rosen, B. C. The achievement syndrome: A psychocultural dimension of social stratification. *American Sociological Review*, 1956, **21**, 203–211.

Samuelson, P. A. *Economics: An introductory analysis*. (4th ed.) New York: McGraw-Hill, 1958.

Staats, A. W. Learning theory and "opposite speech." *Journal of Abnormal and Social Psychology*, 1957, **55**, 268–289.

Staats, A. W. Verbal habit-families, concepts, and the operant conditioning of word classes. *Psychological Review*, 1961, **68**, 190–204.

Staats, A. W. *Human learning*. New York: Holt, Rinehart & Winston, 1964. (a)

Staats, A. W. A case in and a strategy for the extension of learning principles to the problems of human behavior. In A. W. Staats (Ed.), *Human learning*. New York: Holt, Rinehart & Winston, 1964. (b)

Staats, A. W. An integrated-functional approach to complex human behavior. In B. Kleinmuntz (Ed.), *Problem solving: Research, method, and theory*. New York: Wiley, 1966.

Staats, A. W. *Learning, language, and cognition*. New York: Holt, Rinehart & Winston, 1968. (a)

Staats, A. W. Social behaviorism and human motivation: Principles of the A-R-D System. In A. G. Greenwald, T. C. Brock, & T. M. Ostrom (Eds.), *Psychological foundations of attitudes*. New York: Academic Press, 1968. (b)

Staats, A. W., & Butterfield, W. H. Treatment of nonreading in a culturally-deprived juvenile delinquent: An application of a reinforcement principle. *Child Development*, 1965, **36**, 925–942.

Staats, A. W., Finley, J. R., Minke, K. A., & Wolf, M. M. Reinforcement variables in the control of unit reading responses. *Journal of the Experimental Analysis of Behavior*, 1964, 7, 139–149. (a)

Staats, A. W., Minke, K. A., Finley, J. R. Wolf, M. M., & Brooks, L. O. A reinforcer system and experimental procedure for the laboratory study of reading acquisition. *Child Development*, 1964, **35**, 209–231. (b)

Staats, A. W., & Staats, C. K. Attitudes established by classical conditioning. *Journal of Abnormal and Social Psychology*, 1958, **57**, 37–40.

Staats, A. W., & Staats, C. K. A comparison of the development of speech and reading behaviors with implications for research. *Child Development*, 1962, **33**, 831–846.

Staats, A. W. (with contributions by Staats, C. K.). *Complex human behavior*. New York: Holt, Rinehart & Winston, 1963.

Staats, A. W., Staats, C. K., Schutz, R. E., & Wolf, M. M. The conditioning of textual responses utilizing "extrinsic" reinforcers. *Journal of the Experimental Analysis of Behavior*, 1962, **5**, 33–40.

Tate, B. G., & Baroff, G. S. Aversive control of self-injurious behavior in a psychotic boy. *Behaviour Research and Therapy*, 1966, **4**, 281–287.

Trapold, M. A., & Winokur, S. Transfer from classical conditioning and extinction to acquisition, extinction, and stimulus generalization of a positively reinforced instrumental response. *Journal of Experimental Psychology*, 1967, **73**, 517–525.

Ullmann, L. P., & Krasner, L. *Case studies in behavior modification*. New York: Holt, Rinehart & Winston, 1965.

Ullmann, L. P., and Krasner, L. *A psychological approach to abnormal behavior*. New York: Prentice-Hall, 1969.

Walton, D. The application of learning theory to the treatment of a case of neurodermatitis. In H. J. Eysenck (Ed.), *Behavior therapy and the neuroses*. New York: Pergamon, 1960.

Wolf, M. M., Risely, T., & Mees, H. Application of operant conditioning procedures to the behavior problems of an autistic child. *Behaviour Research and Therapy*, 1964, **1**, 305–312.

Zimmerman, D. W. Durable secondary reinforcement: Method and theory. *Psychological Review*, 1957, **64**, 373–383.

THE MEASUREMENT OF PERSONALITY FROM THE WECHSLER TESTS[1]

George H. Frank

DEPARTMENT OF PSYCHOLOGY, NEW YORK UNIVERSITY,
NEW YORK, NEW YORK

I. Introduction

The tests Wechsler developed are ostensibly tests of intelligence (*viz.*, Forms I and II of the Wechsler-Bellevue Intelligence Scale, the Wechsler Adult Intelligence Scale, and the Wechsler Intelligence Scale for Children). However, it seems probable that the forms of the test developed for use with adults are, when employed by psychologists in clinical settings, used to infer aspects of personality functioning as much, if not more than intellective.[2] On the surface, the use of these tests in this way would seem to be inconsistent with their stated *raison d'etre, viz.,* they are tests of *intelligence*. It seems proper (indeed, obligatory) to inquire into the justification of the use of a test of intelligence as a test of personality. This essay will be an attempt to try and answer that question.

In the first edition of Wechsler's test (Wechsler, 1939), no mention was made of the use of the test to infer aspects of personality. At that time, the

---

[1]This paper is dedicated to Solomon Machover who was my first teacher in clinical psychology, from whom it was my privilege and good fortune to learn how to think meaningfully and critically about test data, and who stimulated my initial attempts to conduct research with Wechsler data.

[2]So compelling is this notion with psychologists who test adults that some two decades before Wechsler published his material, another psychologist, reflecting on the extension of the Binet scales for use with adults, wrote, "In conclusion, I would emphasize the value of the Stanford Adult Tests as a direct aid in analysis of an individual's make-up. Within a closely selected group this value would outweigh that of expression of the results in terms of an intelligent quotient" (Downey, 1917, p. 155).

major rationale for the test was as a global, omnibus test of intelligence for adolescents and adults that would be more appropriate and effective than the Binet. However, in the second edition of the test (Wechsler, 1941), there appeared a chapter entitled "Diagnostic and Clinical Features." A number of factors account for this amplification of the use of the Test, some of which we will try to explore.

II. Rationale for the Use of Wechsler Test Data to Infer Personality

In psychology (during the '20's), Gestalt psychologists were emphasizing that factors inside the individual significantly influenced the organization of the perceptual field, which lead to the seminal research in the '30's of such individuals as Murray (1933), Sherif (1935), Sanford (1936, 1937), Sears (1936, 1937), Ansbacher (1937), Neff (1937), and Barker (1938) not only confirming the idea that attitudes did, indeed, influence perception, but encouraged the extension of this idea to the organization of thought processes as well. Then, there was the work of Spearman and his students (e.g., Spearman, 1904, 1923, 1927; Hart & Spearman, 1912, 1914; Webb, 1915; Alexander, 1935) who not only argued that intellective behavior was, in fact, cognitive functioning, but that factors other than cognition and intelligence were being tapped by tests of intelligence, i.e., character and attitudinal factors. This led to the conclusion that personality factors influence performance on tests of intelligence (e.g., Thorndike, Terman, Freeman, Colvin, Pintner, Ruml, & Pressey, 1921), and provided the impetus for a large body of research with the Binet test (see the review of this research by Harris & Shakow, 1937).

Equally important were the attempts to study psychiatric pathology in terms of the psychological functions that were involved and, hence, impaired. In psychiatry, we may cite the early work of Kraepelin (who was a formally trained psychologist in addition to being a psychiatrist; he trained with Wundt at Leipzig in order to initiate such studies). Other early workers were Charcot, Janet, Freud, Bleuler, Adolf Meyer (1906, 1910, 1911, 1912), Storch (1924), Sullivan (1925), and Bychowski (1935). Then there were those pioneering psychologists who used tests to study psychopathology [such as Pressey (1917; Pressey & Cole, 1918), Rawlings (1921), Tendler (1923), Wells and Martin (1923), Babcock (1930), Vigotsky (1934), Hunt (1935), Bolles (1937), Cameron (1938a,b, 1939a,b), Goldstein (1939; Goldstein & Scheerer, 1941), Hanfmann (1939, 1941, 1944; Hanfmann & Kasanin, 1937, 1938; Kasanin & Hanfmann, 1939), and Weigl (1941)].

Thus, from the foregoing, we can see that the trend of events in psychiatry and psychology to study psychopathology from the point of view of the psychological functions involved and impaired (as contrasted with the behavioral facts usually studied in psychiatry), determined that the two major tests of intelligence (e.g., the Binet and the Wechsler) should be used in this way too. For more than twenty years, the Binet test had been used in this way; had Wechsler himself not used his test in this way, it seems probable that other psychologists would have done so anyway. Moreover, we can also see that not only did the currents, outlined above, determine the way in which Wechsler's test would be *used,* but also the form it would take. For example, up until World War I, the need for a test which would, on the one hand, be more appropriate for adults than was the Binet, and, on the other, would be more appropriate for individuals who were not comfortable with or capable of expressing themselves through verbal functions had not been clearly apparent. Particular impetus for the development of such tests of intelligence was generated by the attempts to evaluate the inductees into the army during World War I who were from rural areas, had received little by the way of formal education, or recent immigrants from Europe speaking little, if any, English. To this end, we can note the early work of Woodworth and Wells (1911), Healy (with the picture completion and object assembly tests) (Healy & Fernald, 1911), blocks (Knox, 1914; Kohs, 1923) and mazes (Porteus, 1915). Furthermore, the trend toward the evaluation of several functions at the same time rather than isolated test performances led to the development of such omnibus performance tasks as the Army Beta Test (used during World War I, which included digit symbol, picture completion, picture analogies tests, and tests of spatial relations and form completion), the scale developed by Pintner (Pintner & Paterson, 1917, which was composed of fifteen subtests including the Mare and Foal, the Seguin Formboard, digit symbol, object assembly: manikin and profile, picture completion, and blocks), the scale developed by Grace Arthur (1933) (which included many of the same tasks, e.g., Kohs blocks, Healy picture completion, Seguin formboard, object assembly: manikin and profile, and the Porteus maze), and the scale developed by Cornell and Coxe (1934) (which was composed of seven subtests including the object assembly tasks of the manikin and the profile, block design, picture arrangement, digit symbol, memory for design, picture completion, and cube construction). We should note here the similarity between the Cornell-Coxe and the performance scale of the Wechsler. In the same way, omnibus verbal tests were being developed. Here, we may cite the Army Alpha Test (developed by Bingham, Harnes, Goddard, Terman, Wells,

Whipple, and Yerkes for use during World War I, which included such items as: following directions, disarranged sentences, number completion, arithmetic, judgment, synonyms, analogies, and information), the tests put together by W. M. Brown (1923) (which included such items as following directions, logic, problem-solving, arithmetic, digits, forward and backward, information, synonyms and antonyms, reasoning, comprehension, and object completion), and Thurstone (1931) (which included such tasks as digits, information, syllogisms, analogies, reading comprehension, and number completion). Moreover, the need to evaluate verbal *and* nonverbal aspects of intelligence was already included in the efforts of Thorndike (1920), Whipple (1921), Tendler (1923), Wells and Martin (1923), and Alexander (1935). Even the mode of converting the scores into standard units (i.e., weighted scores) so that the individual's performance on any of the tests might be meaningfully compared was developed beforehand by Yerkes (Yerkes, Bridges, & Hardwick, 1915), who had also developed the whole idea of a point scale evaluating individual cognitive functions (as compared to the age scale evaluation as in the Binet). Conrad (1931) outlined the requisites of a general test of intelligence. In his view, such a test should involve the measurement of both "g" and "s" factors; should include items evaluated in terms of the speed of completion in addition to simple capacity to perform or to reason; should try to measure innate capacity rather than acquired information; should include both verbal as well as nonverbal tasks, but should group them separately; should use an adequate sampling of particular tasks; the scores should be obtained in terms of a scale made up of equal units or scores which should be susceptible to scaling in equal unity, and the test should have a definite zero point. Factor analytic studies of tests of intellective functioning confirmed that the many tests could be grouped into some basic factors defined by different aspects of cognitive functioning (although the resultant factors seemed to vary in number according to the mode of analysis employed by the individual investigator). Thurstone (1936) had isolated eight factors out of the analysis of the intercorrelation of 59 tests [at another time (Thurstone, 1938) it turned out to be nine, while at another time 60 tests produced seven (Thurstone & Thurstone, 1941)]. Thurstone's analyses had isolated such functions as: a numerical ability (arithmetic), memory, induction, verbal reasoning, word fluency (vocabulary), visualizing spatial relations (e.g., blocks and form board), a verbal relations (reading comprehension, opposites, analogies, synonyms), and a factor of speed in perceptual discrimination. Woodrow (1939) had isolated five factors out of the analysis of the intercorrelation of 52 tests [which included a factor of verbal facility (involving such things as definitions, opposites and similarities, judgment in social situations, observations on human behavior, proverbs), a visual-spatial factor (blocks), numerical ability, attention (e.g., arithmetic), and memory (digits)]. Interestingly, Alexander (1935) had taken the verbal tasks of the Binet and the performance tasks of the Pintner-Paterson Scale (Pintner & Paterson, 1917), factor analyzed the data, and, therefrom, derived three factors, *viz.,* a verbal factor, a performance factor, and factor of numerical ability (e.g., digits).

To summarize our work thus far, we have seen that the development of Wechsler's tests and the use of them to infer aspects of personality were a natural outgrowth of the events that preceded it. Of course the Binet had been used to derive clinical factors, but a review of that research (Harris & Shakow, 1937) indicated that there was no real support for the use of the test in this way; clinical (or personality) features could not be derived from a subject's performance with sufficient validity so as to be utilizable clinically. Part of the failure of the research to support the hypothesis that analysis of an individual's performance on the Binet *could* be used to derive inferences regarding personality was attributed to the nature of the instrument itself, and so when Wechsler developed his test, it was hoped that this new tool would enable the psychologist to demonstrate the validity of the hypothesis that personality *could* be inferred from intellective behavior. Despite the failure of the Binet, during the hypothesis-formulating years with the Wechsler (i.e., the late '40's), the literature in experimental psychology continued to lend support to the hypothesis that personality influenced cognitive process (e.g., R. Levine, Chein, & Murphy, 1942; Rokeach, 1943; Schafer & Murphy, 1943; Bruner, 1948; Bruner & Goodman, 1947; Bruner & Postman, 1947a,b, 1948; Postman & Bruner, 1948; Postman, Bruner, & McGinnies, 1948; Atkinson & McClelland, 1948; McClelland & Atkinson, 1948; McClelland & Liberman, 1949; Carter & Schooler, 1949; Frenkel-Brunswik, 1949; Witkin, 1949); all of which lead to the now famous symposia on personality and perception in 1949 at Duke University (Bruner & Krech, 1949), at the University of Texas (Blake & Ramsey, 1951), and at the meetings of the American Psychological Association (Rosenzweig, MacKinnon, Zubin, Snyder, Combs, Roe, & Klein, 1949). There was no reason to question the hypothesis. Encouraged by these data, experience with the administration of the test to the clinical population at Bellevue Hospital, and by the research done in collaboration with his associates (*viz.,* Balinsky, Israel, & Wechsler, 1939; Wechsler, Halpern, & Jaros, 1940; Wechsler, Israel, & Balinsky, 1941) plus the work of Rabin (1941, who had presented a paper at the annual meeting of the then Eastern Section of the A.P.A. reporting his work with the Wechsler at New Hampshire State

Hospital), Wechsler included a chapter on "Diagnostic and Clinical Features" in the second edition of his book (Wechsler, 1941). Hence, we see Wechsler writing,

> Although the primary purpose of an intelligence examination is to give a valid and reliable measure of the subject's global intellectual capacity, it is reasonable to expect any well conceived intelligence scale will furnish its user with something more than an I.Q. or M.A. In point of fact, most intelligence examinations, when administered individually, make available a certain amount of data regarding the testee's mode of reaction, his special abilities and disabilities and, not infrequently, some indicators of his personality traits (Wechsler, 1944, p. 146).

And so it was experience and research with the Wechsler Scales that enabled such psychologists as Wechsler, for example, or Roe (1946; Roe & Shakow, 1942), Machover (1943), Scheerer (1946), or the group at the Menninger Clinic (e.g., Reichard & Schafer, 1943; Schafer & Rapaport, 1944; Rapaport, Gill, & Schafer, 1945; Schafer, 1946; Rapaport, 1946, 1947, 1954; Rapaport, Menninger, & Schafer, 1947; Mayman, Schafer, & Rapaport, 1951) to emphasize that the Wechsler, as a test of intelligence *would* provide the psychologist with more information about a subject than merely his level of intelligence. Having summarized the rationale behind the use of the Wechsler as a measure of personality, we may now examine the empirical validity that this kind of measurement has achieved.

III. Research on the Validity of Wechsler Data in the Assessment of Personality

A. THE WECHSLER AND PSYCHOPATHOLOGY

Because the bulk of the research with the Wechsler tests has explored their use as a means of inferring personality in clinical settings, many of the tests of the validity of these inferences refer to work with individuals who exhibit some form of psychopathology. We may begin our exploration with these data. It should be noted at the outset just how this kind of validity was examined. On the basis of clinical experience and some research at Bellevue Hospital (e.g., Balinsky *et al.,* 1939; Wechsler *et al.,* 1940; Wechsler *et al.,* 1941) and the work of Rabin (1941), Wechsler predicted how various clinical groups would perform on each subtest individually and their patterns of performance over the whole test. For example, he suggested that the neurologically impaired would perform better on verbal tasks than on nonverbal tasks, would do relatively well on Information (I) and Comprehension (C), poorly on Arithmetic (A), Similarities (S), Object Assembly (OA), and Digit Symbol (D Sym), and very poorly on Digits (D) (particularly digits backward) and Block Design (BD); the schizophrenic should also perform better on verbal tasks than on nonverbal; should do well on I and Vocabulary (V), poorly on A, D, S, Picture Arrangement (PA), Picture Completion (PC), D Sym, sometimes well, sometimes poorly on C, and there would be considerable intertest discrepancy (i.e., scatter). Neurotics would also be expected to perform relatively better on verbal tasks than on the nonverbal ones (only psychopaths and mental defectives would be expected to perform relatively better on nonverbal tasks than on verbal ones), that they could be expected to do well on V, I, and S, but poorly on A, D, and OA, etc. Wechsler's description of how each kind of patient might be expected to perform on each subtest was in qualitative and imprecise terminology. On the basis of an accumulated five years of clinical experience and research in the *third* edition of his book (Wechsler, 1944), Wechsler tried to make his predictions much more specific. He converted his qualitative statements into quantitative ones [for example, he set up a range of scatter from 3.0 or more units above or below the mean subtest score (the use of the mean subtest score as a reference point was suggested by Magaret, 1942) represented by the symbols ++ or —— with gradations in between (e.g., scores 1.5 to 2.5 units above or below the mean were symbolized as + or −, and a score within 1.5 units of the mean subtest score was given the symbol O)]. In this manner, Wechsler then stipulated the expectations for the performance of the clinical groups, and on the basis of his notations in the third edition (Wechsler, 1944, pp. 150–151) we can construct a table demonstrating what these predictions would look like (see Table I).

Moreover, Wechsler now began to discuss the psychological rationale underlying each of the subtests, that is, what psychological functions they measured. This discussion of pattern analysis and its psychological rationale was amplified by the work of Rapaport (Rapaport *et al.*, 1945). As time went on, the expectations or hypotheses became more specific and detailed. Accordingly, research began to move to the testing of specific hypotheses.

Literally hundreds of studies have been conducted since 1939, and it would not serve any purpose to explore each individually. Detailed analysis of this research has been done by Rabin and his associates (Rabin, 1945; Rabin & Guertin, 1951; Guertin, Frank, & Rabin, 1956; Guertin, Rabin, Frank, & Ladd, 1962; Guertin, Ladd, Frank, Rabin, & Hiester, 1966), who, approximately every five years, review the research done

TABLE I
PERFORMANCE OF VARIOUS CLINICAL GROUPS ON THE WECHSLER SUBTESTS[a]

Subtests	Clinical Groups			
	Schizophrenics	Neurotics	Psychopaths	Mental defectives
I	+ to ++	+	− to −−	0 to −
C	+ to −	+	0 to −	+
A	0 to −	0 to −	−	−−
D	0 to +	−	0 to −	− to 0
S	+ to −−	+	− to 0	0
V	++	+	0	++
PC	0 to −−	0	+ to 0	− to 0
PA	− to 0	−	++ to +	0
OA	−	−	++ to +	+
BD	0 to +	0	+ to 0	0 to +
D Sym	−	−	0 to −	− to +

[a]This table is simply a compilation of the data found on pages 150 to 151 in the Third Edition of Wechsler's book (Wechsler, 1944).

during that period. It would be a more economic use of our time and energies, therefore, if we utilized these reviews as a basis upon which to determine whether the Wechsler *can* be used to infer personality.

As Wechsler stated them (*viz.,* Table I) the predictions regarding the performance of particular groups were not easy to test. The difficulty lay in their ambiguity. At the same time, the initial research utilized a disarmingly elementary design, i.e., a simple comparison of the performance of one diagnostic group with that of another, or a comparison of verbal (VIQ) and performance (PIQ) discrepancies. Later, research designs became more sophisticated. Following Wechsler's lead, investigators began to make comparisons more in terms of the specific subtests. It soon became apparent to the investigators that in comparing the performance of one clinical group with that of normal controls, there was a risk that they were inadvertently exploring the effect of psychopathology, per se, upon intellective behavior. This consideration led to the study of the performance of different categories of patients compared with each other *and* with controls. It also became apparent that although idiographic factors *were* influencing Wechsler test performance, these were not necessarily personality traits. Systematic exploration revealed that such factors as age, sex, cultural background, and level of socioeconomic status, education, and intelligence, per se, influenced the resultant pattern of subtests. Early studies that attempted to control for the effects of these parameters did so through the use of the random selection of subjects but some employed matched-group design, selecting subjects who are matched (either subject by subject or in terms of group dimensions) on the basis of one or more of these variables. The statistical comparison of the performance of patients likewise increased in sophistication. From the simple two-group comparison (either by t or r), investigators began to utilize techniques of multiple correlation and regression analysis (e.g., Klein, 1948), analyses of variance, and factor analysis. However, what the research was also demonstrating was that although investigators would take great pains to control for these many factors that *were* found to be influencing performance on the Wechsler aside from "personality," the criterion of personality utilized in this kind of research, *viz.,* psychiatric diagnosis, was, in and of itself, an inadequate one. When the Wechsler data of groups of patients diagnosed similarily were compared statistically [either by simple (rank) correlation (Jastak, 1953), analysis of variance (Wittenborn, 1949; Frank, Corrie, & Fogel, 1955), or factor analysis (e.g., Cohen, 1952; Frank, 1956)], it was discovered that grouping patients via psychiatric diagnosis did not enable one to constitute groups of patients with patterns of subtests that resembled each other.

Now knowing that *so* many factors influence performance on the Wechsler over and above the so-called personality factors, and selecting subjects on the basis of *the* criterion for personality used in all of these studies, *viz.,* psychiatric diagnosis, itself did not provide us with homogenous groupings of subjects and subjects' performances, it should not be surprising for us to learn that the results of the studies vary from study to study, so much so that what might be found in one analysis of data can be contradicted in another. The overview of the now more than 25 years of research, therefore, presents us with studies that are inconsistent, contradictory, and hence, inconclusive. What does seem clear, however, is that the specific predictions regarding the performance of subjects in the major diagnostic categories, *viz.,* schizophrenia, neurosis, or the brain-disordered, as postulated by Wechsler and Rapaport, have not received support. Indeed, the research *does* reveal that there is *no* characteristic pattern of performance on the subtests for, for example, the schizophrenic *or* the neurotic. The thought disorder which might be considered *the* characteristic feature of the schizophrenic is manifested to varying degrees by different individuals, and, in consequence, influences the cognitive functioning of that individual according to the degree to which a thought disorder is apparent in *that* individual. The same consequence obtains with regard to the anxiety that might be considered *a* characteristic of many neurotics; obviously, not all neurotics experience the same or even a debilitating degree of anxiety. In the same way, even the more molar kind of analysis (that is the comparison of VIQ to PIQ) does not provide us with a VIQ:PIQ relationship unique for any of the diagnostic categories; i.e., schizophrenics do not always do more poorly on verbal tasks than the performance ones, and individuals with cerebral dysfunction are not always characterized by the "well-known" poor performance on the nonverbal, psychomotor tasks. Research has shown that a VIQ < PIQ relationship could be the product of a lack of cultural or emotional stimulation *or* left-sided cerebral dysfunction, while a PIQ < VIQ relationship could be a function of depression, anxiety, *or* right-sided cerebral dysfunction. As regards schizophrenia, at best one can detect the presence of a thought disturbance *qualitatively*, that is, through an analysis of the problem-solving or associational processes of the individual patient as they might be tapped by either verbal or performance items, or by the *degree* of intra- and/or intertest scatter (a finding that has been found to be reliable since its earliest demonstration, e.g., Rabin, 1944). All of this, however, is a far cry from the degree of specificity that had been originally anticipated.

B. THE WECHSLER AND PERSONALITY TEST DATA

We have sufficient reason, on the basis of these and other data (e.g., Frank, in press), to question the validity of research that has utilized psychiatric diagnosis as the criterion for personality. However we may explore research that has utilized criteria for personality description other than psychiatric diagnosis. In this part of the chapter we will explore research that has compared performance on the Wechsler with performance on personality measures. Since these data do not appear to have been reviewed elsewhere we shall discuss them in detail. The two most frequently used personality measures were the MMPI (Minnesota Multiphasic Personality Inventory) and the Rorschach. We may consider the research with regard to these two tests separately. In addition, some studies have investigated the effect of *induced* affect (via situational, experimental procedures) on Wechsler performance; these shall be reviewed too.

1. MMPI

The primary issue of interest to investigators using data from the MMPI has been the influence of anxiety on performance on the Wechsler. The criterion for anxiety in all of these studies is the MMPI-derived Manifest Anxiety Scale (MAS) (Taylor, 1953). In one study (Calvin, Koons, Bingham, & Fink, 1955), MAS scores were found to relate to Wechsler performance in the following way: −.31 with Full Scale IQ, −.39 with VIQ, −.48 with BD, −.44 with I, −.31 with A and D, and −.29 with V and OA. The authors concluded that anxiety (as measured by MAS) manifests a nonspecific effect on the Wechsler tests; it seemed to pervade much of the test performance in a generalized way. Siegman (1956), on the other hand, found MAS scores to evidence a significant (and negative) relationship with scores on the timed tasks of the Wechsler only (i.e., A, D Sym, PC, PA, BD, and OA). With reference to performance on V, C, BD, and D Sym, Sarason and Minard (1962) found statistically significant relationships only between MAS and V. These studies suggest that there is some observable and statistically significant effect of level of anxiety upon the subject's performance on the Wechsler, although this effect is not consistent (with regard to which subtests are involved) from study to study. In comparison with these findings, other studies report results that seem contradictory. For example, while Siegman found anxiety to effect scores on D Sym, studies by Goodstein and Farber (1957), J. D. Matarazzo and Phillips (1955), and Sarason and Minard (1962) did not; while the study by Calvin et al. (1955) found a significant relationship between anxiety and performance on D, a study by Walker and Spence (1964) did not; while the study by Calvin et al. (1955) demonstrated a significant relationship between MAS and Full Scale IQ, the study by Dana (1957) and Mayzner, Sersen, and Tresselt (1955) did not; and although Siegman (1956) and Calvin et al. (1955) found some broad influence of anxiety on subtest performance, the data in the study by R. G. Matarazzo (1955) failed to demonstrate *any* relationship better than chance with regard to performance on the MAS and performance on any of the Wechsler subtests.

In the previous research, investigators had been attempting to assess the relationship between intelligence and personality through the test of specific hypotheses. In some studies, however, as in that by R. G. Matarazzo (1955), there are tests of this relationship from a broader base. Here, we may note studies by Brower (1947), Winfield (1953), and L'Abate (1962). Brower and Winfield correlated Full Scale IQ (FS IQ) with all the major MMPI variables; Brower found a significant correlation between FS IQ and the Hysteria Scale (of the MMPI) (−.60), Hypochondriasis Scale (−.65) and Psychopathic Deviate Scale (−.57); Winfield only found significance between the correlation of FS IQ and the Masculine-Femininity Scale. L'Abate intercorrelated specific indices of pathology derived from the WAIS (Wechsler Adult Intelligence Scale) (e.g., scatter) and those found on the MMPI and found no significant correlations.

Summary. Research exploring the relationship of performance on Wechsler's test and the MMPI produces little of a definitive nature. There is some suggestion that the research may support the hypothesis that personality factors are reflected in performance on Wechsler's test, but the research, itself, presents us with contradictory and inconsistent specific results from study to study.

2. Rorschach

Several studies have dealt with the relationship between general performance on the Wechsler and specific Rorschach variables. With regard to human movement (M), some investigators have found a low (but, nevertheless, statistically significant) correlation between this factor and IQ score (e.g., Abrams, 1955; M. Levine, Spivack, & Wight, 1959; Spivack, Levine, & Sprigle, 1959). However, some studies (e.g., Williams & Lawrence, 1953) failed to find this result. In a factor analysis of many tests, Singer, Wilensky, and McCraven (1956) found that FS IQ seemed to load, but extremely modestly, with M and other factors of motor inhibition and planfulness, as measured by other tests. Tucker (1950) found a nonsignificant correlation of M and FS IQ; only S yielded a significant correlation with M (.447). Wishner (1948) found no significant correlation between M and FS IQ, but a significant one between it and BD (.363). Levine, Glass, and Meltzoff (1957) found a low but significant correlation between M and the tendency to reverse the "N" in D Sym. From these studies it would appear that whatever M on the Rorschach measures (presumably it is a measure of an ability to defer behavior and to displace energies into ideational activity), it possesses *some* relationship to intelligence, although not an overwhelmingly strong one and certainly not one that is found with consistency from study to study.

Burnham (1949) found no significant relationship between the percent of M and FS IQ, whereas Wishner (1948) did (−.304), and Crookes and Keller (1960) and Tamkin (1959) found no relationship between the tendency to reject cards and FS IQ.

Spaner (1950) presented the results of a study wherein he correlated subtests on the Wechsler with factors on the Rorschach that were presumed to have similar psychological rationale. Spaner tests fifteen such relationships [*viz.*, that I would be significantly correlated with the total number of responses given to the cards (R), C with *good* form responses (F+), A with the number of form responses (F), OA with the number of Animal responses, BD with the number of color responses, and D Sym with the average time per initial response and average time per response]. The statistically significant results that emerged from the intercorrelations were: I with R (.219), C with F+ (.237), V with R (.305), PA with M (.195), PC with the number of popular responses (.138), D Sym and average time for the first response (−.150). In the words of the investigator himself, "The most significant finding of the entire study is the general negative character of the results." In a similar study, Holzberg and Belmont (1952) intercorrelated some of the same Wechsler and Rorschach variables as did Spaner [e.g., C with F+, I with R, white space responses, and number of whole responses (W)] while investigating the relationship of some factors that Spaner had not explored (S with the number of usual large details, D and A with the number of small usual details and the number of human responses, PC with the number of larger and smaller usual details and F+, PC and BD with W, M, and usual large details) offering a rationale for each hypothesized relationship. The results of their correlations revealed that nothing seemed to be strongly related to anything; none of the correlation coefficients was above .30.

Summary. Here, as with the research exploring the relationship between factors on the Wechsler and those of the MMPI, the research leaves us in the unenviable position of being able to find studies which support as well as reject the very same hypotheses. Moreover, wherever statistical significance has been found, the actual magnitude of the relationship (i.e., the correlation coefficient) is usually so small as to be virtually meaningless; this forces us to view even the few uncontested positive results as not being definite supports of whatever hypotheses they were geared to test.

C. The Effect of Experimentally Induced Affect

It would appear that few studies have involved a test of the hypothesis that personality factors are reflected in Wechsler data using a research design other than that of the traditional test-test correlation. A few studies have explored the effect of situational stimulation of affect and its effect on responsiveness to Wechsler material. Moldawsky and Moldawsky (1952) exposed college students to what they felt would be an anxiety-inducing experience for the students (*viz.*, the students were questioned by an "apprehensive" examiner who suggested recording the subject's attitudes manifested during the examination; the subject was told he had been selected because "there was something odd" about his answers on a test taken previously during the semester; and the examination was taken with an "assistant" seated behind the subject). The subject's performance on D was significantly influenced by these procedures, but not the V performance. Wiener (1957) measured mistrustfulness via questionnaire and also gave his subjects instructions which were geared to increase such a feeling (e.g., the examiner announced he had lied regarding the original purpose stated for the experiment). Scores on PC and S were seen to be influenced (lowered) by degree of distrustfulness as measured by the questionnaire; the situational variable was not a significant influence. Too few studies have been done for any conclusions to be drawn with regard to experiments of this nature; the studies are presented primarily for the edification of the reader and the hopes that they might generate research.

IV. Discussion

As we stop to review what we have found herein, it would be understandable that we might end this survey by developing a feeling of dismay and a sense of painful frustration, for it would appear that the fruit of our labor is to confirm a growing dissatisfaction with tests, and an increasing sense of doubt regarding some of the most cherished assumptions made by the clinician. It would not be surprising for some to point to the review article by Harris and Shakow (1937) and those by Rabin and co-workers (Rabin, 1945; Rabin & Guertin, 1951; Guertin *et al.*, 1956, 1962, 1966) and conclude that the research (clearly) indicates that the assumption that even the omnibus tests of intelligence (e.g., the Binet and the Wechsler) can be used to infer or measure anything but intelligence has not been stoutly supported. Despite the efforts to convert the scores on the Wechsler into something more amenable to statistical analysis as by Jastak (1953) who recommended using raw scores, Barnett (1950) who offered a Z-score transformation of the scores, the various referrant points suggested with which the scores might be compared (e.g., average mean subtest score, verbal and performance mean subtest scores computed individually, or vocabulary score), or the attempts to analyse the tests through clinical impression, factor analysis, or regression equation, the research yield with the Wechsler strongly suggests that it is *not* an effective method of measuring personality. Whatever studies *can* be cited to support the contention that personality *can* be inferred from tests of intelligence must be viewed in relation to those studies which refute the thesis. But it is just this latter point which may make us hesitate to write the Wechsler off so quickly and to reject the hypothesis that the clinician can derive valid inferences about personality from performance on a test of intelligence. It is true that inferences cannot be made with the kind of specificity that was once hoped for. Moreover, one must recognize the sheer difficulty of conducting research in the area of personality, of which clinical psychology is a part, as, for example, discussed by Rosenzweig (1950), Garfield (1957), and Frank (1963). Moreover, to review the *results* of research without examining the research methodology seems unwise.

In regard to the research design employed in the studies reviewed herein, the main defect has been the tendency to ignore the complexity of man and to assume that because something has been isolated and labeled (even operationally) that this variable may be studied apart from the rest of the organism. It is perhaps an axiom that everything in the universe of things (from the smallest unicellular structure to the meta galaxies) exists and functions in interaction with everything else; what varies only is the degree to which the many parameters influence a given phenomenon. The recognition that one cannot really study man's psychological functions in isolation led to the concept of organismic integration (as, for example, by Sherrington) and research in the "new look" in perception (e.g., Postman, 1953). It is perhaps equally axiomatic, as Thorndike stated, that everything that exists can be measured, but we tend to act when measuring some aspect of behavior as though it exists in splendid isolation. Both experimental *and* clinical psychologists have been guilty of this error, and the field has suffered by virtue of the state of affairs of our most important research. Psychologists, both experimental and clinical, who have studied personality, have tended to regard their criteria measures (whether with regard to other test data, clinical impression, or psychiatric diagnosis) as valid. This is not always the case. It leads to attempts to study the relationship between a personality variable and some other aspect of behavior without considering all the other factors that might influence the same behavior. Any student of personality who takes this position insures that his study will minimize the possibility of reliably exploring the effect of personality on behavior and maximizes the possibility of contributing a study that some time in the future might be contradicted by the results of some other study. This has been the fate of much of the research with the Wechsler that has not *measured* the effects of *all* the parameters *known* to effect performance on a test of intelligence, from the idiographic to the situational (Masling, 1960). A review of research with the Wechsler ends up with contradictory results because investigators have either not been motivated to or able to control for the effects of all the parameters, and it is the random variation in these factors from study to study that causes the results of one study to vary from the results of another. On the other hand, when one is faced with conceptualizing the *critical* research, one notes that to measure the influence of *all* the factors we already know influence an individual's performance on the Wechsler, we would end up with a monumental and virtually unconductable piece of research. For even limiting ourselves to the variables of age, sex, socioeconomic status, level of education, and level of intelligence, we could end up with a $3 \times 2 \times 3 \times 4 \times 4$ design, or 288 cells. In order to insure the meaningfulness of the results, thereby placing the requirement of having a conservative number of subjects in each cell, e.g., 30, we would, then, need 8680 subjects for the research. To the extent that this reasoning is correct, to that extent we will probably not be able to conduct *the* critical piece of research, and we will have to content ourselves with research that is always going to be far from ideal.

However, even if we accept the limitation upon our research endeavors imposed upon us by the reality of the nature of that which we are studying, we should examine the nature of the instrument we are employing in this area of study. Schofield (1952) has reminded us that the extent to which a test is loaded with a given factor, it precludes the measurement of other factors. In this regard, the degree to which the Wechsler subtests are loaded with intelligence (both g and s), to that degree is the factor of personality precluded from being able to play a role in the subtest. Here, we note that just with regard to the age 35–49, the correlation of each test with all the other subtests (less itself) is: I (.705), C (.682), D (.517), A (.671), PA (.625), PC (.604), OA (.508), BD (.727), D Sym (.697) (Wechsler, 1944, p. 225) (Wechsler's data here do not include computations for V.) These are fairly high correlations. However, they might be reduced by factoring out that which is due to the idiographic parameters mentioned previously other than personality, so that it would appear the more appropriate the statistical technique perhaps the greater the possibility of being able to abstract that degree of influence contributed by personality.

Another set of caveats of which to take note are those posed by Lorr and Meister (1941). In general, the clinician assesses the patterning of the subtest and either clinically or statistically attempts to extract something meaningful from a comparison of one set of subtest patterns with another. It was in this way that the original thinkers in the field, such as Wechsler and Rapaport, attempted to derive their hypotheses regarding the characteristic performance of different groups. However, Lorr and Meister have reminded us that there are many factors which are involved in the production of scatter in the subtests over and above personality. For example, they note that variable correlation of one subtest with another, variable correlation between each subtest and the criterion, the lack of uniform increase of difficulty of items within subtests, and so-called "chance" variation (that is, factors which we have not or cannot measure), all serve to produce scatter. From Wechsler's data (Wechsler, 1944) we already know that the subtests vary considerably in the degree to which they correlate with each other and even with the major criterion, and Rabin (Rabin, Davis, & Sanderson, 1946), very early discovered the degree to which the subtests are not composed of items in always the correct order of difficulty. Finally, to the extent that we accept the hypothesis that a test of intelligence is really a test of cognitive functions (Spearman, 1923), we should take note of the fact that factor analytic studies of Wechsler data (e.g., Balinsky, 1941; Berger, Bernstein, Klein, Cohen, & Lucas, 1964; Birren, 1952; Cohen, 1952, 1957, 1959; Davis, 1956; Frank, 1956; Hammer, 1949; Maxwell, 1959, 1960, 1961; Riegel & Riegel, 1962) have, by and large, extracted only three factors, viz., a verbal factor, a performance factor, and a memory factor. However, we noted previously that factor analyses of intellective behavior produced more than just three factors (again, depending on the method used and criterion for determining when simple structure has been arrived at, the number tends to vary), with three factors being, conservatively, half the number of "actual" cognitive factors that do "exist." Therefore, another problem may be that the Wechsler tests do not provide a broad enough sampling of the spectrum of cognitive functions, thereby limiting the opportunity to witness the influence of personality on these functions.

V. Summary

Although the tests Wechsler developed are entitled tests of "intelligence," it is apparent that in most clinical situations, certainly as regards the evaluation of adolescents and adults, the psychologist is equally (if not more) interested in deriving some hypotheses regarding the personality of the individual he is testing as he is his level of intelligence, per se. We have explored some of the factors in clinical and experimental psychology that have lent support to the use of the Wechsler data from which to infer personality, as well as the research which pertains to the validity of this assumption. By and large, we have to admit that the research does not seem to lend support to the use of Wechsler data as that from which to infer personality, certainly not in the specific manner in which it was hoped for and even postulated. Personality variables *do* seem to be reflected in Wechsler data, but in a very *qualitative* manner. For example, instead of being able to isolate characteristic patterns of subtest performance for *any* group which would help us in identifying personality variables, we must, rather, look to the verbalizations and the performance of the subject to determine whether the thought disorder of the schizophrenic or the characteristic quality of thinking of the obsessive-compulsive is revealed in the pattern of thinking tapped by the test, or whether the *degree* of (overall) (intra-and/or intertest) scatter is significant thereby reflecting a serious degree of internal disorganization. Yet, to do justice to the data, we also had to explore the nature of the test itself as a (presumably) multivariate test of cognitive functions, the way it has been used (that is, the design of the research), the many factors characteristic of the individual, over and above "personality" which are known to influence his performance on the Wechsler (such as age, sex, socioeconomic-cultural status, level of education, and intelligence, per se) *as well as* the sheer difficulty of conducting research in this area in general. The overall conclusion is that it is not fair to take the research at face value, since the design of some of the research leaves much to be desired, so that we should not condemn the use of the Wechsler as a tool from which we might infer personality, but, rather, see its limitations, and, in light of these limitations, derive what we *can* from the data in the manner in which we can, hoping that in the future, a better test will be developed. Ah, but there's the rub. Clinical work began under the pressure of practical exigencies (Frank, 1963), and clinical psychologists, like other individuals in the mental health professions, continue to be pressed to gain competence in working with their tools so that they might be able to meet the ever-increasing needs of the community. As such, the programs developed to train psychologists for this task, even if they have striven to reflect the Boulder model of the scientist-professional, have succeeded only to the extent of encouraging the clinician to do *some* research (usually only that which he needs to get his degree) and to have a sound theoretical-conceptual basis for the clinical work in which he will be engaging. However, not only have we been witness to a recent trend to deprecate the role of testing (Rosenwald, 1963) but we have reduced the degree to which, even if we teach testing, we teach the principles and methods of test *construction*. Hence, we seemed to have programmed our own future with a considerable degree of failure, for not only have we virtually stopped teaching how to construct the very thing we seem to need, *viz.,* better tests, but even the research that needs to be done if done by students may be either perfunctory (to satisfy the degree requirements) or done by individuals who, as Holt (1968) points out, might not have the sagacity (by virtue of their professional and scientific youth) to conceptualize the really meaningful research.

However, in conclusion, we can state that Wechsler data do seem to be able to reflect personality data; the problem seems to be that in its present form, the capacity to derive such information from the test is limited. It would appear that we are in need of an omnibus test of intelligence which, in fact, provides us with *statistically* independent subtests, and one which would permit the exploration of *many* facets of cognition *in depth*. Perhaps only then will the factor of personality be able to be revealed with clarity in intelligence test data. Therefore, in spite of the hundreds of studies in this area, it seems painfully apparent that we need more research, but much more basic research than perhaps had been anticipated, e.g., the development of a new intelligence test and the exploration of the relationship of the cognitive factors involved in tests of intelligence and basic personality factors *before* we attempt to utilize the test to explore the nature of psychopathology. Finally, it would appear that if we really appreciate and respect the complexity of man, we cannot indulge ourselves in the kinds of studies which attempt to explore psychological processes out of the total context of the human situation. This would suggest that our studies will have to take into consideration many more parameters than they sometimes have; we need studies which explore the multivariate nature of man's behavior (motoric or cognitive) through multivariate designs and multivariate statistical techniques. In the face of some of the findings when we review large segments of the research in clinical psychology, it seems as though we have to start all over again from the beginning, with a whole new approach to the systematic exploration of the nature of man. Perhaps then some of our clinical techniques can be placed on a sounder footing, more adequately reflecting the nature of man. This might, perhaps, enable us to conduct better research from which either to develop new ideas or better tests of the validity of those current hypotheses on which our work is based.

References

Abrams, E. N. Predictions of intelligence from certain Rorschach factors. *Journal of Clinical Psychology*, 1955, 11, 81–83.

Alexander, W. P. Intelligence, concrete and abstract. *British Journal of Psychology, Monograph Supplement*, 1935, No. 19.

Ansbacher, H. Perception of numbers as affected by the monetary value of the objects. *Archives of Psychology*, 1937, No. 215.

Arthur, G. *A point scale of performance tests.* New York: Commonwealth Fund, 1933.

Atkinson, J. W., & McClelland, D. C. The projective expression of needs: II. The effect of different intensities of the hunger drive on thematic apperception. *Journal of Experimental Psychology*, 1948, 38, 643–655.

Babcock, H. An experiment in the measurement of mental deterioration. *Archives de Psychologie*, 1930, No. 117.

Balinsky, B. An analysis of the mental factors of various age groups from nine to sixty. *Genetic Psychology Monographs*, 1941, 23, 191–234.

Balinsky, B., Israel, H., & Wechsler, D. Relative effectiveness of the Stanford-Binet and Bellevue Scale in diagnosing mental deficiency. *American Journal of Orthopsychiatry*, 1939, 9, 798–801.

Barker, R. G. The effect of frustration upon cognitive ability. *Character and Personality*, 1938, 7, 145–150.

Barnett, I. The use of Z scores in equating the Wechsler-Bellevue subtests. *Journal of Clinical Psychology*, 1950, 6, 184–188.

Berger, L., Bernstein, A., Klein, E., Cohen, J., & Lucas, G. Effects of aging and pathology on the factorial structure of intelligence. *Journal of Consulting Psychology*, 1964, 28, 199–207.

Birren, J. E. A factorial analysis of the Wechsler-Bellevue Scale given to an elderly population. *Journal of Consulting Psychology*, 1952, 16, 399–405.

Blake, R. R., & Ramsey, G. V. (Eds.) *Perception—An approach to personality.* New York: Ronald Press, 1951.

Bolles, M. M. The basis of pertinence: A study of the test performance of aments, dements, and normal children of the same mental age. *Archives de Psychologie*, 1937, No. 212.

Brower, D. The relation between intelligence and Minnesota Multiphasic Personality Inventory scores. *Journal of Social Psychology*, 1947, 25, 243–245.

Brown, R. R., & Partington, J. E. A psychometric comparison of narcotic addicts with hospital attendants. *Journal of Genetic Psychology*, 1942, **27**, 71–79.

Brown, W. M. Character traits as factors in intelligence test performance. *Archives de Psychologie*, 1923, No. 65.

Bruner, J. S. Perceptual theory and the Rorschach test. *Journal of Personality*, 1948, **17**, 157–168.

Bruner, J. S., & Goodman, C. C. Value and need as organizing factors in perception. *Journal of Abnormal and Social Psychology*, 1947, **42**, 33–44.

Bruner, J. S., & Krech, D. (Eds.) *Perception and personality.* Durham, N.C.: Duke University Press, 1949.

Bruner, J. S., & Postman, L. Emotional selectivity in perception and reaction. *Journal of Personality*, 1947, **16**, 69–77. (a)

Bruner, J. S., & Postman, L. Tension and tension release as organizing factors in perception. *Journal of Personality*, 1947, **15**, 300–308. (b)

Bruner, J. S., & Postman, L. Symbolic value as an organizing factor in perception. *Journal of Social Psychology*, 1948, **27**, 203–205.

Bruner, J. S., & Postman, L. 1948

Burnham, C. A. A study of the degree of relationship between Rorschach H% and Wechsler-Bellevue Picture Arrangement scores. *Journal of Projective Techniques*, 1949, **13**, 206–209.

Bychowski, G. Certain problems of schizophrenia in the light of cerebral pathology. *Journal of Nervous and Mental Diseases*, 1935, **81**, 280–298.

Calvin, A. D., Koons, P. B., Bingham, J. L., & Fink, H. H. A further investigation of the relationship between manifest anxiety and intelligence. *Journal of Consulting Psychology*, 1955, **19**, 280–282.

Cameron, N. Reasoning, regression and communication in schizophrenia. *Psychological Monographs*, 1938, **50**, Whole No. 221. (a)

Cameron, N. A study of thinking in senile deterioration and schizophrenic disorganization. *American Journal of Psychology*, 1938, **51**, 650–664. (b)

Cameron, N. Deterioration and regression in schizophrenic thinking. *Journal of Abnormal and Social Psychology*, 1939, **34**, 265–270. (a)

Cameron, N. Schizophrenic thinking in a problem-solving situation. *Journal of Mental Science*, 1939, **85**, 1012–1035. (b)

Carter, L., & Schooler, E. Value, need and other factors in perception. *Psychological Review*, 1949, **56**, 200–208.

Cohen, J. Factors underlying Wechsler-Bellevue performance of three neuropsychiatric groups. *Journal of Abnormal and Social Psychology*, 1952, **47**, 359–365.

Cohen, J. The factorial structure of the WAIS between early adulthood and old age. *Journal of Consulting Psychology*, 1957, **21**, 283–290.

Cohen, J. The factorial structure of the WISC at ages 7–6, 10–6, and 13–6. *Journal of Consulting Psychology*, 1959, **23**, 285–299.

Conrad, H. S. The measurement of adult intelligence and the requisites of a general intelligence test. *Journal of Social Psychology*, 1931, **2**, 72–85.

Cornell, E. L., & Coxe, W. W. *A performance ability scale.* Yonkers, N.Y.: World Book, 1934.

Crookes, T. G., & Keller, A. J. Rorschach card rejection and IQ. *Journal of Clinical Psychology*, 1960, **16**, 424–426.

Dana, R. H. Manifest anxiety, intelligence, and psychopathology. *Journal of Consulting Psychology*, 1957, **21**, 38–40.

Davis, P. C. A factor analysis of the Wechsler-Bellevue Scale. *Educational and Psychological Measurement*, 1956, **16**, 127–146.

Downey, J. E. The Stanford Adult Intelligence Tests. *Journal of Delinquency*, 1917, **2**, 144–155.

Frank, G. H. The Wechsler-Bellevue and psychiatric diagnosis: A factor analytic approach. *Journal of Consulting Psychology*, 1956, **20**, 67–69.

Frank, G. H. On the nature of clinical psychology. *Journal of General Psychology*, 1963, **69**, 119–124.

Frank, G. H. Psychiatric diagnosis: A review of research. *Journal of General Psychology*, in press.

Frank, G. H., Corrie, C. C., & Fogel, J. An empirical critique of research with the Wechsler-Bellevue in differential psychodiagnosis. *Journal of Clinical Psychology*, 1955, **11**, 291–293.

Frenkel-Brunswik, E. Intolerance of ambiguity as an emotional and perceptual personality variable. *Journal of Personality*, 1949, **18**, 108–143.

Garfield, S. L. *Introductory clinical psychology*. New York: Macmillan, 1957.

Goldstein, K. The significance of special mental tests for diagnosis and prognosis in schizophrenia. *American Journal of Psychiatry*, 1939, **96**, 575–588.

Goldstein, K., & Scheerer, M. Abstract and concrete behavior. *Psychological Monographs*, 1941, **53**, Whole No. 239.

Goodstein, L., & Farber, I. E. On the relation between A-scale scores and digit symbol performance. *Journal of Consulting Psychology*, 1957, **21**, 152–154.

Guertin, W. H., Frank, G. H., & Rabin, A. I. Research with the Wechsler-Bellevue Intelligence Scale: 1950–1955. *Psychological Bulletin*, 1956, **53**, 235–257.

Guertin, W. H., Ladd, C. E., Frank, G. H., Rabin, A. I., & Hiester, D. E. Research with the Wechsler Intelligence Scales for Adults: 1960–1965. *Psychological Bulletin*, 1966, **66**, 385–409.

Guertin, W. H., Rabin, A. I., Frank, G. H., & Ladd, C. E. Research with the Wechsler Intelligence Scales for Adults: 1955–60. *Psychological Bulletin*, 1962, **59**, 1–26.

Hammer, A. G. A factorial analysis of the Bellevue intelligence tests. *Australian Journal of Psychology*, 1949, **1**, 108–114.

Hanfmann, E. Analysis of thinking disorder in a case of schizophrenia. *A.M.A. Archives of Neurology and Psychiatry*, 1939, **41**, 568–579.

Hanfmann, E. A study of personal patterns in an intellectual performance. *Character and Personality*, 1941, **9**, 315–325.

Hanfmann, E. Approaches to the intellective aspects of personality. *Transactions of the New York Academy of Sciences*, 1944, **6**, 229–235.

Hanfmann, E., & Kasanin, J. A method for the study of concept formation. *Journal of Psychology*, 1937, **3**, 521–540.

Hanfmann, E., & Kasanin, J. Disturbances in concept formation in schizophrenia. *A.M.A. Archives of Neurology and Psychiatry*, 1938, **40**, 1276–1282.

Harris, A., & Shakow, D. The clinical significance of numerical measures of scatter on the Stanford-Binet. *Psychological Bulletin*, 1937, **34**, 134–150.

Hart, B., & Spearman, C. General ability, its existence and nature. *British Journal of Psychology*, 1912, **5**, 51–84.

Hart, B., & Spearman, C. Mental tests of dementia. *Journal of Abnormal Psychology*, 1914, **9**, 217–264.

Healy, W., & Fernald, G. M. Tests for practical mental classification. *Psychological Monographs*, 1911, **8** (Whole No. 54).

Holt, R. R. Editor's foreword. In D. Rapaport, M. M. Gill, & R. Schafer (Eds.), *Diagnostic psychological testing*. New York: International Universities Press, 1968.

Holzberg, J., & Belmont, L. The relationship between factors on the Wechsler-Bellevue and

Rorschach having common psychological rationale. *Journal of Consulting Psychology,* 1952, 16, 23–29.

Hunt, J. McV. Psychological loss in paretics and schizophrenics. *American Journal of Psychology,* 1935, 47, 458–463.

Jastak, J. Ranking Bellevue subtest scores for diagnostic purposes. *Journal of Consulting Psychology,* 1953, 17, 403–410.

Kasanin, J., & Hanfmann, E. An experimental study of concept formation in schizophrenia. I. Quantitative analysis of the results. *American Journal of Psychiatry,* 1939, 95, 35–52.

Klein, G. S. An application of the multiple regression principle to clinical prediction. *Journal of General Psychology,* 1948, 38, 159–179.

Knox, H. A. A scale based on the work at Ellis Island for estimating mental defect. *Journal of the American Medical Association,* 1914, 52, 741–747.

Kohs, S. C. *Intelligence measurement.* New York: Macmillan, 1923.

L'Abate, L. The relationship between WAIS-derived indices of maladjustment and MMPI in deviant groups. *Journal of Consulting Psychology,* 1962, 26, 441–445.

Levine, M., Glass, H., & Meltzoff, J. The inhibition process, Rorschach human movement responses, and intelligence. *Journal of Consulting Psychology,* 1957, 21, 41–45

Levine, M., Spivack, G., & Wight, B. The inhibition process, Rorschach human movement responses, and intelligence: Some further data. *Journal of Consulting Psychology,* 1959, 23, 306–312.

Levine, R., Chein, I., & Murphy, G. The relation of the intensity of a need to the amount of perceptual distortion: A preliminary report. *Journal of Psychology,* 1942, 13, 283–293.

Lorr, M., & Meister, R. K. The concept of scatter in light of mental test theory. *Educational and Psychological Measurement,* 1941, 1, 303–310.

McClelland, D. C., & Atkinson, J. W. The projective expression of needs: I. The effect of different intensities of the hunger drive on perception. *Journal of Psychology,* 1948, 25, 205–222.

McClelland, D. C., & Liberman, A. M. The effect of need for achievement on recognition of need-related words. *Journal of Personality,* 1949, 18, 236–251.

Machover, S. *Cultural and racial variations in patterns of intellect: Performance of Negro and white criminals on the Bellevue Adult Intelligence Scale.* New York: Teachers College, Columbia University Press, 1943.

Magaret, A. Parallels in the behavior of schizophrenics, paretics and presenile non-psychotic patients. *Journal of Abnormal and Social Psychology,* 1942, 37, 511–528.

Masling, J. The influence of situational and interpersonal variables in objective testing. *Psychological Bulletin,* 1960, 57, 65–85.

Matarazzo, J. D., & Phillips, J. S. Digit symbol performance as a function of increasing levels of anxiety. *Journal of Consulting Psychology,* 1955, 19, 131–134.

Matarazzo, R. G. The relationship of manifest anxiety to Wechsler-Bellevue performance. *Journal of Consulting Psychology,* 1955, 19, 218.

Maxwell, A. E. A factor analysis of the Wechsler Intelligence Scale for children. *British Journal of Educational Psychology,* 1959, 29, 237–241.

Maxwell, A. E. Obtaining factor scores on the Wechsler Adult Intelligence Scale. *Journal of Mental Science,* 1960, 106, 1060–1062.

Maxwell, A. E. Trends in cognitive ability in the older age ranges. *Journal of Abnormal and Social Psychology,* 1961, 63, 449–452.

Mayman, M., Schafer, R., & Rapaport, D. Interpretation of the Wechsler-Bellevue Intelligence Scale in personality appraisal. In H. H. Anderson & G. L. Anderson (Eds.), *An introduction to projective techniques.* New York: Prentice-Hall, 1951.

Mayzner, M. S., Sersen, E., & Tresselt, M. E. The Taylor Manifest Anxiety Scale and intelligence. *Journal of Consulting Psychology,* 1955, 19, 401–403.

Meyer, A. The relation of emotional and intellectual functions in paranoia and in obsession. *Psychological Bulletin*, 1906, 3, 255–274.

Meyer, A. The dynamic interpretation of dementia praecox. *American Journal of Psychiatry*, 1910, 21, 385–403.

Meyer, A. The nature and conception of dementia praecox. *Journal of Abnormal Psychology*, 1911, 5, 274–285.

Meyer, A. Pathopsychology and psychopathology. *Psychological Bulletin*, 1912, 9, 129–145.

Moldawsky, S., & Moldawsky, P. C. Digit span as an anxiety indicator. *Journal of Consulting Psychology*, 1952, 16, 115–118.

Murray, H. A. The effect of fear upon estimates of the maliciousness of other personalities. *Journal of Social Psychology*, 1933, 4, 310–329.

Neff, W. S. Perceiving and symbolizing: An experimental study. *American Journal of Psychology*, 1937, 49, 376–418.

Pintner, R., & Paterson, D. G. *A scale of performance tests.* New York: Appleton-Century, 1917.

Porteus, S. D. Mental tests for the feeble-minded: A new series. *Journal of Psycho-asthenics*, 1915, 19, 200–213.

Postman, L. Perception, motivation, and behavior. *Journal of Personality*, 1953, 22, 17–31.

Postman, L., & Bruner, J. S. Perception under stress. *Psychological Review*, 1948, 55, 314–323.

Postman, L., Bruner, J. S., & McGinnies, E. M. Personal values as selective factors in perception. *Journal of Abnormal and Social Psychology*, 1948, 43, 142–154.

Pressey, S. L. Distinctive features in psychological test measurements made upon dementia praecox and chronic alcoholic patients. *Journal of Abnormal Psychology*, 1917, 12, 130–139.

Pressey, S. L., & Cole, L. W. Irregularity in a psychological examination as a measure of mental deterioration. *Journal of Abnormal Psychology*, 1918, 13, 285–294.

Rabin, A. I. Test score patterns in schizophrenic and nonpsychotic states. *Journal of Psychology*, 1941, 12, 91–100.

Rabin, A. I. Fluctuations in mental level of schizophrenic patients. *Psychiatric Quarterly*, 1944, 18, 78–92.

Rabin, A. I. The use of the Wechsler-Bellevue Scales with normal and abnormal persons. *Psychological Bulletin*, 1945, 42, 410–422.

Rabin, A. I., Davis, J. C., & Sanderson, M. H. Item difficulty of some Wechsler-Bellevue subtests. *Journal of Applied Psychology*, 1946, 30, 493–500.

Rabin, A. I., & Guertin, W. H. Research with the Wechsler-Bellevue Test: 1945–1950. *Psychological Bulletin*, 1951, 48, 211–248.

Rapaport, D. Principles underlying nonprojective tests of personality. *Annals of the New York Academy of Sciences*, 1946, 46, 643–652.

Rapaport, D. Psychological testing: Its practical and its heuristic significance. *Samiksa*, 1947, 1, 245–262.

Rapaport, D. The theoretical implications of diagnostic testing procedures. In R. P. Knight & C. R. Friedman (Eds.), *Psychoanalytic psychiatry and psychology.* New York: International Universities Press, 1954. Pp. 173–195.

Rapaport, D., Gill, M., & Schafer, R. *Diagnostic psychological testing.* Chicago: Year Book Publ., 1945.

Rapaport, D., Menninger, K. M., & Schafer, R. The new role of psychological testing in psychiatry. *American Journal of Psychiatry*, 1947, 103, 473–476.

Rawlings, E. Intellectual status of patients with paranoid dementia praecox: Its relation to organic changes. *A.M.A. Archives of Neurology and Psychiatry*, 1921, 5, 283–295.

Reichard, S., & Schafer, R. The clinical significance of scatter on the Bellevue Scale. *Bulletin of the Menninger Clinic*, 1943, 9, 93–99.

Riegel, R. M., & Riegel, K. F. A comparison and reinterpretation of factor structures of the W-B, the WAIS, and the HAWIE on aged persons. *Journal of Consulting Psychology*, 1962, 26, 31–37.

Roe, A. Non-projective personality tests. *Annals of the New York Academy of Sciences*, 1946, 46, 631–678.

Roe, A., & Shakow, D. Intelligence in mental disorders. *Annals of the New York Academy of Sciences*, 1942, 42, 361–490.

Rokeach, M. Generalized mental rigidity as a factor in ethnocentrism. *Journal of Abnormal and Social Psychology*, 1943, 48, 259–278.

Rosenwald, G. C. Psychodiagnostics and its discontents. *Psychiatry*, 1963, 26, 222–240.

Rosenzweig, S. Imbalance in clinical psychology. *American Psychologist*, 1950, 5, 678–680.

Rosenzweig, S., MacKinnon, D. W., Zubin, J., Snyder, W. U., Combs, A. W., Roe, A., & Klein, G. S. Clinical practice and personality theory: A symposium. *Journal of Abnormal and Social Psychology*, 1949, 44, 3–49.

Sanford, R. N. The effect of abstinence from food upon imaginal processes. *Journal of Psychology*, 1936, 2, 129–136.

Sanford, R. N. The effect of abstinence from food upon imaginal processes: A further experiment. *Journal of Psychology*, 1937, 3, 145–159.

Sarason, I. G., & Minard, J. Test anxiety, experimental instructions, and the Wechsler Adult Intelligence Scale. *Journal of Educational Psychology*, 1962, 53, 299–302.

Schafer, R. The expression of personality and maladjustment in intelligence test results. *Annals of the New York Academy of Sciences*, 1946, 46, 609–623.

Schafer, R., & Murphy, G. The role of autism in a visual figure-ground relationship. *Journal of Experimental Psychology*, 1943, 32, 335–343.

Schafer, R., & Rapaport, D. The scatter: In diagnostic intelligence testing. *Character and Personality*, 1944, 12, 275–284.

Scheerer, M. Problems of performance analysis in the study of personality. *Annals of the New York Academy of Sciences*, 1946, 46, 653–675.

Schofield, W. Critique of scatter and profile analysis of psychometric data. *Journal of Clinical Psychology*, 1952, 8, 16–22.

Sears, R. R. Experimental studies of projection: I. Attribution of traits. *Journal of Social Psychology*, 1936, 7, 151–163.

Sears, R. R. Experimental studies of projection: II. Ideas of reference. *Journal of Social Psychology*, 1937, 8, 389–400.

Sherif, M. A study of some social factors in perception. *Archives of Psychology*, 1935, No. 187.

Siegman, A. W. The effect of manifest anxiety on a concept formation task, a nondirected learning task, and on timed and untimed intelligence tests. *Journal of Consulting Psychology*, 1956, 20, 176–178.

Singer, J. L., Wilensky, H., & McCraven, V. G. Delaying capacity, fantasy, and planning ability: A factorial study of some basic ego functions. *Journal of Consulting Psychology*, 1956, 20, 375–383.

Spaner, F. E. An analysis of the relationship between some Rorschach Test determinants and subtest scores on the Wechsler-Bellevue Adult Scale. Unpublished doctoral dissertation, Purdue University, 1950.

Spearman, C. "General intelligence," objectively determined and measured. *American Journal of Psychology*, 1904, 15, 201–287.

Spearman, C. *The nature of intelligence and the principles of cognition.* New York: Macmillan, 1923.

Spearman, C. *The abilities of man.* New York: Macmillan, 1927.

Spivack, G., Levine, M., & Sprigle, H. Intelligence test performance and the delay function of the ego. *Journal of Consulting Psychology,* 1959, **23**, 428-431.

Storch, A. The primitive archaic forms of inner experiences and thought in schizophrenia. *Nervous and Mental Disease Monographs,* 1924, No. 36.

Sullivan, H. S. Peculiarity of thought in schizophrenia. *American Journal of Psychiatry,* 1925, **5**, 21-86.

Tamkin, A. S. Intelligence as a determinant of Rorschach card rejection. *Journal of Clinical Psychology,* 1959, **15**, 63-64.

Taylor, J. A. A personality scale of manifest anxiety. *Journal of Abnormal and Social Psychology,* 1953, **48**, 285-290.

Tendler, A. D. The mental status of psychoneurotics. *Archives of Psychology,* 1923, No. 60.

Thorndike, E. L. Intelligence examinations for college entrance. *Journal of Educational Research,* 1920, **1**, 329-337.

Thorndike, E. L., Terman, L. M., Freeman, F. N., Colvin, S. S., Pintner, R., Ruml, B., & Pressey, S. L. Intelligence and its measurement: A symposium. *Journal of Educational Psychology,* 1921, **12**, 123-147.

Thurstone, L. L. A cycle-omnibus intelligence test for college students. *Journal of Educational Research,* 1931, **4**, 265-278.

Thurstone, L. L. The factorial isolation of primary abilities. *Psychometrika,* 1936, **1**, 175-182.

Thurstone, L. L. *Primary mental abilities.* Chicago: University of Chicago Press, 1938.

Thurstone, L. L., & Thurstone, T. G. *Factorial studies of intelligence.* Chicago: University of Chicago Press, 1941.

Tucker, J. E. Rorschach human and other movement responses in relation to intelligence. *Journal of Consulting Psychology,* 1950, **14**, 283-286.

Vigotsky, L. S. Thought in schizophrenia. *A.M.A. Archives of Neurology and Psychiatry,* 1934, **31**, 1063-1077.

Walker, R. E., & Spence, J. T. Relationship between digit span and anxiety. *Journal of Consulting Psychology,* 1964, **28**, 220-223.

Webb, E. Character and intelligence. *British Journal of Psychology,* 1915 (Monogr. Suppl. 3).

Wechsler, D. *Measurement of adult intelligence.* Baltimore: Williams & Wilkins, 1939.

Wechsler, D. Nonintellective factors in general intelligence. *Psychological Bulletin,* 1940, **37**, 444-445.

Wechsler, D. *The measurement of adult intelligence.* (2nd ed.) Baltimore: Williams & Wilkins, 1941.

Wechsler, D. Nonintellective factors in general intelligence. *Journal of Abnormal Psychology,* 1943, **38**, 101-103.

Wechsler, D. *The measurement of adult intelligence.* (3rd ed.) Baltimore: Williams & Wilkins, 1944.

Wechsler, D. Cognitive, conative, and non-intellective intelligence. *American Psychologist,* 1950, **5**, 78-83.

Wechsler, D., Halpern, F., & Jaros, E. Psychometrics study of insulin-treated schizophrenics. *Psychiatric Quarterly,* 1940, **14**, 466-476.

Wechsler, D., Israel, H., & Balinsky, B. A study of the subtests of the Bellevue Intelligence

Scale in borderline and defective cases. *American Journal of Mental Deficiency*, 1941, **45**, 555-558.

Weigl, E. On the psychology of so-called processes of abstraction. *Journal of Abnormal Psychology*, 1941, **36**, 3-33.

Wells, F. L., & Martin, H. A. A. A method of memory examination suitable for psychotic cases. *American Journal of Psychiatry*, 1923, **3**, 243-257.

Whipple, G. M. The National Intelligence Tests. *Journal of Educational Research*, 1921, **4**, 16-31.

Wiener, G. The effect of distrust on some aspects of intelligence test behavior. *Journal of Consulting Psychology*, 1957, **21**, 127-130.

Williams, H. L., & Lawrence, J. F. Further investigation of Rorschach determinants subjected to factor analysis. *Journal of consulting Psychology*, 1953, **17**, 261-264.

Winfield, D. The relationship between IQ scores and Minnesota Multiphasic Personality Scores. *Journal of Social Psychology*, 1953, **38**, 299-300.

Wishner, J. Rorschach intellectual indicators in neurotis. *American Journal of Orthopsychiatry*, 1948, **18**, 265-279.

Witkin, H. A. The nature and importance of individual differences in perception. *Journal of Personality*, 1949, **18**, 145-170.

Wittenborn, J. R. An evaluation of the use of Bellevue-Wechsler subtest scores as an aid in psychiatric diagnosis. *Journal of Consulting Psychology*, 1949, **13**, 433-439.

Woodrow, H. The common factors in fifty-two mental tests. *Psychometrika*, 1939, **4**, 99-108.

Woodworth, R. S., & Wells, F. L. Association tests. *Psychological Monographs,* 1911, **8**, Whole No. 5.

Yerkes, R. M., Bridges, J. W., & Hardwick, R. S. *A point scale for measuring mental ability*. Baltimore: Warwick & York, 1915.

AUTHOR INDEX

Numbers in italics refer to the pages on which the complete references are listed.

A

Abrams, E. N., 180, *187*
Agnew, M., 44, *63*
Agnew, N., 44, *63*
Ajmone Marsan, C., 22, *32*
Akers, R. L., 128, *166*
Alexander, W. P., 170, 172, 173, *187*
Allen, K. E., 148, *166*
Amsel, A., 100, *105*
Andrews, T. G., 78, *107*
Ansbacher, H., 170, *187*
Aronson, E., 68, *106*
Arthur, G., 171, *187*
Atkinson, J. W., 58, 68, 69, 70, 71, 72, 73, 74, 75, 77, 78, 79, 82, 83, 90, 95, 96, 97, 98, 104, *106, 107,* 173, *187, 190*
Ayllon, T., 113, 114, 147, 152, *166*
Azrin, N., 114, *166*

B

Babcock, H., 170, *187*
Balinsky, B., 173, 174, 184, *187, 193*
Balonov, L. Y. A., 24, *34*
Bandura, A., 132, 138, *166*
Bannister, D., 21, *30*
Barker, R. G., 170, *187*
Barnett, I., 182, *187*
Baroff, G. S., 156, *168*
Bastian, J. R., 71, *106*
Bateson, G., 3, *30*
Beck, L. H., 22, *33*
Belmont, L., 180, *189*
Berg, P. S., 39, *65*
Berger, L., 184, *187*
Berkowitz, L., 103, *106*
Berlyne, D., 42, *63*
Bernstein, A., 184, *187*
Bingham, J. L., 178, 179, *188*
Birch, D., 83, *106*

Birdsall, T. G., 51, *66*
Birnbrauer, J. S., 152, *166*
Birren, J. E., 184, *187*
Blake, R. R., 173, *187*
Bleuler, E., 1, 4, *30,* 37, *63*
Blewett, D. B., 14, 15, *34,* 50, *66*
Bolles, M. M., 170, *187*
Boring, E. G., 49, *64*
Borinsky, M., 60, *63*
Boudreau, D., 25, *30*
Bowers, M. V., 6, *30*
Bransome, E. D., 22, *33*
Breger, L., 155, *166*
Bridges, J. W., 172, *194*
Broadbent, D. E., 11, *30,* 42, *63*
Broen, W. E., 60, *63*
Brooks, L. O., 114, 152, *167*
Brosgole, L., 47, *63*
Brower, D., 179, *187*
Brown, G. W., 3, *30,* 40, *63*
Brown, J. C., 51, *63*
Brown, P. A., 96, *107*
Brown, R. R., *188*
Brown, W. M., 172, *188*
Bruner, J. S., 20, *30,* 173, *188, 191*
Bruning, J. L., 44, *66*
Bryant, A. R. P., 21, *30*
Buell, J. S., 148, *166*
Burgess, R. L., 128, *166*
Burnham, C. A., 180, *188*
Buss, A. H., 45, *63, 64*
Butterfield, W. H., 114, 122, 139, 152, 163, *167*
Bychowski, G., 170, *188*
Bzhalava, I. T., 18, 19, *30*

C

Caird, W. K., 8, *33,* 59, *65*
Callaway, E., 43, *63*
Calvin, A. D., 178, 179, *188*

195

SUBJECT INDEX

A

Ability grasping, 95
Achievement motivation, *see* Motivation
Achievement-risk preference scale, 68
Agoraphobia, 145
Alcoholism, 144, 146, 150, 155, 160
Amyl nitrate, 43
Anxiety
  MMPI, 178, 179
  motivation, 72, 77–80, 85, 86, 95, 96, 98,
    99, 103, 124
  schizophrenia, 78
  Wechsler tests, 177
Approach-avoidance conflict, 68–71, 79, 87,
    88, 97, 145
Army Alpha Test, 171, 172
Army Beta Test, 171
Arousal, 22–27, 43–45
  arousal and schizophrenia, 43–45, 49, 56,
    60, 61
  autonomic arousal, 26
  cortical arousal, 26
Asthma, 142
Atkinson's theory of achievement motiva-
    tion, *see* Motivation
Attitude-Reinforcer-Discrimative (A-R-D)
    System, 119-169, *see also* Motivation
  behavior therapy and behavior modifica-
    tion, 141–149
  controlling function of, 131–134
  deficits and inappropriacies in, 134–139
  deprivation and satiation, 127, 128
  formation and change of, 119–121
  hierarchical nature of its functions,
    125–129
  implications and extensions, 159–163
  interactions of A-R-D and instrumental
    behavior repertoires, 139–141
  limitations in relation to learning theory,
    149–159
  reinforcing function of, 121–125
  rules of application of reinforcers,
    128–131

Attribution theory, 101, 102
Autism, 148, 160
Aversion therapy, *see* Behavior therapy

B

Behavior modification, 146–148
  implications, 161, 162
  limitations, 151, 152
  relationship to behavior therapy, 148, 149
    see also Behavior therapy
Behavior therapy, 114, 116, 141, 163
  behavior modification, 146–148
  implications and extensions, 159–163
  instrumental conditioning 145, 146
  limitations in relation to learning theory,
    150–159
  as procedure for changing A-R-D,
    142–145
  relationship to behavior modification,
    148, 194
Binet Test, 170, 171, 173, 182
Broadbent's theory of limited capacity deci-
    sion channel, 11

C

Cardiovascular system, 45
Chemotherapy, 39, 50
Choice, studies of, 71, 72
Classical conditioning, 116–121, 124, 126,
    131, 133, 141–145, 149, 151, 154–156,
    159, 160, 163
Chlorpromazine, 22
Cognitive control, 20, 21, 45–48
Cold Pressor Test, 43
Competing information tasks, 58, 59
Conceptual performance, 59, 60
Conditional stimuli, 116–118, 120, 122,
    131–134, 152
Continuous Performance Test (CPT), 22,
    23
Counterconditioning, 126, 127, 143, 144